Computer Basics

Windows® 8.1

ABSOLUTE BEGINNER'S GUIDE

Michael Miller

800 East 96th Street,
Indianapolis, Indiana 46240

Seventh Edition

Computer Basics Absolute Beginner's Guide, Seventh Edition

ISBN-13: 978-0-7897-5233-8
ISBN-10: 0-7897-5233-6

Library of Congress Control Number: 2013955272

Printed in the United States of America

Second Printing: January 2014

Trademarks

All terms mentioned in this book that are known to be trademarks or service marks have been appropriately capitalized. Que Publishing cannot attest to the accuracy of this information. Use of a term in this book should not be regarded as affecting the validity of any trademark or service mark.

Warning and Disclaimer

Every effort has been made to make this book as complete and as accurate as possible, but no warranty or fitness is implied. The information provided is on an "as is" basis. The author and the publisher shall have neither liability nor responsibility to any person or entity with respect to any loss or damages arising from the information contained in this book.

Special Sales

For information about buying this title in bulk quantities, or for special sales opportunities (which may include electronic versions; custom cover designs; and content particular to your business, training goals, marketing focus, or branding interests), please contact our corporate sales department at corpsales@pearsoned.com or (800) 382-3419.

For government sales inquiries, please contact governmentsales@pearsoned.com.

For questions about sales outside the U.S., please contact international@pearsoned.com.

Editor in Chief
Greg Wiegand

Acquisitions Editor
Michelle Newcomb

Development Editor
William Abner

Managing Editor
Sandra Schroeder

Project Editor
Mandie Frank

Indexer
Cheryl Lenser

Proofreader
Gill Editorial Services

Technical Editor
Vince Averello

Publishing Coordinator
Cindy Teeters

Designer
Mark Shirar

Compositor
Trina Wurst

Contents at a Glance

Table of Contents

Part III: Setting Up the Rest of Your Computer System

Part V: Communicating Online

Part VII: Doing Fun and Useful Things with Your PC

About the Author

Michael Miller is a successful and prolific author with a reputation for practical advice and technical accuracy and an unerring empathy for the needs of his readers.

Mr. Miller has written more than 150 best-selling books over the past two decades. His books for Que include *Easy Computer Basics*, *My Windows 8.1 Computer for Seniors*, *My Facebook for Seniors*, *Facebook for Grown-Ups*, *Easy Facebook*, *My Pinterest*, and *The Ultimate Digital Music Guide*. He is known for his casual, easy-to-read writing style and his practical, real-world advice—as well as his ability to explain a wide variety of complex topics to an everyday audience.

You can email Mr. Miller directly at abg@molehillgroup.com. His website is located at www.molehillgroup.com. Follow him on Twitter: @molehillgroup.

Dedication

To Sherry—finally and forever.

Acknowledgments

Thanks to the usual suspects at Que Publishing, including but not limited to Greg Wiegand, Michelle Newcomb, William Abner, Todd Brakke, Mandie Frank, and long-time technical editor Vince Avarello.

We Want to Hear from You!

As the reader of this book, *you* are our most important critic and commentator. We value your opinion and want to know what we're doing right, what we could do better, what areas you'd like to see us publish in, and any other words of wisdom you're willing to pass our way.

We welcome your comments. You can email or write to let us know what you did or didn't like about this book—as well as what we can do to make our books better.

Please note that we cannot help you with technical problems related to the topic of this book.

When you write, please be sure to include this book's title and author as well as your name and email address. We will carefully review your comments and share them with the author and editors who worked on the book.

Email: feedback@quepublishing.com

Mail: Que Publishing
         ATTN: Reader Feedback
         800 East 96th Street
         Indianapolis, IN 46240 USA

Reader Services

Visit our website and register this book at www.informit.com/title/9780789752338 for convenient access to any updates, downloads, or errata that might be available for this book.

INTRODUCTION

Because this is the *Computer Basics Absolute Beginner's Guide*, let's start at the absolute beginning, which is this: Computers aren't supposed to be scary. Intimidating? Sometimes. Difficult to use? Perhaps. Inherently unreliable? Most definitely. (Although they're much better than they used to be.)

But scary? Definitely not.

Computers aren't scary because there's nothing they can do to hurt you (unless you drop your notebook PC on your foot, that is). And there's not much you can do to hurt them, either. It's kind of a wary coexistence between man and machine, but the relationship has the potential to be beneficial—to you, anyway.

Many people think that they're scared of computers because they're unfamiliar with them. But that isn't really true.

You see, even if you've never actually used a computer before, you've been exposed to computers and all they can do for the past three decades or so. Whenever you make a deposit at your bank, you're working with computers. Whenever you make a purchase at a retail store, you're working with computers. Whenever you watch a television show or read a newspaper article or look at a picture in a magazine, you're working with computers.

That's because computers are used in all those applications. Somebody, somewhere, is working behind the scenes with a computer to manage your bank account and monitor your credit card purchases.

In fact, it's difficult to imagine, here in the 21st century, how we ever got by without all those keyboards, mice, and monitors. (Or, for that matter, the Internet.)

However, just because computers have been around for a while doesn't mean that everyone knows how to use them. It's not unusual to feel a little trepidation the first time you sit down in front of that intimidating display and keyboard. Which keys should you press? What do people mean by double-clicking the mouse? And what are all those little pictures onscreen?

As foreign as all this might seem at first, computers really aren't that hard to understand—or use. You have to learn a few basic concepts, of course (all the pressing and clicking and whatnot), and it helps to understand exactly what part of the system does what. But once you get the hang of things, computers really are easy to use.

Which, of course, is where this book comes in.

Computer Basics Absolute Beginner's Guide, Windows 8.1 Edition, will help you figure out how to use your new computer system. You'll learn how computers work, how to connect all the pieces and parts (if your computer has pieces and parts, that is; not all do), and how to start using them. You'll learn about computer hardware and software, about the Microsoft Windows 8.1 operating system, and about the Internet. And after you're comfortable with the basic concepts (which won't take too long, trust me), you'll learn how to actually do stuff.

You'll learn how to do useful stuff, such as writing letters and scheduling appointments; fun stuff, such as listening to music, watching movies and TV shows, and viewing digital photos; online stuff, such as searching for information, sending email, and keeping up with friends and family via Facebook and other social networks; and essential stuff, such as copying files, troubleshooting problems, and protecting against malware and computer attacks.

All you have to do is sit yourself down in front of your computer, try not to be scared (there's nothing to be scared of, really), and work your way through the chapters and activities in this book. And remember that computers aren't difficult to use, they don't break easily, and they let you do all sorts of fun and useful things once you get the hang of them. Really!

How This Book Is Organized

This book is organized into eight main parts, as follows:

- **Part I, "Understanding Computers and Similar Devices,"** discusses all the different types of computers available today; describes all the pieces and parts of desktop, notebook, and tablet PCs; and talks about how to connect everything to get your new system up and running.

- **Part II, "Using Windows,"** introduces the backbone of your entire system, the Microsoft Windows operating system—in particular, Windows 8.1. You'll learn how Windows 8.1 works, how it's different from previous versions of Windows, and how to find things on the Start screen and beyond. You'll also learn how to use Windows to perform basic tasks, such as copying and deleting files and folders.

- **Part III, "Setting Up the Rest of Your Computer System,"** talks about all those things you connect to your computer—printers, external hard drives, USB thumb drives, and the like. You'll also learn how to connect your new PC to other computers and devices in a home network.

- **Part IV, "Using the Internet,"** is all about going online. You'll discover how to connect to the Internet and surf the Web with Internet Explorer. You'll also learn how to search for information, do research, shop, and even sell things online. This is the fun part of the book.

- **Part V, "Communicating Online,"** is all about keeping in touch. You'll find out how to send and receive email, of course, but also how to get started with social networking, on Facebook, Pinterest, Twitter, and other social networks. It's how everyone's keeping in touch these days.

- **Part VI, "Working with Apps,"** tells you everything you need to know about using what we used to call software programs and now call "apps." You'll learn how apps work, which apps are included in Windows 8.1, and where to find more apps. (This last bit covers Microsoft's Windows Store, which is where a lot of fun apps can be had.)

- **Part VII, "Doing Fun and Useful Stuff with Your PC,"** brings more fun—and a little work. You'll learn all about getting productive with Microsoft Office, as well as how to manage your schedule with the Windows Calendar app. You'll also discover how to use your PC to manage, edit, and view digital photos; listen to music, both on your PC and over the Internet; and watch movies and TV shows online. Like I said, fun and useful stuff.

- **Part VIII, "Keeping Your System Up and Running,"** contains all the boring (but necessary) information you need to know to keep your new PC in tip-top shape. You'll learn how to protect against Internet threats (including viruses, spyware, and spam), as well as how to perform routine computer maintenance. You'll even learn how to troubleshoot problems and, if necessary, restore, refresh, or reset your entire system.

Taken together, the 30 chapters in this book will help you progress from absolute beginner to experienced computer user. Just read what you need, and before long you'll be using your computer like a pro!

Which Version of Windows?

This edition of *Computer Basics Absolute Beginner's Guide* is written for computers running the latest version of Microsoft's operating system, dubbed Windows 8.1. If you're running previous versions of Windows, you'll be better off with previous editions of this book. There are editions out there for Windows 8, Windows 7, Windows Vista, even Windows XP. If you can't find a particular edition at your local bookstore, look for it online.

Conventions Used in This Book

I hope that this book is easy enough to figure out on its own, without requiring its own instruction manual. As you read through the pages, however, it helps to know precisely how I've presented specific types of information.

Menu Commands

Most computer programs operate via a series of pull-down menus. You use your mouse to pull down a menu and then select an option from that menu. This sort of operation is indicated like this throughout the book:

Select File, Save

or

Right-click the file and select Properties from the pop-up menu.

All you have to do is follow the instructions in order, using your mouse to click each item in turn. When submenus are tacked onto the main menu, just keep clicking the selections until you come to the last one—which should open the program or activate the command you want!

By the way, because Windows 8.1 is optimized for touchscreen devices, I also include touchscreen instructions where practical. As you'll learn throughout the book, if you have a touchscreen PC, there's a whole host of screen-based gestures and commands you can use to do what you need to do.

Shortcut Key Combinations

When you're using your computer keyboard, sometimes you have to press two keys at the same time. These two-key combinations are called *shortcut keys* and are shown as the key names joined with a plus sign (+).

For example, Ctrl+W indicates that you should press the W key while holding down the Ctrl key. It's no more complex than that.

Web Page Addresses

This book contains a lot of web page addresses. (That's because you'll probably be spending a lot of time on the Internet.)

Technically, a web page address is supposed to start with http:// (as in http:// www.molehillgroup.com). Because Internet Explorer and other web browsers automatically insert this piece of the address, however, you don't have to type it—and I haven't included it in any of the addresses in this book.

Special Elements

This book also includes a few special elements that provide additional information not included in the basic text. These elements are designed to supplement the text to make your learning faster, easier, and more efficient.

 TIP   A *tip* is a piece of advice—a little trick, actually—that helps you use your computer more effectively or maneuver around problems or limitations.

 NOTE   A *note* is designed to provide information that is generally useful but not specifically necessary for what you're doing at the moment. Some are like extended tips—interesting, but not essential.

 CAUTION   A *caution* tells you to beware of a potentially dangerous act or situation. In some cases, ignoring a caution could cause you significant problems—so pay attention to them!

Let Me Know What You Think

I always love to hear from readers. If you want to contact me, feel free to email me at abg@molehillgroup.com. I can't promise that I'll *answer* every message, but I do promise that I'll *read* each one!

If you want to learn more about me and any new books I have cooking, check out my Molehill Group website at www.molehillgroup.com. Who knows, you might find some other books there that you would like to read.

HOW PERSONAL COMPUTERS WORK

Chances are you're reading this book because you just bought a new computer, are thinking about buying a new computer, or maybe even had someone give you his old computer. (Nothing wrong with high-tech hand-me-downs!) At this point you might not be totally sure what it is you've gotten yourself into. Just what is this mess of boxes and cables, and what can you—or *should* you—do with it?

This chapter serves as an introduction to the entire concept of personal computers in general—what they do, how they work, that sort of thing—and computer hardware in particular. It's a good place to start if you're not that familiar with computers or want a brief refresher course in what all those pieces and parts are and what they do.

Of course, if you want to skip the background and get right to using your computer, that's okay, too. For step-by-step instructions on how to connect and configure a new desktop PC, go directly to Chapter 2, "Setting Up and Using a Desktop Computer." Or, if you have a new notebook or tablet PC, go to Chapter 3, "Setting Up and Using a Notebook or Tablet Computer." Everything you need to know should be in one of those two chapters.

What Your Computer Can Do

What good is a personal computer, anyway?

Everybody has one, you know. (Including you, now!) In fact, it's possible you bought your new computer just so that you wouldn't feel left out. But now that you have your very own personal computer, what do you do with it?

Good for Getting Online

Most of what we do on our computers these days is accomplished via the Internet. We find and communicate with our friends online; we find useful information online; we watch movies and listen to music online; we play games online; we even shop and do our banking online. Most of these activities are accomplished by browsing something called the World Wide Web (or just the "Web"), which you do from something called a web browser. Now that you have a new computer and (hopefully) an Internet connection at home, you won't feel left out when people start talking about "double-u double-u double-u" this and "dot-com" that—because you'll be online, too.

 NOTE Learn more about getting online in Chapter 12, "Connecting to the Internet—at Home and on the Road."

Good for Social Networking

One of the most popular online activities these days involves something called social networking. A *social network* is a website where you can keep informed as to what your friends and family are doing, and they can see what you're up to, too. There are several social networks you can use, but the most popular are Facebook, Pinterest, Twitter, and LinkedIn. You can join one or more of these and start sharing your life online.

 NOTE Learn more about Facebook, the most popular social network, in Chapter 17, "Social Networking with Facebook." Learn more about other social networks in Chapter 18, "More Social Networking with Pinterest, LinkedIn, and Twitter."

Good for Communicating

Your new computer is also great for one-to-one communication. Want to send a note to a friend? Or keep your family informed of what's new and exciting? It's easy enough to do, thanks to your new computer and the Internet. You can drop a note via email or keep 'em posted via Facebook or some similar social networking site.

 NOTE   Learn more about communicating with email in Chapter 16, "Sending and Receiving Email."

Good for Sharing Photos and Home Movies

You can also use your computer to store and share your favorite photos and home movies. When you upload a picture, your friends can view it online. You can even touch up the photo before you share it. Pretty nifty.

 NOTE   Learn more about digital photos in Chapter 26, "Viewing and Sharing Digital Photos."

Good for Keeping in Touch

There are a number of ways to use your new computer to keep in touch with absent family and friends. You can communicate over the Internet, via email. You can communicate via Facebook and other social networks. You can even participate in video chats in real time, using your computer's webcam and the Skype video chatting service. It's just like being there!

 NOTE   Learn more about online video chats in Chapter 20, "Video Chatting with Friends and Family."

Good for Entertainment

For many people, a personal computer is a hub for all sorts of entertainment. You can use your computer to watch movies on DVDs, listen to music on CDs, or—even better—go online to watch TV shows and movies. You can also go online to purchase and download new music or listen to all your favorite tunes in real time via streaming music services.

 NOTE   Learn more about listening to music with your PC in Chapter 27, "Playing Music." Learn more about watching TV and movies on your PC in Chapter 28, "Watching Movies, TV Shows, and Other Videos."

Good for Keeping Informed

Entertainment is fun, but it's also important to stay informed. Your computer is a great gateway to tons of information, both old and new. You can search for just about anything you want online or use your computer to browse the latest news headlines, sports scores, and weather reports. All the information you can think of is online somewhere, and you use your computer to find and read it.

 NOTE Learn more about staying informed online in Chapter 13, "Using Internet Explorer to Surf the Web."

Good for Work

A lot of people use their home PCs for work-related purposes. You can bring your work (reports, spreadsheets, you name it) home from the office and finish it on your home PC. Or, if you work at home, you can use your computer to pretty much run your small business—you can use it to do everything from typing memos and reports to generating invoices and setting budgets.

In short, anything you can do with a normal office PC, you can probably do on your home PC.

 NOTE Learn more about using your computer for office work in Chapter 24, "Doing Office Work."

Good for Play

All work and no play make Jack a dull boy, so there's no reason not to have a little fun with your new PC. There are a lot of cool games (from Angry Birds to Candy Crush Saga) online, plus you can purchase all manner of computer games to play, if that's what you're into. There's a lot of fun to be had with your new PC!

 NOTE This book is written for users of relatively new personal computers—in particular, PCs running the Microsoft Windows 8.1 operating system. If you have an older PC running an older version of Windows, most of the advice here is still good, although not all the step-by-step instructions will apply.

Inside a Personal Computer

As we'll discuss momentarily, there are lots of different types of personal computers—desktops, notebooks, tablets, and the like. What they all have in common is a core set of components—the computer *hardware*. Unlike computer *software,* which describes the programs and applications you run on your computer, the hardware is composed of those parts of your system you can actually see and touch.

Well, you could see the parts if you opened the case, which you can't always do. Let's take a virtual tour inside a typical PC, so you can get a sense of how the darned thing works.

The Motherboard: Home to Almost Everything

Inside every PC are all manner of computer chips and circuit boards. Most of these parts are connected to a big circuit board called a *motherboard*, so named because it's the "mother" for the computer's microprocessor and memory chips, as well as for all other internal components that enable your system to function. On a traditional desktop PC, the motherboard is located near the base of the computer, as shown in Figure 1.1; on an all-in-one desktop, it's built into the monitor unit; on a notebook PC, it's just under the keyboard; and on a tablet or hybrid model, it's built into the touchscreen display.

FIGURE 1.1

What a typical desktop PC looks like on the inside   a big motherboard with lots of add on boards attached.

On a traditional desktop PC, the motherboard contains several slots, into which you can plug additional *boards* (also called *cards*) that perform specific functions. All-in-one and notebook PC motherboards can't accept additional boards, and thus aren't expandable like PCs that have separate system units.

Most traditional desktop PC motherboards contain multiple slots for add-on cards. For example, a video card enables your motherboard to transmit video signals to your monitor. Other available cards enable you to add sound and modem/fax capabilities to your system. (On an all-in-one or notebook PC, these video and audio functions are built into the motherboard, rather than being on separate cards.)

Microprocessors: The Main Engine

We're not done looking at the motherboard just yet. That's because, buried somewhere on that big motherboard, is a specific chip that controls your entire computer system. This chip is called a *microprocessor* or a *central processing unit (CPU)*.

The microprocessor is the brains inside your system. It processes all the instructions necessary for your computer to perform its duties. The more powerful the microprocessor chip, the faster and more efficiently your system runs.

Microprocessors carry out the various instructions that let your computer compute. Every input and output device connected to a computer—the keyboard, printer, monitor, and so on—either issues or receives instructions that the microprocessor then processes. Your software programs also issue instructions that must be implemented by the microprocessor. This chip truly is the workhorse of your system; it affects just about everything your computer does.

Different computers have different types of microprocessor chips. Desktop and notebook computers running the Windows operating system use chips manufactured by either Intel or AMD. (Apple Macintosh computers also use Intel chips, although they're different from the chips used in Windows PCs.)

In addition to having different chip manufacturers (and different chip families from the same manufacturer), you'll run into microprocessor chips that run at different speeds. CPU speed today is measured in *gigahertz (GHz)*. A CPU with a speed of 1GHz can run at one *billion* clock ticks per second! The bigger the gigahertz number, the faster the chip runs.

It gets better. Many chips today incorporate so-called *dual-core* or *quad-core* chips. What this means is that a single chip includes the equivalent of two (dual-core) or four (quad-core) CPUs. That's like doubling or quadrupling your processing power! The more cores, the better—especially for processor-intensive tasks, such as editing digital video files.

If you're shopping for a new PC, look for one with the combination of a powerful microprocessor and a high clock speed for best performance. And don't forget to count all the cores; a dual-core chip with two 1.8GHz CPUs is more powerful than a single-core chip with a 2.0GHz CPU.

Computer Memory: Temporary Storage

Before a CPU can process instructions you give it, your instructions must be stored somewhere, in preparation for access by the microprocessor. These instructions—along with other data processed by your system—are temporarily held in the computer's *random access memory (RAM)*. All computers have some amount of memory, which is created by a number of memory chips. The more memory that's available in a machine, the more instructions and data that can be stored at one time.

Memory is measured in terms of *bytes*. One byte is equal to approximately one character in a word processing document. A unit equaling approximately one thousand bytes (1,024, to be exact) is called a *kilobyte (KB)*, and a unit of approximately one thousand (1,024) kilobytes is called a *megabyte (MB)*. A thousand megabytes is a *gigabyte (GB)*.

Most computers today come with at least 4GB of memory, some with much more. To enable your computer to run as many programs as quickly as possible, you need as much memory installed in your system as it can accept—or that you can afford. You can add extra memory to a computer by installing new memory modules, which is as easy as plugging a "stick" directly into a slot on your system's motherboard.

If your computer doesn't possess enough memory, its CPU must constantly retrieve data from permanent storage on its hard disk. This method of data retrieval is slower than retrieving instructions and data from electronic memory. In fact, if your machine doesn't have enough memory, some programs will run very slowly (or you might experience random system crashes), and other programs won't run at all!

Hard Disk Drives: Long-Term Storage

Another important physical component inside your system unit is the *hard disk drive*. The hard disk permanently stores all your important data. Some hard disks today can store up to 4 *terabytes* (TB) of data—that's 4,000GB—and even bigger hard disks are on the way. (Contrast this to your system's RAM, which temporarily stores only a few gigabytes of data.)

A hard disk consists of numerous metallic platters. These platters store data *magnetically*. Special read/write *heads* realign magnetic particles on the platters, much like a recording head records data onto magnetic recording tape.

However, before data can be stored on a disk, including your system's hard disk, that disk must be *formatted*. A disk that has not been formatted cannot accept data. When you format a hard disk, your computer prepares each track and sector of the disk to accept and store data magnetically. Fortunately, hard disks in new PCs are preformatted, so you don't have to worry about this. (And, in most cases, your operating system and key programs are preinstalled.)

 CAUTION   If you try to reformat your hard disk, you'll erase all the programs and data that have been installed—so don't do it!

Solid-State Drives: Faster Long-Term Storage

Not all long-term storage is hard disk-based, however. Many of the smaller portable PCs today (called *ultrabooks*) don't have traditional hard disk storage. Instead, they use solid-state flash memory for long-term storage.

A solid-state drive has no moving parts. Instead, data is stored electronically on an integrated circuit. This type of storage is both lighter and faster than traditional hard disk storage; data stored on a solid-state drive can be accessed pretty much instantly. Plus, notebooks with solid-state drives are considerably lighter than notebooks with traditional hard drives.

The downside of solid-state storage is that it's more expensive than hard drive storage. This typically results in less storage capacity for a similar price. For example, most ultrabooks today come with no more than 128GB solid-state storage capacity. Compare this to similarly priced notebooks with 500GB or more capacity on a traditional hard drive, and you see the issue.

So if it's important for your computer to be fast and lightweight, consider a model with solid-state storage. If you prefer a lower-priced model or need more storage space, stick with a traditional hard disk PC.

CD/DVD Drives: Storage on a Disc

Not all the storage on your PC is inside the system unit. As you can see in Figure 1.2, most PCs feature a combination *CD/DVD drive* that lets you play audio CDs and movie DVDs, install CD- or DVD-based software programs, and burn music, movies, or data to blank CD or DVD discs.

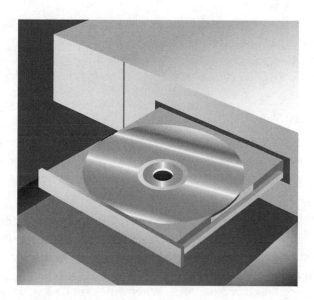

FIGURE 1.2

Store tons of data on a shiny CD or DVD data disc.

Computer CD discs, called CD-ROM discs (the ROM stands for "read-only memory), look just like the compact discs you play on your audio system. They're also similar in the way they store data (audio data in the case of regular CDs; computer data in the case of CD-ROMs).

 NOTE The *ROM* part of CD-ROM means that you can only read data from the disk; unlike normal hard disks and diskettes, you can't write new data to a standard CD-ROM. However, most PCs include recordable (CD-R) and rewritable (CD-RW) drives that *do* let you write data to CDs—so you can use your CD drive just like a regular disk drive.

If you need even more storage, consider writing to blank DVD discs. A DVD can contain up to 4.7GB of data (for a single-layer disc) or 8.5GB of data (for a double-layer disc). Compared to 700MB of storage for a typical CD-ROM, this makes DVDs ideally suited for large applications or games that otherwise would require multiple CDs. Similar to standard CD-ROMs, most DVDs are read-only—although all DVD drives can also read CD-ROMs.

Some high-end PCs do the standard DVD one step better and can read and write high-definition DVDs in the *Blu-ray* format, which lets you store 25GB or more of data on a single disc. Although that storage for PC data might be overkill, it might be nice to play high-definition Blu-ray movies on your PC.

By the way, those smaller ultrabook PCs and tablets get smaller and lighter by leaving out the CD/DVD drives. You can always add an external CD/DVD drive, but in most cases you can get by without the drive at all; just about anything you can find on CD or DVD is also available online for downloading.

Keyboards: Fingertip Input

Computers receive data by reading it from disk, accepting it electronically over a modem, or receiving input directly from you, the user. You provide your input by way of what's called, in general, an *input device*; the most common input device you use to talk to your computer is the keyboard.

A computer keyboard, similar to the one in Figure 1.3, looks and functions just like an old-fashioned typewriter keyboard, except that computer keyboards have a few more keys. Some of these keys (such as the arrow, Pg Up, Pg Dn, Home, and End keys) enable you to move around within a program or file. Other keys provide access to special program features. When you press a key on your keyboard, it sends an electronic signal to your system unit that tells your machine what you want it to do.

FIGURE 1.3

A keyboard for a desktop PC.

Most keyboards that come with desktop PCs hook up via a cable to the back of your system unit, although some manufacturers make *wireless* keyboards that connect to your system unit via radio signals—thus eliminating one cable from the back of your system. Keyboards on notebook PCs are built into the main unit, of course, and are typically a little smaller than desktop PC keyboards; most notebook keyboards, for example, lack a separate numeric keypad for entering numbers.

On a Windows PC, there are a few extra keys in addition to the normal letters and numbers and symbols and such. Chief among these is the Windows key (sometimes called the *Winkey*), like the one shown in Figure 1.4, which has a little Windows logo on it. In Windows 8 and 8.1, many operating functions are initiated by pressing the Windows key either by itself or along with another key on the keyboard.

FIGURE 1.4

The Windows key on a computer keyboard.

 NOTE On some tablet and hybrid PCs, there's a Windows button instead of a Windows key.

Mice and Touchpads: Point-and-Click Input Devices

It's a funny name but a necessary device. A computer *mouse*, like the one shown in Figure 1.5, is a small handheld device. Most mice consist of an oblong case with a roller underneath and two or three buttons on top. When you move the mouse along a desktop, an onscreen pointer (called a *cursor*) moves in response. When you click (press and release) a mouse button, this motion initiates an action in your program.

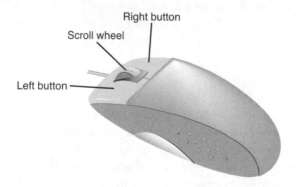

FIGURE 1.5

Roll the mouse back and forth to move the onscreen cursor.

Mice come in all shapes and sizes. Some have wires, and some are wireless. Some are relatively oval in shape, and others are all curvy to better fit in the palm of your hand. Some have the typical roller ball underneath, and others use an optical sensor to determine where and how much you're rolling. Some even have extra buttons that you can program for specific functions or a scroll wheel you can use to scroll through long documents or web pages.

Some newer mice also double as touch input devices. That is, you can tap and squeeze your fingers on a touch mouse much as you can on a touchscreen display. Obviously, you can also use a touch mouse like a traditional rolling and clicking mouse; the touch functionality is just a nice extra.

If you have a notebook PC, you don't have a separate mouse. Instead, most notebooks feature a *touchpad* pointing device that functions like a mouse. You move your fingers around the touchpad to move the onscreen cursor and then click one of the buttons underneath the touchpad the same way you'd click a mouse button.

 TIP If you have a portable PC, you don't have to use the built-in touchpad. Most portables let you attach an external mouse, which you can use in addition to the internal device.

If you're using a tablet or hybrid computer with a touchscreen display, you don't need a mouse at all. Instead, you control your computer by tapping and swiping the screen, using specific motions to perform specific operations. With a touchscreen computer, operation is fairly intuitive.

 TIP How do you enter information if your tablet or touchscreen PC doesn't have a traditional keyboard? By using the Windows virtual onscreen keyboard, which pops up automatically when input is needed on a touchscreen device.

Network Connections: Getting Connected

If you have more than one computer in your home, you might want to connect them to a home network. A network enables you to share files between multiple computers, as well as connect multiple PCs to a single printer or scanner. In addition, you can use a home network to share a broadband Internet connection so that all your computers are connected to the Internet.

You can connect computers via either wired or wireless networks. Most home users prefer a wireless network, as there are no cables to run from one room of your house to another. Fortunately, connecting a wireless network is as easy as buying a wireless router, which functions as the hub of the network, and then connecting wireless adapters to each computer on the network. (And if you have a notebook PC, the wireless adapter is probably built in.)

 NOTE Learn more about wireless networks in Chapter 11, "Setting Up a Home Network."

Sound Cards and Speakers: Making Noise

Every PC comes with some sort of speaker system. Most traditional desktop systems let you set up separate right and left speakers, sometimes accompanied by a subwoofer for better bass. (Figure 1.6 shows a typical right-left-subwoofer speaker system.) All-in-one desktops and notebook PCs typically come with right and left speakers built in, but with the option of connecting external speakers if you want. You can even get so-called 5.1 surround sound speaker systems, with five satellite speakers (front and rear) and the ".1" subwoofer—great for listening to movie soundtracks or playing explosive-laden video games.

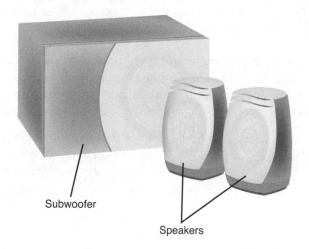

Subwoofer

Speakers

FIGURE 1.6

A typical set of right and left external speakers, complete with subwoofer.

All speaker systems are driven by a sound card or chip that is installed inside your system unit. If you upgrade your speaker system, you also might need to upgrade your sound card accordingly. (You can easily switch sound cards on a traditional desktop PC, but it's really not an option on a notebook or all-in-one.)

Video Cards and Monitors: Getting the Picture

Operating a computer would be difficult if you didn't constantly receive visual feedback showing you what your machine is doing. This vital function is provided by your computer's monitor.

Most computer monitors today are built around an LCD display. On a notebook PC, this display is built into the unit; on a desktop PC, you connect a separate external monitor. You measure the size of a monitor from corner to corner, diagonally. Today's freestanding LCD monitors start at 15" or so and run up to 21" or larger.

A flat-screen LCD display doesn't take up a lot of desk space or use a lot of energy, both of which are good things. Many LCD monitors today come with a widescreen display that has the same 16:9 (or 16:10) aspect ratio used to display widescreen movies—which makes them ideal for viewing or editing movies on your PC.

 NOTE   Older computer monitors were built around a cathode ray tube, or CRT, similar to the picture tube found in normal television sets.

Know, however, that your computer monitor doesn't generate the images it displays. Instead, screen images are electronically crafted by a *video card* or chip installed inside your system unit. To work correctly, both the video card and monitor must be matched to display images of the same resolution.

Resolution refers to the size of the images that can be displayed onscreen and is measured in pixels. A *pixel* is a single dot on your screen; a full picture is composed of thousands of pixels. The higher the resolution, the sharper the resolution—which lets you display more (smaller) elements onscreen.

Resolution is expressed in numbers of pixels, in both the horizontal and vertical directions. Older video cards and monitors could display only 640×480 or 800×600 pixel resolution; you want a card/monitor combination that can display at least 1024×768 resolution—or, in the case of a widescreen monitor, 1280×800.

For most users, the video card or chip installed in their new PC works just fine. However, if you do a lot of heavy-duty gaming—especially with some of the newer graphics-intensive games—you might want to consider upgrading the video card in a desktop PC to one with more on-board memory, to better reproduce those cutting-edge graphics. Serious gamers seek out video cards with separate *graphics processing units (GPUs)*, which take the graphics processing load off the PC's main CPU. The more graphics processing power, the better your system looks.

Other Parts of Your Computer System

The computer hardware itself is only part of your overall computer system. A typical PC has additional devices—such as printers—connected to it, and it runs various programs and applications to perform specific tasks.

Providing Additional Functionality with Peripherals

There are lots of other devices, called *peripherals*, you can connect to your computer. These items include

- **Printers**—A printer lets you make hardcopy printouts of documents and pictures.

   NOTE Learn more about printers and scanners in Chapter 9, "Working with Printers."

- **Scanners**—These devices convert printed documents or pictures to electronic format.

- **Webcams**—These are small cameras (typically with built-in microphones) that let you send live video of yourself to friends and family.

- **Joysticks and gamepads**—These are alternatives to mice that let you play the most challenging computer games.

- **External storage**—These are just like the hard disks inside your computer, but they connect externally to help you back up your precious data.

   NOTE Learn more about using external hard disks in Chapter 10, "Adding Storage and Backup."

You can also hook up all manner of portable devices to your PC, including digital cameras, camcorders, smartphones, and portable music players. You can even add the appropriate devices to connect multiple PCs in a network, which is useful if you have more than one computer in your house.

Fortunately, connecting a new device is as easy as plugging in a single cable. Whether you have a desktop or notebook PC, or even a tablet, most printers connect using a special type of cable called a USB cable. Almost all computers have multiple USB connections (sometimes called *ports*), so you can connect multiple peripherals via USB at the same time.

Doing What You Need to Do with Software and Apps

By themselves, the beige and black boxes that comprise a typical computer system aren't that useful. You can connect them and set them in place, but they won't do anything until you have some software to make things work.

As discussed earlier, computer hardware refers to those things you can touch—the keyboard, monitor, system unit, and the like. Computer *software*, on the other hand, is something you *can't* touch because it's nothing more than a bunch of electronic bits and bytes. These bits and bytes, however, combine into computer programs—sometimes called *applications* or just *apps*—that provide specific functionality to your system.

For example, if you want to crunch some numbers, you need a piece of software called a *spreadsheet* program. If you want to write a letter, you need a *word processing* program. If you want to make changes to some pictures you took with your digital camera, you need *graphics editing* software. And if you want to surf the Internet, you need a *web browser*.

In other words, you need separate software for each task you want to do with your computer. Fortunately, most new computer systems come with a lot of this software already installed. You might have to buy a few specific programs, but it shouldn't set you back a lot of money.

 NOTE Learn more about computer software and apps in Part VI of this book, "Working with Apps."

Making Everything Work—with Windows

Whatever program or app you're using at any given point in time, you interface with your computer via a special piece of software called an *operating system*. As the name implies, this program makes your system operate; it's your gateway to the hardware part of your system.

The operating system is also how your application software interfaces with your computer hardware. When you want to print a document from your word processor, that software works with the operating system to send the document to your printer.

Most computers today ship with an operating system called *Microsoft Windows*. This operating system has been around in one form or another for more than 25 years and is published by Microsoft Corporation.

Windows isn't the only operating system around, however. Computers manufactured by Apple Computing use a different operating system, called the *Mac OS*. Therefore, computers running Windows and computers by Apple aren't totally compatible with each other. Then there's _Linux_, which is compatible with most PCs sold today, but it's used primarily by über-techie types; it's not an operating system I would recommend for general users.

But let's get back to Windows, of which there have been several different versions over the years. The newest version is called _Microsoft Windows 8.1_; Windows 8 was the eighth major version of the operating system, and Windows 8.1 is a minor revision (what we call a "point upgrade") of that. If you've just purchased a brand-new PC, this is probably the version you're using. If your PC is a little older, you might be running _Windows 7_, the immediate predecessor to Windows 8, or maybe even _Windows Vista_ or _Windows XP_, both of which are much older.

To some degree, Windows is Windows is Windows; all the different versions do pretty much the same things. Windows 8 and 8.1, however, look and function much differently than previous versions; Windows 8 was the first version designed for touchscreen operation, and it and Windows 8.1 look more like what you'd find on a smartphone than what you're used to on a computer desktop. In any case, you use Windows—whichever version you have installed—to launch specific programs and to perform various system maintenance functions, such as copying files and turning off your computer.

 NOTE You can learn more about Windows 8.1 in Chapter 4, "Getting to Know Windows 8.1."

Different Types of Computers

Although all computers consist of pretty much the same components and work in pretty much the same way, there are several different types to choose from. You can go with a traditional desktop computer, a smaller, more portable notebook model, a touchscreen tablet—or one that combines some or all of these features.

Let's look at the different types of computers you can choose from.

Desktop PCs

A _desktop PC_ is one with a separate monitor that's designed to sit on your desktop, along with a separate keyboard and mouse. This type of PC is stationary; you can't take it with you. It sits on your desktop, perfect for doing the requisite office work.

Although all desktop PCs sit on your desktop, there are actually two different types of desktop units:

- **Traditional desktops**—A traditional desktop system, like the one shown in Figure 1.7, has a separate system unit that sits either on the floor or beside the monitor.

- **All-in-one desktops**—This newer type of desktop PC builds the system unit into the monitor for a more compact system, like the one shown in Figure 1.8. Some of these all-in-one PCs feature touchscreen monitors, so you can control them by tapping and swiping the monitor screen itself.

FIGURE 1.7

A traditional desktop PC, complete with monitor, keyboard, mouse, and separate system unit. (Photo courtesy Acer.)

FIGURE 1.8

An all-in-one desktop system, with the system unit built into the monitor. (Photo courtesy Lenovo.)

A lot of folks like the easier setup (no system unit or speakers to connect) and smaller space requirements of all-in-one systems. The only drawbacks to these all-in-one desktops are the price (they're typically a bit more costly than traditional desktop PCs) and the fact that if one component goes bad, the whole system is out of commission. It's a lot easier to replace a single component than an entire system!

 NOTE   Learn more about desktop PCs in Chapter 2.

Notebook PCs

A *notebook PC*, sometimes called a *laptop*, combines a monitor, keyboard, and system unit in a single, compact case. This type of portable PC, like the one shown in Figure 1.9, can operate via normal electrical power or via a built-in battery; when using battery power, a notebook can be taken with you and used just about anywhere you choose to go.

FIGURE 1.9

A typical notebook PC. (Photo courtesy Toshiba.)

Just as there are several types of desktop PCs, there are several types of notebooks, including the following:

- **Traditional notebooks**—These units have screens that run in the 14" to 16" range and include decent-sized hard drives (200GB and up) and a combo CD/DVD drive. These are typically the least expensive notebooks because there's a lot of competition; this category is the most popular.

- **Desktop-replacement notebooks**—These are larger notebooks, with screens in the 17" range. They're not only bigger; they're also heavier, and the batteries don't last as long. As such, these notebooks really aren't designed for true portable use, but rather they replace traditional desktop PCs. Plus, these desktop-replacement models typically cost a bit more than traditional notebooks.

- **Ultrabooks**—An ultrabook is a smaller, thinner, and lighter notebook. Most ultrabooks have screens in the 12" to 14" range, don't have CD/DVD drives, and use solid-state flash storage instead of hard disk storage. All this makes an ultrabook very fast and very easy to carry around without necessarily sacrificing computing power and functionality. However, all this new technology means ultrabooks cost a bit more than more traditional notebooks.

 NOTE Learn more about notebook, tablet, and hybrid computers in Chapter 3.

With all these choices available, which type of notebook should you buy? It all depends.

Most users choose traditional notebooks, because they do everything you need them to do at a reasonable price. If you need more computing power but don't plan on taking your PC out of the house, then a desktop-replacement model might make sense. If you're a die-hard road warrior who likes to travel light, consider a more expensive but lighter weight ultrabook.

Tablet PCs

A tablet PC is a self-contained computer you can hold in one hand. Think of a tablet as the real-world equivalent of one of those communication pads you see on *Star Trek*; it doesn't have a separate keyboard, so you operate it by tapping and swiping the screen with your fingers.

No question about it, the most popular tablet today is the Apple iPad; no other model comes close in terms of number of users. The iPad, however, runs its own proprietary operating system (called iOS) and is thus incompatible with the hundreds of millions of Windows-based computers currently in use. That might not be important if all you do with your tablet is browse the Web, read books, and watch movies, but if you want to do more serious work—or read or work on documents created on a Windows computer—then using the iPad is somewhat problematic.

Sensing a need in the market (and wanting to grab some of that tablet revenue for itself), Microsoft designed the original Windows 8 operating system for touchscreen tablet use, and there are now a lot of tablets running the new Windows 8.1 system. A Windows tablet, such as the one in Figure 1.10, looks and works just like a Windows desktop or notebook PC; it's the same tiled interface, the same taps and swipes, the same everything.

FIGURE 1.10

Microsoft's Surface tablet computer, complete with optional external keyboard.

NOTE Tablet PCs can run either the full-blown Windows operating system or a "lighter" version dubbed Windows RT. The only difference between Windows RT and normal Windows 8.1 is that RT does not run traditional desktop software; it only runs newer Windows apps.

Tablets are great for consuming media and information, and they're pretty good for web-based tasks, but they're not that great if you have to get serious work done; the lack of a true keyboard is a killer when you need to type long pieces of text and enter lots of numbers. Still, a Windows tablet can easily supplement a more traditional PC for many types of tasks and is a strong competitor to Apple's iPad.

Hybrid PCs

A hybrid PC is the newest type of personal computer, a blend of the ultrabook and tablet form factors—literally. Think of a hybrid PC as an ultrabook with a touchscreen, or a tablet with a keyboard.

Most hybrid PCs, like the one in Figure 1.11, come with a swivel or fully removable keyboard, so you can type if you need to or get rid of the keyboard and use the touchscreen display as you would a tablet. Windows 8.1 is optimized for this new type of PC, as many functions are touch enabled.

FIGURE 1.11

A hybrid ultrabook/tablet PC. (Photo courtesy Lenovo.)

With a hybrid PC, you use it like a touchscreen tablet when you're watching movies or browsing the Web, and like a notebook PC when you have office work to do. For many users, it's the best of both worlds.

NOTE Microsoft's Surface and Surface Pro tablets are kind of hybrid PCs, especially when you consider the keyboard built into the tablet's case. Use the Surface without the keyboard and it's a tablet; open up the case and start typing on the keyboard, and it's kind of an ultrabook. Which, technically, makes it a hybrid—if old definitions are to be applied.

Which Type of PC Should You Choose?

Which type of PC is best for you? It depends on how you think you'll use your new computer:

- If all you plan to do is check your Facebook feed, view some photos and movies, and maybe send the occasional email, then you don't really need a full keyboard and can make do with a tablet or hybrid PC.

- If you need to do more serious work, then a traditional desktop or notebook PC, complete with keyboard and mouse, is a must.

- If you plan to do all your computing in one spot, such as your home office, then a desktop PC can do the job.

- If you want more flexibility—and the ability to take your computer with you—then a notebook or hybrid model is a necessity.

As you can see, there are lots of choices, and even within these general types, more specific considerations to make. The price depends a lot on the amount of hard disk storage you get, the size of the display, the amount of internal memory, the speed of the microprocessor, and other technical details. And don't forget the design; make sure you choose a model you can personally live with, in terms of both style and functionality.

Don't Worry, You Can't Screw It Up—Much

I don't know why, but a lot of people are afraid of their computers. They think if they press the wrong key or click the wrong button they'll break something or have to call an expensive repairperson to put things right.

This really isn't true.

The important thing to know is that it's difficult to break your computer system. Yes, it's possible to break something if you drop it, but in terms of breaking your system through normal use, it just doesn't happen that often.

It *is* possible to make mistakes, of course. You can click the wrong button and accidentally delete a file you didn't want to delete or turn off your system and lose a document you forgot to save. You can even take inadequate security precautions and find your system infected by a computer virus. But in terms of doing serious harm just by clicking your mouse, it's unlikely.

So don't be afraid of the thing. Your computer is a tool, just like a hammer or a blender or a camera. After you learn how to use it, it can be a very useful tool. But it's *your* tool, which means *you* tell it what to do—not vice versa. Remember that you're in control and that you're not going to break anything, and you'll have a lot of fun—and maybe even get some real work done!

THE ABSOLUTE MINIMUM

Here are the key points to remember from this chapter:

- There are four main types of computer systems available today: desktops, notebooks, tablets, and hybrid models.

- Regardless of type, all personal computers are composed of various hardware components; in a desktop PC, they're separate devices, whereas notebook and tablet PCs combine them all into a single portable unit.

- You interface with your computer hardware via a piece of software called an operating system. The operating system on your new computer is probably some version of Microsoft Windows—Windows 8.1, Windows 7, Windows Vista, or Windows XP, depending on when you purchased the computer.

- You use specific software programs or apps to perform specific tasks, such as writing letters and editing digital photos.

- The brains and engine of your system is the system unit, which contains the microprocessor, memory, disk drives, and all the connections for your other system components.

- To make your system run faster, get a faster microprocessor or more memory.

- Data is temporarily stored in your system's memory; you store data permanently on some type of disk drive—either a hard disk or solid-state drive.

SETTING UP AND USING A DESKTOP COMPUTER

Chapter 1, "How Personal Computers Work," gave you the essential background information you need to understand how your computer system works. With that information in hand, it's now time to connect all the various pieces and parts of your computer system—and get your PC up and running!

Of course, how you set up your computer depends on what type of computer you have. We examine notebook and tablet PCs in Chapter 3, "Setting Up and Using a Notebook or Tablet Computer"; in this chapter, we address the proper way to connect all the components of a traditional desktop PC.

Understanding the Components of a Desktop Computer System

A desktop PC is composed of several different pieces and parts. You have to properly connect all these components to make your computer system work.

On a traditional desktop PC, the most important piece of hardware is the *system unit*. This is the big, ugly box that houses your disk drives and many other components. Most system units, like the one in Figure 2.1, stand straight up like a kind of tower—and are, in fact, called either *tower* or *mini-tower* PCs, depending on the size.

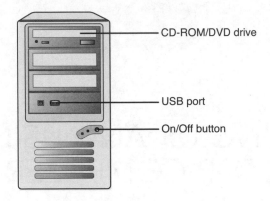

CD-ROM/DVD drive

USB port

On/Off button

FIGURE 2.1

A desktop PC system unit in a mini-tower configuration.

Know, however, that some desktop systems combine the system unit and the monitor into a single unit. These all-in-one desktops take up less space and, in some instances, provide touch-screen functionality that lets you use your fingers (instead of a mouse) to navigate the screen.

The system unit is where everything connects; it truly is the central hub for your entire system. For this reason, the back of the system unit typically is covered with all types of connectors. Because each component has its own unique type of connector, you end up with the assortment of jacks (called *ports* in the computer world) that you see in Figure 2.2.

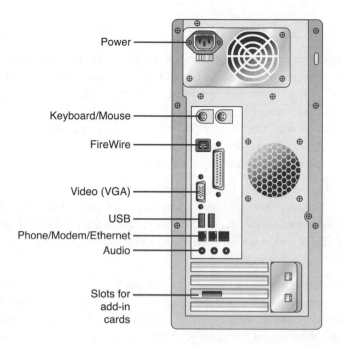

FIGURE 2.2

The back of a typical desktop PC system unit—just look at all those different connectors!

As you've probably noticed, some PCs put some of these connectors on the front of the case, in addition to the back. This makes it easier to connect portable devices, such as an iPod music player or a digital video camcorder, without having to muck about behind your PC.

The connections are on the outside, but all the good stuff in your system unit is inside the case. With most system units, you can remove the case to peek and poke around inside.

To remove your system unit's case, make sure the unit is unplugged, and then look for some big screws or thumbscrews on either the side or the back of the case. (Even better—read your PC's instruction manual for instructions specific to your unit.) With the screws loosened or removed, you should then be able to either slide off the entire case or pop open the top or back.

 CAUTION Always turn off and unplug your computer before attempting to remove the system unit's case—and be careful about touching anything inside. If you have any built-up static electricity, you can seriously damage the sensitive chips and electronic components with an innocent touch.

Before You Get Started

It's important to prepare the space where you'll be putting your new PC. Obviously, the space has to be big enough to hold all the components—though you don't have to keep all the components together. You can, for example, spread out your left and right speakers, place your subwoofer on the floor, and separate the printer from the main unit. Just don't put anything so far away that the cables don't reach. (And make sure you have a spare power outlet—or even better, a multioutlet power strip—nearby.)

You also should consider the ergonomics of your setup. You want your keyboard at or slightly below normal desktop height, and you want your monitor at or slightly below eye level. Make sure your chair is adjusted for a straight and firm sitting position with your feet flat on the floor, and then place all the pieces of your system in relation to that.

Wherever you put your computer, you should make sure that it's in a well-ventilated location free of excess dust and smoke. (The moving parts in your computer don't like dust and dirt or any other such contaminants that can muck up the way they work.) Because your computer generates heat when it operates, you must leave enough room around the system unit for the heat to dissipate. *Never* place your computer (especially a desktop PC's system unit) in a confined, poorly ventilated space; your PC can overheat and shut down if it isn't sufficiently ventilated.

For extra protection to your computer, connect the PC's power cable to a surge suppressor rather than directly into an electrical outlet. A *surge suppressor*—which looks like a power strip but has an On/Off switch and a circuit breaker button—protects your PC from power-line surges that could damage its delicate internal parts. When a power surge temporarily spikes your line voltage (causing the voltage to momentarily increase above normal levels), a surge suppressor helps to keep the level of the electric current as steady as possible. Most surge suppressors also include circuit breakers to shut down power to your system in the event of a severe power spike.

TIP When you unpack your PC, be sure you keep all the manuals, discs, cables, and so forth. Put the ones you don't use in a safe place in case you need to reinstall any software or equipment at a later date.

CAUTION Before you connect *anything* to your computer, make sure that the peripheral is turned off.

Connecting a Traditional Desktop PC

Now it's time to get connected—which can be a bit of a chore for a traditional desktop computer system. (It's a lot easier for an all-in-one model, as you'll see in a moment.)

Connect in Order

Start by positioning your system unit so that you easily can access all the connections on the back. Then you need to carefully run the cables from each of the other components so that they're hanging loose at the rear of the system unit. Now you're ready to get connected.

It's important that you connect the cables in a particular order. To make sure that the most critical devices are connected first, follow these steps:

1. Connect your mouse to an open USB port on your computer.

2. Connect your keyboard to an open USB port on your computer.

NOTE   Some older mice and keyboards connect to separate mouse and keyboard connections on the back of your PC. Most newer mice and keyboards, however, connect via USB.

3. Connect your video monitor to the video connector on the back of your PC. Most monitors connect via a standard VGA connector, although some LCD monitors can connect via a digital DVI or HDMI connector, if one of those is present.

4. Connect the phono jack from your speaker system to the "audio out" or "sound out" connector on the back of your PC. Run the necessary cables between your right and left speakers and your subwoofer, as directed by the manufacturer. (If your speaker system connects via USB, which many newer ones do, just connect the USB cable from the main speaker to an open USB port on your computer.)

5. If you're connecting your computer to a wired router for network and Internet access, connect an Ethernet cable between the router and the Ethernet connector on the back of your computer. (If you're connecting to a wireless router and network, you can skip this step.)

6. If you have a printer, connect it to an open USB port on your computer.

NOTE   Some older printers connect to a parallel port connector, sometimes labeled "printer" or "LPT1." Most newer printers, however, connect via USB.

7. Connect any other external devices to open USB ports on your PC.

8. Plug the power cable of your video monitor into a power outlet.

9. If your system includes powered speakers, plug them into a power outlet.

10. Plug any other powered external components, such as your printer, into a power outlet.

11. Connect the main power cable to the power connector on the back of your PC.

12. Plug your PC's power cable into a power outlet.

 CAUTION Make sure that every cable is *firmly* connected—both to the system unit and to the specific piece of hardware. Loose cables can cause all sorts of weird problems, so be sure they're plugged in really well.

Connect by Color

Most PC manufacturers color-code the cables and connectors to make the connection even easier—just plug the blue cable into the blue connector, and so on. If you're not sure what color cable goes to what device, take a look at the standard cable color coding in Table 2.1.

TABLE 2.1 Connector Color Codes

Connector	Color
VGA (analog) monitor	Blue
Digital monitor (DVI)	White
Video out	Yellow
Mouse	Green
Keyboard	Purple
Serial	Teal or turquoise
Parallel (printer)	Burgundy
USB	Black
FireWire (IEEE 1394)	Gray
Audio line out (right)	Red
Audio line out (left)	White
Audio line out (headphones)	Lime

Connector	Color
Speaker out/subwoofer	Orange
Right-to-left speaker	Brown
Audio line in	Light blue
Microphone	Pink
Gameport/MIDI	Gold
HDMI	Black

Connecting an All-in-One Desktop

Connecting an all-in-one desktop is somewhat easier than connecting one with a separate system unit simply because you have fewer components to deal with. You don't have to worry about connecting the monitor to the system unit because they're all one unit. Same thing typically with speakers, which are usually built into the monitor/system unit.

All you need to worry about connecting, then, are the keyboard and mouse, as well as any peripherals you might have. Follow these steps:

1. Connect your mouse to an open USB port on your computer.

2. Connect your keyboard to an open USB port on your computer.

3. If you're connecting your computer to a wired router for network and Internet access, connect an Ethernet cable between the router and the Ethernet connector on the back of your computer. (If you're connecting to a wireless router and network, you can skip this step.)

4. If you have a printer, connect it to an open USB port on your computer.

5. Connect any other external devices to open USB ports on your PC.

6. Plug any powered external components, such as your printer, into a power outlet.

7. Connect the main power cable to the power connector on the back of your PC.

8. Plug your PC's power cable into a power outlet.

Pretty simple—which is one of the advantages of all-in-one units.

Turning It On and Setting It Up

Now that you have everything connected, sit back and rest for a minute. Next up is the big step—turning it all on.

Getting the Right Order

It's important that you turn on things in the proper order. For a traditional desktop PC, follow these steps:

1. Turn on your video monitor.

2. Turn on your speaker system—but make sure the speaker volume knob is turned down (toward the left).

3. Turn on any other system components that are connected to your system unit—such as your printer, scanner, and so on. (If your PC is connected to an Ethernet network, make sure that the network router is turned on.)

4. Turn on your system unit.

Note that your system unit is the *last* thing you turn on. That's because when it powers on, it has to sense the other components of your system—which it can do only if the other components are plugged in and turned on.

For an all-in-one desktop, there's less to worry about. Just turn on any peripherals connected to the PC, such as your printer, and then press your PC's power button. It's a snap.

Powering On for the First Time

The first time you turn on your PC is a unique experience. A brand-new, out-of-the-box system has to perform some basic configuration operations, which include asking you to input some key information.

 NOTE   For full installation, activation, and registration, your PC needs to be connected to the Internet—typically via a cable or DSL modem connected either to your PC or to a network hub or router.

This first-time startup operation differs from manufacturer to manufacturer, but it typically includes one or both of the following steps:

- **Windows Product Activation**—You might be asked to enter the long and nonsensical product code found on the label attached to the rear of a desktop PC system unit. Your system then connects to the Microsoft mother ship (via the Internet), registers your system information, and unlocks Windows for you to use. (Note that some manufacturers "preactivate" Windows at the factory, so you might not have to go through this process.)

- **Windows Configuration**—During this process, Windows asks a series of questions about your location, the current time and date, and other essential information. You also might be asked to create a username and password.

Many computer manufacturers supplement these configuration operations with setup procedures of their own. It's impossible to describe all the different options that might be presented by all the different manufacturers, so watch the screen carefully and follow all the onscreen instructions.

After you have everything configured, Windows finally starts, and then *you* can start using your system.

 NOTE Some installation procedures require your computer to be restarted. In most cases, this happens automatically; then the installation process resumes where it left off.

THE ABSOLUTE MINIMUM

Here are the key points to remember when connecting and configuring your new computer:

- Most peripherals connect to any USB port on your computer.

- Connecting an all-in-one unit is easier than connecting one with a separate system unit.

- Make sure your cables are firmly connected; loose cables are the cause of many computer problems.

- Connect all the cables to your system unit before you turn on the power.

- Remember to turn on your printer and monitor before you turn on the system unit.

- For full registration and activation, your computer needs to be connected to the Internet.

SETTING UP AND USING A NOTEBOOK OR TABLET COMPUTER

Setting up a notebook or tablet PC is considerably easier than setting up a traditional desktop system. Because everything is built into the unit's case, there's much, much less to connect!

Understanding Notebook and Hybrid PCs

Although desktop systems used to dominate the market, the most popular type of computer today is the notebook PC. A notebook PC does everything a larger desktop PC does, but in a more compact package.

A typical notebook PC combines all the various elements found in a desktop PC system into a single case and then adds a battery so that you can use it on the go. Many users find that portability convenient, even if it's just for using the computer in different rooms of the house.

As you can see in Figure 3.1, a notebook PC looks like a smallish keyboard with a flip-up LCD screen attached. That's what you see, anyway; beneath the keyboard is a full-featured computer, complete with motherboard, CPU, memory chips, video and audio processing circuits, hard drive, and battery. (And possibly a CD/DVD drive, depending on the notebook.)

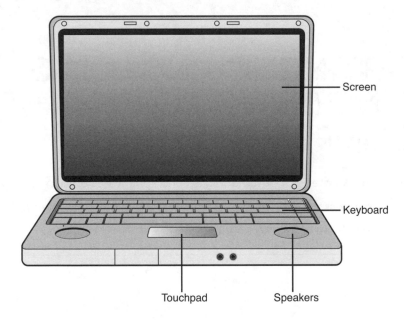

FIGURE 3.1

The important parts of a notebook PC.

When the screen is folded down, the keyboard is hidden and the PC is easy to carry from place to place; when the screen is flipped up, the keyboard is exposed. On the keyboard is some sort of built-in pointing device, like a touchpad, which is used in place of a standalone mouse.

On hybrid PCs, the screen may flip or fold in a way to hide the keyboard and make the unit look like and function as a tablet. (It may be the keyboard doing the flipping, on some models.) In some instances, the screen detaches from the keyboard for tablet use. Hybrid PCs have touchscreen displays, which you can operate with your fingers in either notebook or tablet mode.

If you look closely at a notebook or hybrid PC, you also see two built-in speakers, typically just above the top edge of the keyboard. Most notebooks also have an earphone jack, which you can use to connect a set of headphones or earbuds, the better to listen to music in a public place. (When you connect a set of headphones or earbuds, the built-in speakers are automatically muted.)

Somewhere on the notebook—either on the side or along the back edge—should be a row of connecting ports, like what's shown in Figure 3.2. Most notebooks have two or more USB connectors, an Ethernet connector (for connecting to a wired network), a VGA video connector (for connecting to an external display monitor), and perhaps an HDMI connector (for connecting to a living room TV).

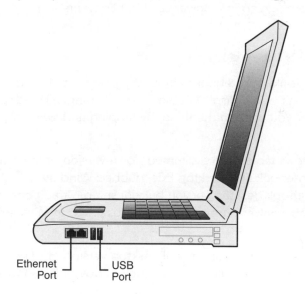

Ethernet Port | USB Port

FIGURE 3.2

Connecting ports on a notebook PC.

 NOTE Some notebooks include a DisplayPort port, which can be used to connect the PC to an external monitor. To do so, you use a special adapter that connects to the DisplayPort connector on one end and to a VGA, DVI, or HDMI connector on the other.

In addition, most traditional notebooks (but not ultrabooks or hybrids) have a built-in CD/DVD drive, typically on the side of the case. Some notebooks up the ante and include Blu-ray capability as well. Press the little button to open the drive and insert a disc; push the drive back in to begin playing the CD or DVD.

Inside the notebook case are the guts of the computer—everything you have in a desktop PC's system unit but more compact. In fact, most notebooks have *more* inside than a typical desktop does; in particular, most notebook PCs have a built-in Wi-Fi adapter so that the notebook can connect to a wireless home network or public Wi-Fi hotspot.

In addition, virtually all notebook PCs come with some sort of built-in battery. That's because a portable PC is truly portable; in addition to running on normal AC power, a notebook PC can operate unplugged, using battery power. Depending on the PC (and the battery), you might be able to operate a laptop for three or four hours or more before switching batteries or plugging the unit into a wall outlet. That makes a notebook PC great for use on airplanes, in coffee shops, or anywhere plugging in a power cord is inconvenient.

Understanding Tablet PCs

A tablet PC is like a notebook without the keyboard. That is, you have a single, nonhinged unit with a display in the 7" to 10" range. The display is a touchscreen, which is how you operate the thing, by tapping and swiping your fingers across the screen.

Some Windows tablets run a slimmed-down version of the same operating system found on notebook and desktop PCs, dubbed Windows RT. Window RT looks just like the notebook/desktop version but doesn't run traditional desktop software programs, only newer purpose-specific apps found in Microsoft's online Windows Store.

Other tablets, however, run the full desktop version of Windows. These tablets can run not only the newer full-screen Windows apps, but also older desktop software.

Unlike the competing Apple iPad, Windows tablets feature a small selection of ports along the side of the unit. Depending on the model, you're likely to find one or more USB ports, as well as a headphone connector and full-size or mini HDMI connector. You can use the USB ports to connect all manner of peripherals, from printers to external hard drives. You use the headphone connector to connect a set of headphones or earbuds, of course. And you use the HDMI port to connect your tablet to an external monitor or living room TV.

Connecting Peripherals and Powering On

One nice thing about notebook PCs is that you don't have nearly as many pieces to connect to get your system up and running. Because the monitor, speakers, keyboard, mouse, and Wi-Fi adapter are all built into the notebook unit, the only things you really have to connect are a printer and a power cable. (And not even a printer, if you already have one connected elsewhere on your home network.)

Getting Connected

To get your notebook PC up and running, all you have to do is connect your printer or any other desired peripherals to a USB port on your computer. Then connect your notebook's power cable to a power strip or surge suppressor and press the power button. (You can even skip connecting to a power strip if you're running on internal batteries.)

Getting a tablet up and running is even simpler, as you probably won't have any peripherals to connect. Because the tablet runs on battery power, all you have to do is turn it on—after you've charged it up, of course.

Powering On for the First Time

As with a desktop PC, the first time you turn on a notebook or tablet computer is different from what you'll experience in later use. There are some basic configuration operations you need to perform.

 NOTE   For full installation, activation, and registration, your PC needs to be connected to the Internet—typically via the unit's built-in Wi-Fi connection.

This first-time startup operation differs from manufacturer to manufacturer, but it typically includes one or both of the following steps:

- **Windows Product Activation**—You might be asked to input the long and nonsensical product code found on the label attached to the bottom of a notebook PC or back of a tablet. Your system then connects to Microsoft (via the Internet), registers your system information, and unlocks Windows for you to use. (Note that some manufacturers "preactivate" Windows at the factory, so you might not have to go through this process.)

- **Windows Configuration**—During this process, Windows asks a series of questions about your location, the current time and date, and other essential information. You also might be asked to create a username and password.

It's also possible that the computer manufacturer might supplement these configuration operations with setup procedures of its own. Just make sure you follow the onscreen instructions as best you can. After you have everything configured, Windows finally starts, and then you can begin using your system.

THE ABSOLUTE MINIMUM

Here are the key points to remember when connecting and configuring your new computer:

- Notebook PCs contain all the components of a desktop PC, but in a smaller, more portable case—complete with battery.

- A tablet PC is just like a notebook, but without the keyboard.

- You don't have to connect anything to your notebook or tablet to get it up and running—save for the power cord, at least until the internal battery is charged up.

- Turning on a notebook or tablet is as simple as pressing the power button.

- For full registration and activation, your notebook or tablet needs to be connected to the Internet.

4

GETTING TO KNOW WINDOWS 8.1

As you learned in Chapter 1, "How Personal Computers Work," the software and operating system make your hardware work. The operating system for most personal computers is Microsoft Windows, and you need to know how to use Windows to use your PC. Windows pretty much runs your computer for you; if you don't know your way around Windows, you won't be able to do much of anything on your new PC.

Introducing Microsoft Windows

Microsoft Windows is a type of software called an *operating system*. An operating system does what its name implies—*operates* your computer *system*, working in the background every time you turn on your PC.

Equally important, Windows is what you see when you first turn on your computer, after everything turns on and boots up. Windows is your gateway to every program and app you run on your computer and to all the documents and files you view and edit.

Welcome to Windows 8.1—If You've Used an Older Version of Windows

If you've recently purchased a new PC, the version of Windows on your PC is probably Windows 8.1. Microsoft has released different versions of Windows over the years, and Windows 8.1 (released in October 2013) is the latest—which is why it comes preinstalled on most new PCs.

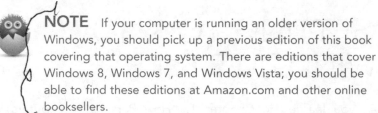 **NOTE**   If your computer is running an older version of Windows, you should pick up a previous edition of this book covering that operating system. There are editions that cover Windows 8, Windows 7, and Windows Vista; you should be able to find these editions at Amazon.com and other online booksellers.

If you are moving to Windows 8.1 from a version of Windows prior to Windows 8 (Windows 7, Windows Vista, or Windows XP), you're in for a big surprise— Windows 8.1 looks and acts completely different from what you're used to. Don't worry, though; everything that was in the old Windows is still in the new Windows—it's just in a slightly different place, and you have to do something different to get to it.

 NOTE   You can upgrade a computer running an older version of Windows to Windows 8.1—but you probably don't want to. Basic operation is so different in Windows 8.1 that you'll face significant retraining time if you move to the new version.

So what did Microsoft change in Windows 8? Lots! Here's a short list of changes from older versions of Windows:

- The Start button and Start menu were removed from the traditional desktop.

- A new Start screen was introduced to launch all applications—part of what Microsoft dubbed the "Modern" interface.

- Full-screen Modern apps were introduced, along with a new online Windows Store to purchase and download them.

- Touchscreen operation was introduced for the Modern interface (actually, Microsoft designed the Modern interface for touchscreen use).

- The desktop's translucent "Aero" interface was changed to a flatter, nontransparent look.

- All the "gadgets" from the traditional desktop were removed.

- The concept of online user accounts was introduced, so you could log into Windows using your Microsoft account information.

- Microsoft's SkyDrive cloud storage service was integrated into the Windows operating system.

- Internet Explorer 10 was included, in both desktop and full-screen Modern versions.

- Windows Explorer was renamed to File Explorer, with a new ribbon interface.

- The Task Manager tool was completely overhauled to make it more functional.

- The Windows Defender antivirus/antispyware tool was included, free of charge.

- Options to both refresh and reset the operating system in case of severe system problems were added.

Naturally, all these Windows 8 changes carry over to Windows 8.1.

For most users, the most different part of Windows 8/8.1 is the graphical user interface, or GUI. Where versions of Windows prior to Windows 8 operated from something called the Windows desktop, Windows 8 and Windows 8.1 hide the desktop (it's still there, just buried) and the old Start menu and instead rely on a tile-based Start screen. The new Windows puts everything front and center; launching an app or opening a file is as easy as scrolling to the right tile and then clicking or tapping it.

The new Windows 8/8.1 interface isn't just for computers, by the way; it looks right at home on a touchscreen device, such as a tablet PC or smartphone—in fact, it's touch enabled. That means you can just as easily operate Windows 8.1 with a tap and a swipe of your finger (on a touchscreen device, that is) as you can with a mouse or keyboard.

If you're a brand-new computer user, you'll find the Windows 8.1 interface easy to understand and even easier to use. If you've used other versions of Windows in the past, however, you might find the Windows 8.1 interface to be a little confusing; nothing looks the same, and nothing is where you expect it to be. It requires a bit of relearning, but after you get past that, Windows 8.1 is actually quite easy to use.

Welcome to Windows 8.1—If You've Used Windows 8

If you're moving to Windows 8.1 from Windows 8, its immediate predecessor, you won't see a lot of dramatic differences between the two versions. That said, Windows 8.1 includes a number of incremental improvements that should make it a little easier to use your computer.

For those of you who were early adopters of Windows 8, you know that it represented a major change from older versions of Windows—too big a change for most people. Windows 8's new Modern interface alienated a lot of users, who resented having to change the way they worked with their computers.

Segue to Windows 8.1, which was released just about a year after Windows 8. Windows 8.1 is a minor update to the Windows 8 operating system, but one that fixes a lot of the problems that bugged people about its predecessor. The changes primary affect the Modern interface and help users work more consistently in a single environment (either Modern or traditional desktop) without having to needlessly shift between the two.

So if you've been using Windows 8, here's what you'll find new and improved in Windows 8.1:

- The Start button is returned to the desktop, although there's still no Start menu; instead, clicking the Start button displays the Modern Start screen.

- You can now "boot" directly to the desktop on startup, bypassing the Start screen.

- The Start screen is more customizable, including the introduction of two new tile sizes.

- You can use the desktop background as the background for the Start screen, so the switch between desktop and Modern environments is less jarring.

- The Lock screen can now display a photo slideshow.

- There are more system configuration options within the Modern interface, so you don't have to open the desktop Control Panel to make most changes.

- Bing web search is added to the traditional Windows file/system search.

- Microsoft's SkyDrive cloud storage is more fully integrated throughout the operating system.

- There are additional "snap" options for displaying multiple Modern apps onscreen at the same time.

- The Windows Store is completely revamped to make it easier to use.

- The Xbox Music, Xbox Video, and Photos apps are also much improved.

- There are several new Modern apps, including Calculator, Alarm, Health & Fitness, and Food & Drink.

- Internet Explorer 11 is included, in both desktop and Modern versions—with major interface changes to the Modern version.

Some of these changes are relatively minor, some more noticeable, but all are designed to make Windows 8.1 more useable on either a touchscreen or a traditional computing device. If you've been complaining about Windows 8, you'll find that the Windows 8.1 update addresses most of your issues.

Different Versions of Windows 8.1

Not to confuse you, but there are four different versions of Windows 8.1, each with a slightly different feature set. Which version you have depends on which was installed by your PC's manufacturer.

Most consumer-oriented PCs should be running the basic version, called simply Windows 8.1. This version is designed for home use and comes with all the functionality the average user needs.

Windows 8.1 Pro is designed for professional and business users. The primary additions to this version are features for large businesses and professional IT folks, such as BitLocker drive encryption and an encrypting file system (for greater security), as well as a group policy editor (for managing multiple PCs from a single location). There's also a Windows 8.1 Enterprise edition, with even more corporate IT-oriented features.

If you're running Windows on a tablet PC, you could be running either basic Windows 8.1 or the tablet-oriented Windows 8.1 RT. This version of Windows is designed for this type of limited-functionality device, not for full-featured notebook and desktop computers. It's a lot like the basic Windows 8.1 version, but it lacks the ability to run traditional desktop computer software.

It's likely, then, that your personal computer is running the basic Windows 8.1 version. That's also the version we focus on throughout this book.

TIP You can upgrade the basic version of Windows 8.1 to the Pro version within Windows itself. Open the Control Panel, click System and Security, then System, then Get More Features with a New Edition of Windows. Select the version you want, enter your payment information (the upgrade costs $100, sorry), and then prepare to download and install the new version.

Starting and Logging into Windows

Starting your computer and logging into Windows 8.1 is a simple affair, albeit a bit different than in older versions of Windows. It all starts when you push the power button on your PC.

Each time you turn on your computer, you see a series of short, perhaps indecipherable text messages flash across your screen. These messages are there to let you know what's going on as your computer *boots up.*

NOTE Technical types call the procedure of starting up a computer *booting* or *booting up* the system. Restarting a system (turning it off and then back on) is called *rebooting.*

After a few seconds (during which your system unit beeps and whirrs a little bit), the Windows Lock screen appears. As you can see in Figure 4.1, the Lock screen provides some basic information—today's date and the current time, Internet connection status, and power status—against a pretty photographic background while Windows waits for you to log on.

To log onto your Windows account, all you have to do is press any key on your keyboard, click the mouse, or tap the screen. This displays your username, as shown in Figure 4.2.

Enter your password and then press the Enter key or click/tap the right-arrow button. After you're past this Lock screen, you're taken directly to the Windows Start screen, and your system is ready to use.

FIGURE 4.1

The first thing you see in Windows 8.1—the Lock screen.

FIGURE 4.2

Select your username and enter your password to proceed.

 NOTE It's easy to configure Windows 8.1 for multiple users, each with their own account and settings; we'll discuss that in Chapter 5, "Using the New Windows 8.1 Interface." If you only have a single user on the machine, only one name appears from the Lock screen.

Using Windows with a Mouse

To use Windows efficiently on a desktop or notebook PC, you must master a few simple operations with your mouse or touchpad, such as pointing and clicking, dragging and dropping, and right-clicking. (If you have a touchscreen PC, you can perform many of these same operations with your finger—which we discuss later in this chapter.) When you're using your mouse or touchpad in this fashion, you're moving the onscreen *cursor*—that pointer thing that looks like a little arrow.

Pointing and Clicking

The most common mouse operation is *pointing and clicking*. Simply move your computer's mouse or, on a notebook PC, drag your finger across the touchpad or other pointing device so that the cursor is pointing to the object you want to select, and then click the left mouse button once. Pointing and clicking is an effective way to select tiles, menu items, and the like.

Double-Clicking

In some instances, single-clicking doesn't launch or open an item; it merely selects it. In these instances, you need to *double-click* an item to activate an operation. This involves pointing at something onscreen with the cursor and then clicking the left mouse button twice in rapid succession.

Right-Clicking

Here's one of the secret keys to efficient Windows operation. When you select an item and then click the *right* mouse button, you often see a pop-up menu. This menu, when available, contains commands that directly relate to the selected object. So, for example, if you right-click a file icon, you see commands related to that file—copy, move, delete, and so forth.

Refer to your individual programs to see whether and how they use the right mouse button.

Dragging and Dropping

Dragging is a variation of clicking. To drag an object, point at it with the cursor and then press and hold down the left mouse button. Move the mouse without releasing the mouse button and drag the object to a new location. When you're finished moving the object, release the mouse button to drop it onto the new location.

You can use dragging and dropping to move files from one location to another.

Mouse Over

When you position the cursor over an item without clicking your mouse, you *mouse over* that item. (This is sometimes called *hovering*.) Many operations require you to mouse over an item to display additional options or information.

Using Windows with a Touchscreen Display

If you're using Windows on a computer or tablet with a touchscreen display, you use your fingers instead of a mouse to do what you need to do. To that end, it's important to learn some essential touchscreen operations.

Tapping

The touchscreen equivalent of clicking an item is tapping that item. That is, you tap a tile or button or menu item with the tip of your finger. Just tap and release to open an app or select an option.

Pressing and Holding

As you've learned, right-clicking an item with your mouse often displays additional information or options. The touchscreen equivalent of the right-click is pressing and holding an item. Simply touch an item onscreen with your finger and hold it there until a complete circle appears on the display. You can then lift your finger, and a shortcut menu appears.

Swiping

With a touchscreen display, you can perform many common tasks with a simple swipe of your finger across the screen, typically from one edge or corner into the center of the screen. For example, swiping from the right side of the screen inward to the left displays the Charms bar.

Panning

You use panning to scroll down or through a long page or series of screens. Simply touch and drag the page with one or more fingers in the direction you want to pan.

Zooming

You use two fingers to zoom into or out of a given screen that is, to make a selection larger (zooming in) or smaller (zooming out) onscreen.

To zoom out, use two fingers (or your thumb and first finger) to touch two points on the item, and then move your fingers in toward each other, as if you're pinching the screen. To zoom in, use your fingers to touch two points on the item, and then move your fingers apart from each other, as if you're stretching the screen.

Rotating

You can use your fingers to rotate a picture or other item on the screen in a circular motion, either clockwise or counterclockwise. Simply use two fingers to touch two points on the item, and then turn your fingers in the direction you want to rotate it.

Learning Important Windows Operations

Now that you know how to use your mouse or touchscreen to get around Windows, it's time to learn some important Windows operations. Most of these actions can be initiated with either a mouse or a keyboard—or, on a touchscreen display, with your fingers—as detailed in Table 4.1.

TABLE 4.1 Essential Windows 8.1 Operations

Operation	Keyboard	Mouse	Touchscreen
Close currently running app or window	None	Drag the top of the app to the bottom of the screen; for desktop apps, click the X button in the top-right corner of the window.	Touch the top edge of the screen and swipe down about halfway through the screen.
Display Apps screen	From Start screen, press Ctrl+Tab	From the Start screen, click the Apps (down arrow) button.	From the Start screen, swipe up from the bottom toward the middle of the screen.
Display Charms bar	Windows+C	Mouse over the upper- or lower-right corner of screen.	Touch the right edge of the screen and swipe to the left.
Display context-sensitive options menu	Application (menu) key	Right-click.	Press and hold the item with your finger.
Display Options bar	Windows+Z	Right-click anywhere on the screen.	Touch the top or bottom of the screen and swipe toward the middle.

Operation	Keyboard	Mouse	Touchscreen
Display Start screen	Windows key	Click the Start button.	From the Charms bar, tap Start.
Display two or more Modern apps side-by-side (snap the apps)	N/A	Mouse over the top-left corner of the screen and then move the cursor down to display thumbnails of all open apps; select the app to snap and drag its (large) thumbnail to either the left or the right side of the screen and then release the mouse button.	Touch the left edge of the screen, drag your finger to the right, and then quickly drag it back to the left to display the switcher panel; press and drag the app you'd like to snap to the right and then drop it on either the left or the right edge of the screen.
Lock computer	Win+L	From the Start screen, click username, Lock (where user-name is the username you use).	From the Start screen, tap username, Lock (where username is the username you use).
Move an item to a new location	N/A	Click and drag, and then release.	Press and hold, drag to new location, and then release.
Open a program or document	Enter	Click (sometimes double-click).	Tap.
Open Windows Help	Windows+F1	From the Charms bar, click Settings, Help.	From the Charms bar, tap Settings, Help.
Scroll down	Pg Dn or down arrow	Click and drag the scrollbar or click the scroll arrows; use the mouse scroll wheel.	Swipe up.
Scroll left	Pg Up or left arrow	Click and drag the scrollbar or click the scroll arrows; use the mouse scroll wheel.	Swipe right.
Scroll right	Pg Dn or right arrow	Click and drag the scrollbar or click the scroll arrows; use the mouse scroll wheel.	Swipe left.
Scroll up	Pg Up or up arrow	Click and drag the scrollbar or click the scroll arrows; use the mouse scroll wheel.	Swipe down.
Search	Windows+Q or Windows+S	Display the Charms bar and click Search.	Display the Charms bar and tap Search.

Operation	Keyboard	Mouse	Touchscreen
Shut down Windows	Alt+F4	Right-click the Start button to display the Quick Access menu; then select Shut Down, Shut Down.	From the Charms bar, tap Settings, Power, Shut Down.
Switch to previous application	N/A	N/A	Touch the left edge of the screen and swipe rapidly to the right.
View or switch to other open apps	Alt+Tab	Mouse over the top-left corner of the screen and then move the cursor downward to display thumbnails of all open documents; click a thumbnail to switch to that item.	Touch the left edge of the screen, drag your finger to the right, and then quickly drag it back to the left. You can then tap any app thumbnail to switch to that app.
Zoom in to the Start screen	N/A	Click anywhere on the zoomed-out screen; or press the Ctrl key and then use the mouse scroll wheel.	Use two fingers to touch two adjacent points on the screen and then move your fingers apart.
Zoom out of the Start screen	N/A	Click the – button in the lower-right corner of the Start screen; or press the Ctrl key and then use the mouse scroll wheel.	Use two fingers at two distant points on the screen and then pinch your fingers in toward each other.

Getting Help in Windows

When you can't figure out how to perform a particular task, it's time to ask for help. In Windows 8.1, you get help through the Help and Support Center.

To launch the Help and Support Center, follow these steps:

1. Click the Start button or press the Windows key to display the Start screen.

2. Right-click anywhere on the Start screen to display the App Bar at the bottom of the screen.

3. Click or tap All Apps.

4. When the Apps screen appears, scroll to the Windows System section and tap or click Help and Support.

A Help and Support window opens on the Windows desktop, as shown in Figure 4.3. From here you can search for specific answers to your problems, browse the table of contents, connect to another computer for remote assistance, go online for additional help, and troubleshoot any problems you might be having. Click the type of help you want, and follow the onscreen instructions from there.

FIGURE 4.3

The Windows Help and Support Center.

Shutting Down Windows—and Your Computer

You've probably already noticed that Windows starts automatically every time you turn on your computer. Although you see lines of text flashing onscreen during the initial startup, Windows loads automatically and goes on to display the Windows desktop.

CAUTION Do *not* turn off your computer from your computer's main power button without first shutting down Windows. You could lose data and settings that are temporarily stored in your system's memory.

When you want to turn off your computer, you do it through Windows. In fact, you don't want to turn off your computer any other way—you *always* want to turn off things through the official Windows procedure.

To shut down Windows and turn off your PC, follow these steps:

1. Right-click the Start button to display the Quick Access menu, shown in Figure 4.4.

2. Select Shut Down to display all the shut down options.

3. Click Shut Down to shut down your computer.

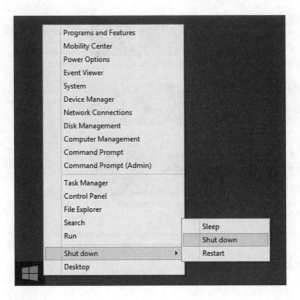

FIGURE 4.4

Powering off from the Quick Access menu.

That's it. If you have a desktop PC, you then need to manually turn off your monitor, printer, and other peripherals.

THE ABSOLUTE MINIMUM

This chapter gave you a lot of background about Windows 8.1—your new PC's operating system. Here are the key points to remember:

- You use Windows to manage your computer system and run apps and programs.

- Windows 8.1 is a slight update to Windows 8, which itself was a major upgrade to the Windows operating system.

- When you start your computer, you see the Windows Lock screen; click or tap this screen to log into your account and enter Windows.

- You can complete most operations in Windows 8.1 using your computer keyboard, mouse, or—on touchscreen displays—a tap or swipe of your finger on the touchscreen.

- To exit Windows and turn off your computer, right-click the Start button and select Shut Down, Shut Down.

5

USING THE NEW WINDOWS 8.1 INTERFACE

Window 8 revolutionized the way Windows looks and works. Windows 8.1 picks up on those changes and adds a few more tweaks and refinements— all of which you need to learn to get the most out of your new PC.

Working Your Way Around the Start Screen

Everything in Windows 8.1 revolves around the Start screen. That's where you start out and where you launch apps and software programs.

 NOTE While the Start screen appears by default when you boot up your PC, Windows 8.1 lets you bypass the Start screen and go directly to the traditional desktop. You can also opt to display the Apps screen (which displays all the apps on your PC) instead of the Start screen when you click the Start button. Both these options are discussed later in this chapter.

Examining the Parts of the Start Screen

As you can see in Figure 5.1, the main area of the Start screen consists of a series of *tiles*. Each tile represents a particular app, program, document, or function.

FIGURE 5.1

The Windows 8.1 Start screen.

 NOTE Your Start screen probably looks a little different from the one in Figure 5.1, in particular the tiles you see. That's because every person's system is different, depending on the particular programs and apps they have installed on their PC.

The tiles in Windows 8.1 are big and colorful, ideal for viewing on a portable or touchscreen device. Tiles vary in size, with some spanning half a column and some spanning two columns; there's no real difference between a large tile and a small tile, other than the size.

At the top-left corner of the screen is the screen name—Start. Clicking this name doesn't do anything; the name just tells you where you are.

At the top-right corner of the screen is your name and profile picture. Click or tap your name to sign out of Windows, lock the screen, or change your account picture.

The bottom of the Start screen is empty until you move your mouse to this area or tap your finger here (if you have a touchscreen display). Then, as shown in Figure 5.2, you see three things—the horizontal scrollbar, a big down arrow on the left, and the Zoom button on the right.

FIGURE 5.2

The navigation elements at the bottom of the Start screen.

You use the scrollbar to scroll left and right through additional tiles on the Start screen. You can also do this with the Pg Up and Pg Dn keys on your keyboard — or by swiping left or right on a touchscreen display.

You click the down arrow to display the Apps screen, which lists all the apps and utilities installed on your system. The Apps screen is useful because the Start screen doesn't necessarily display all your apps, at least by default.

You click the Zoom button when you want to zoom out to see all the screens of tiles on your Start screen, in a minimized mode, as shown in Figure 5.3.

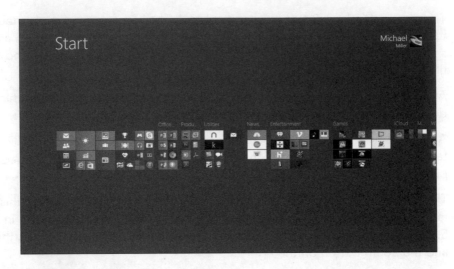

FIGURE 5.3

Zooming out to see the entire Start screen.

NOTE   Microsoft calls this ability to view the entire Start screen in minimized mode *semantic zoom*. If you have a touchscreen display, you can perform this semantic zoom by "pinching" your thumb and first finger together to zoom out or by "spreading" your thumb and finger to return to normal view. When you're zoomed out on the Start screen, you can then click or tap any individual screen of tiles to go to that screen.

Displaying the Start Screen

Obviously, the Start screen is important; it's where you launch everything you want to do in Windows. Fortunately, it's easy to display the Start screen at any time.

Actually, there are several different ways to return to the Start screen from any running app. The easiest is to click the Start button that displays on just about every screen in Windows.

The Start button is fixed permanently to the left end of the taskbar on the Windows desktop. When you're using new Modern apps, you display the Start button by mousing over the lower-left corner of the screen, as shown in Figure 5.4. Clicking the Start button returns you to the Start screen.

FIGURE 5.4

The Start button in Windows 8.1.

 NOTE The Windows 8.1 Start button is different from the Start button in older versions of Windows. Clicking the old Start button displayed the Start menu. Unfortunately, the Start menu was removed from Window 8 and 8.1, so clicking this new Start button displays the Start screen instead.

You can also display the Start screen by pressing the Windows key on your computer keyboard or the Windows button on a tablet. Another way to get back to Start is to display the Charms bar and then click or tap Start.

Scrolling Through the Tiles

There are probably more tiles on your Start or Apps screen than will fit on a single screen of your computer display. To view all your Start tiles, you need to scroll the screen left or right. There are several ways to do this:

- **With your mouse**—Click and drag the horizontal scrollbar at the bottom of the screen, or click the right and left scroll arrows on either side of the scrollbar. If your mouse has a scroll wheel, you can use the scroll wheel to scroll right (down) or left (up) through the tiles.

- **With your keyboard**—To scroll one screen at a time, press the Page Down button (scroll right) or the Page Up button (scroll left). To scroll one tile at a time, press the left arrow or right arrow buttons.

- **With a touchscreen display**—Swipe the screen with your finger right to left to scroll right, or left to right to scroll left.

Opening a Tile

Remember that each tile on the Start screen represents a specific app or document. There are three ways to launch an app or open a document from these tiles:

- **With your mouse**—Click the tile, using the left mouse button.

- **With your keyboard**—Use your keyboard's arrow keys to highlight that tile and then press the Enter key.

- **With a touchscreen display**—Tap the tile with your finger.

Find Additional Apps on the Apps Screen

The Start screen is where you find most of your favorite apps and utilities. When you install a new app, however, it doesn't automatically appear on the Start screen; you have to manually add the app to it.

If you want to view *all* the apps and utilities installed on your PC, you use Windows 8.1's Apps screen instead. You can easily access this screen from the Start screen by clicking the Apps (down arrow) button or, on a touchscreen display, swiping up from the bottom of the screen.

The resulting Apps screen, shown in Figure 5.5, displays every application and program installed on your computer. Click an app to launch it.

FIGURE 5.5

Viewing all your apps on the Apps screen.

TIP   To add an app to the Start screen, right-click the app on the Apps screen to display the Options bar, and then click Pin to Start.

Using the Charms Bar

Windows 8.1 has more functions up its sleeve, although they're not obvious during normal use. These are a series of system functions, called *Charms*, which are accessed from the Charms bar that appears on the right side of the screen.

There are three ways to display the Charms bar:

- **With your mouse**—Move your mouse to either the top-right or the bottom-right corner of the screen.

- **With your keyboard**—Press Windows ⌐ C.

- **On a touchscreen display**—Swipe your finger from the right edge of the screen (to the left).

As you can see in Figure 5.6, the Charms bar consists of the following icons:

- **Search**—Click this icon to search your computer for apps and documents. (We discuss the search function later in this chapter.)

- **Share**—If you're using a specific application, click this icon to share the content of the app with other users via email and other services.

- **Start**—Click this icon to return to the Start screen from any other location in Windows.

- **Devices**—Click this icon to configure the settings of any external devices connected to your computer.

- **Settings**—Click this icon to access and configure various Windows settings.

FIGURE 5.6

The Windows Charms bar.

 NOTE Whenever the Charms bar is displayed, Windows also displays a notification panel (at the bottom left of the screen) with the current date and time, Internet connection status, and power status. This panel pretty much duplicates the information shown on the Lock screen.

Note that you can access the Charms bar from *any* screen in Windows 8.1, even if you have an app displayed full screen. All you have to do is click or tap appropriately, and the Charms bar appears. (And the content of the Charms bar changes depending on what app you're using; it offers app-specific configuration options.)

TIP   You can access more advanced system options, such as Network Connections, Power Options, and Device Manager, by moving your mouse to the lower-left corner of the screen and then right-clicking. A Quick Access menu of advanced options displays; click an item to open it.

Personalizing the Start Screen

When you first turn on your new computer, you see the Windows Start screen as Microsoft (or your computer manufacturer) set it up for you. If you like the way it looks, great. If not, you can change it.

Windows presents a lot of different ways to personalize the look and feel of your system. In fact, one of the great things about Windows is how quickly you can make Windows look like *your* version of Windows, different from anybody else's.

Let's start by learning how to configure your personal Start screen. You can easily change the background color of the Start screen, choose to display your desktop background as the background for the Start screen, and determine which tiles are displayed—and how.

Changing the Background Color and Pattern

When you configured Windows when you first turned on your new computer, you were asked to choose a color scheme. This color scheme is what you see when you display the Windows Start screen.

Fortunately, you're not locked into your initial choice. You can change the color scheme for your Start screen (and various subsidiary screens) at any time. Just follow these steps:

1. Display the Charms bar and click or tap Settings to display the Settings panel.

2. Click or tap Personalize to display the Personalize panel, shown in Figure 5.7.

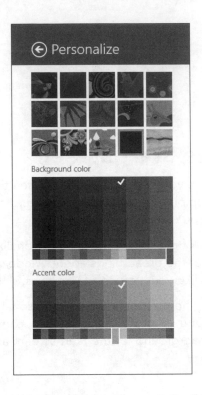

FIGURE 5.7

Personalizing the Start screen.

3. Select a background color from the Background Color chooser.

4. Select an accent color from the Accent Color chooser *or...*

5. ...select a background theme from the selection at the top of the bar. (This option preselects background and accent colors to match the selected pattern.)

That's it. The changes you make are immediate and interactive. You don't have to "save" them; they're applied automatically.

Displaying Your Desktop Background on the Start Screen

In Windows 8.1, you can display the same background picture on the Start screen as you do on the Windows desktop. This makes the transition from the desktop environment to the Modern Start screen less visually jarring.

1. From the Start screen, click the Desktop tile to display the Windows desktop.

2. Right-click an open area of the taskbar and select Properties to display the Taskbar and Navigation Properties dialog box.

3. Click the Navigation tab, shown in Figure 5.8.

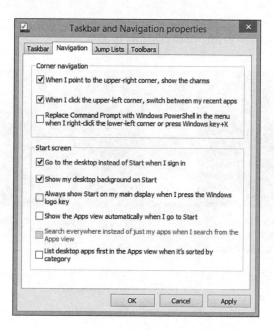

FIGURE 5.8

Displaying the desktop background on the Start screen.

4. Go to the Start Screen section and check Show My Desktop Background on Start.

5. Click the OK button.

 NOTE To change the background picture on the desktop (and the Start screen, if you have them linked), right-click the desktop and select Personalize.

Making a Tile Larger or Smaller

The Start screen is composed of dozens of individual tiles, each representing an app, program, operation, or file. There are four sizes of tiles to choose from—small, medium, wide, and large.

1. Right-click the tile (or press and hold it on a touchscreen) you want to change. This adds a check mark to the tile and displays the Options bar at the bottom of the screen, as shown in Figure 5.9.

2. Click Resize.

3. Click the new size you want for this tile.

FIGURE 5.9

Changing the size of a tile.

Rearranging Tiles

If you don't like where a given tile appears on the Start screen, you can rearrange the order of your tiles. To move a tile, use your mouse (or, on a touchscreen display, your finger) to click and drag a given tile to a new position.

You can also move tiles from one Start screen group to another. (We'll discuss groups in the next section.) To do so, just click and drag the tile from one group to another.

Organize Tiles into Groups

You can organize tiles on the Start screen into multiple groups of like tiles. For example, you might want to group the tiles for all the Office apps into a Microsoft Office group. You can create new tile groups at any time. Follow these steps:

1. Click and drag an existing tile to the right of its current group until you see a shaded vertical bar.

2. Drop the tile onto that bar. This creates a new group with that tile as the first tile.

TIP You can shrink the Start screen to see more tiles and complete groups. Move your cursor to the bottom-right corner of the Start screen and click the Zoom (–) button. (Or, on a touchscreen device, pinch the screen to shrink it.) Then, with the Start screen shrunk, you can rearrange your tile groups by clicking and dragging a complete group from one position to another.

Name Groups of Tiles

You can give each tile group a name so that you know what's where. For example, you might want to organize all your media-related (photos, music, and video) tiles into one group and call it Media. Follow these steps:

1. Right-click any empty area of the Start screen to display the Options bar.

2. Click Customize.

3. Move the cursor to the text box above the group of tiles, as shown in Figure 5.10, enter a name for that group, and press Enter.

FIGURE 5.10

Naming a group of tiles.

NOTE   To remove the name from a tile group, right-click the Start screen to display the Options bar, click Customize, mouse over the current name, and then click the X next to the name.

Removing a Tile

You might find that there are one or more tiles on your Start screen that you never use. You can remove unused tiles to get them out of your way and make room for additional titles. Follow these steps:

1. Right-click the tile (or press and hold it on a touchscreen) you want to delete. This adds a check mark to the tile and displays the pop-up bar at the bottom of the screen.

2. Click or tap Unpin from Start.

Adding a New Tile

If you accidently remove a tile from the Start screen, or you want to add a tile for an app that isn't already there, you can do so. To add a new tile, follow these steps:

1. Click the Apps button at the bottom left of the Start screen to display the Apps screen.

2. Right-click the item you want to add; this displays the Options bar at the bottom of the screen, as shown in Figure 5.11.

3. Click or tap Pin to Start.

FIGURE 5.11

Adding a new tile to the Start screen.

The new tile appears at the end of your existing tiles on the Start screen. You can move it to a new position by clicking and dragging it with your mouse or finger.

Turning On or Off a Live Tile

Many tiles are "live," meaning that they display the current information or a selected document for that app. For example, the Weather tile displays the current weather conditions; the Photos tile displays a slide show of photographs stored on your computer.

As useful as that sounds, all the blinking and shifting of the live tiles can be distracting. If you don't like the constant action of a live tile, you can turn it off—that is, display a default tile icon instead. Follow these steps:

1. Right-click the tile (or press and hold it on a touchscreen) you want to change; this adds a check mark to the tile and displays the Options bar at the bottom of the screen.

2. Click or tap Turn Live Tile Off.

To turn on a live tile, repeat these steps but select Turn Live Tile On.

Show the Apps Screen Instead of the Start Screen

Because not all apps automatically appear on the Start screen, some users will find the Apps screen (that displays all installed apps) more useful. You can configure Windows to display the Apps screen instead of the Start screen when you click the Start button.

Here's how to do it.

1. Open the Windows desktop, right-click the taskbar, and click Properties to display the Taskbar and Navigation Properties dialog box.

2. Click the Navigation tab.

3. Go to the Start Screen section and check Show the Apps View Automatically When I Go to Start.

4. Click the OK button.

Personalizing the Lock Screen

You can also personalize the Lock screen that you see when you first start or begin to log into Windows. You can change the background picture of the Lock screen, turn the Lock screen into a photo slide show, and add informational apps to the screen.

Changing the Lock Screen Background

To change the background picture you see on the Lock screen, follow these steps:

1. Display the Charms bar and click or tap Settings to display the Settings panel.

2. Click or tap Change PC Settings to display the PC Settings page.

3. Click or tap PC & Devices in the left column.

3. Click or tap Lock Screen to display the screen shown in Figure 5.12.

FIGURE 5.12

Personalizing the Lock screen.

4. Go to the Background section and click or tap the thumbnail for the picture you want to use.

5. Alternatively, click the Browse button to use your own picture as the background. Navigate to and select the picture you want to use, and then click the Choose Image button.

Displaying a Slide Show on the Lock Screen

Windows 8.1 lets you turn your computer into a kind of digital picture frame by displaying a slide show of your photos on the Lock screen while your PC isn't being used. Follow these steps:

1. Display the Charms bar and then click or tap Settings to display the Settings panel.

2. Click or tap Change PC Settings to display the PC Settings page.

3. Click or tap PC & Devices in the left column.

4. Click or tap Lock Screen.

5. Click "on" the Play a Slide Show on the Lock Screen switch.

6. Click or tap Add a Folder to select the picture folder you want to display in your slide show.

7. Alternatively, if you'd rather let Windows pick your slide show pictures, click "on" the Let Windows Choose Pictures for My Slide Show switch.

8. Use the Turn Off Screen After Slide Show Has Played For control to have Windows turn off the slide show (and dim the screen) after a set period of time. Select a time period—30 minutes, 1 hour, or 3 hours. To keep the slide show playing indefinitely, select Don't Turn Off.

Adding Apps to the Lock Screen

The Lock screen can display a number of apps that run in the background and display useful or interesting information, even while your computer is locked. By default, you see the date/time, power status, and connection status, but it's easy to add other apps and information (such as weather conditions and unread email messages) to the Lock screen. Just follow these steps:

1. Display the Charms bar and click or tap Settings to display the Settings panel.

2. Click or tap Change PC Settings to display the PC Settings page.

3. Click or tap PC & Devices in the left column.

4. Click or tap Lock Screen.

5. Scroll down the Lock Screen panel to the Lock Screen Apps section and click or tap a + button to display the Choose an App panel.

6. Click or tap the app you want to add.

 TIP   You can also opt for one of the apps to display detailed live information. For example, you might want the Lock screen to display current weather conditions from the Weather app or upcoming appointments from the Calendar app. To select which app displays detailed information, click or tap the app button in the Choose an App to Display Detailed Status section.

Changing Your Account Picture

When you first configured Windows, you picked a default image to use as your profile picture. You can, at any time, change this picture to something more to your liking. Follow these steps:

1. From the Start screen, click or tap your account name in the top-right corner to display the pop-up menu.

2. Click or tap Change Account Picture.

3. When the Your Account page appears, as shown in Figure 5.13, go to the Account Picture section and click one of the images displayed there, *or...*

FIGURE 5.13

Changing your account picture.

4. Click or tap the Browse button to display the Files screen.

5. Navigate to and click or tap the picture you want.

6. Click or tap the Choose Image button.

TIP If your computer has a webcam, you can take a picture with your webcam to use for your account picture. From the Account Picture page, click or tap the Camera button and follow the onscreen directions from there.

Making Windows 8.1 More Like Windows 7

One of the big complaints people had about Windows 8 was how different it was from Windows 7. Microsoft listened and made some changes to Windows 8.1 that let you configure the new operating system to more closely work and look like the older one. Doing so, however, requires a small amount of customization.

Reconfiguring Windows

Here's what you can change:

- Boot directly to the desktop, bypassing the Start screen.
- Display the desktop background image as the background image on the Start screen, so the transition between desktop and Start screen isn't so jarring.
- Display desktop apps first on the Apps screen.
- Disable "live" corners, so that you don't accidentally activate Modern features when you mouse over them.

You make all these changes from the traditional Windows desktop. Follow these steps:

1. From the Windows desktop, right-click the taskbar and click Properties to display the taskbar and Navigation Properties dialog box.

2. Click the Navigation tab.

3. Go to the Start Screen section and check the following options:

   - When I Sign In or Close All Apps on a Screen, Go to the Desktop Instead of Start
   - Show My Desktop Background on Start
   - List Desktop Apps First in the Apps View When It's Sorted By Category

4. Go to the Corner Navigation section and *uncheck* the following options:

- When I Point to the Upper-Right Corner, Show the Charms

- When I Click the Upper-Left Corner, Switch Between My Recent Apps

5. Click the OK button.

Installing a Start Menu Replacement Tool

If you've been using Windows for a while, it's hard to understand why Microsoft made so many changes in Windows 8 and 8.1—especially removing the Start menu. These changes force us to relearn how to do many tasks we've been doing the same way for years, and most people—especially seniors—don't particularly like having to relearn this sort of stuff. I know I don't.

There are, however, some options for replacing the absent Start menu in Windows 8.1. These options don't come from Microsoft, but rather from third parties who have created add-on utilities that return the functionality of the old Start menu to the new Windows 8.1 desktop. Most of these utilities are free, and they're all relatively easy to download and install on your Windows 8.1 PC.

I recommend the following Start menu replacement programs:

- Classic Shell (www.classicshell.net)

- IOBit StartMenu8 (www.iobit.com/iobitstartmenu8.php)

- Pokki (www.pokki.com/windows-8-start-menu)

- Start8 (www.stardock.com/products/start8/)

With one of these Start menu replacements installed, you never have to back out to the Start screen to launch new programs. Just log into Windows 8.1, open the desktop, and stay there—using the Start menu replacement just as you did the old Start menu before.

Setting Up Additional User Accounts

Chances are you're not the only person using your computer; it's likely that you'll be sharing your PC with your spouse or kids, at least to some degree. Fortunately, you can configure Windows so that different people using your computer sign on with their own custom settings—and access to their own personal files.

The way to do this is to assign each user in your household her own password-protected *user account*. Anyone trying to access another user's account and files without the password is denied access.

Windows 8.1 lets you create two different types of user accounts—online and local. The default is the online account, which comes with some unique benefits.

 NOTE When you set up an account, you can choose from three different ways to log in. You can log into an account with a traditional password, with a PIN code, or with a picture password that you sketch onscreen with your finger or mouse.

Setting Up a New Account with a Microsoft Account

An online account is linked to a new or existing Microsoft Account (previously known as a Windows Live account), and it lets you synchronize your account settings between multiple computers. (That is, you can log into another Windows 8.1 computer with your Microsoft Account and see the same Start screen, apps, and favorites you have on your home computer.) The only downside to this type of account is that your computer has to be connected to the Internet for you to log on.

In addition, when you use a Microsoft Account on your computer, Windows displays information from other Microsoft sites you use. For example, Windows displays the latest weather conditions in the Weather app, the latest news headlines in the News app, and the latest stock quotes in the Stock app—all based on settings you make when you configure your Microsoft Account. Local accounts cannot access this personalized data.

By default, Windows uses an existing Microsoft Account to create your new Windows user account. So if you have an Outlook.com, Hotmail, Windows Live Mail, Xbox Live, Windows Phone, or other Microsoft account, you can use that account to sign into Windows on your computer. And if you don't yet have a Microsoft Account, it's easy enough to create one while you're setting up a new user account on your PC.

1. Display the Charms bar and click or tap Settings to display the Settings panel.
2. Click or tap Change PC Settings to display the PC Settings page.
3. Click or tap Accounts in the left column to display the Accounts page.
4. Click or tap Other Accounts in the left column.
5. Click or tap the Add a User button.

6. This displays the How Will This Person Sign In page, shown in Figure 5.14. Enter the person's email address into the Email Address box. If this person currently has a Microsoft Account, such as an Outlook.com or Xbox Live account, use that email address for that account. Click or tap Next when you're done.

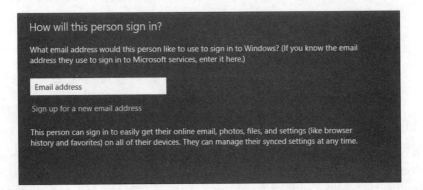

How will this person sign in?

What email address would this person like to use to sign in to Windows? (If you know the email address they use to sign in to Microsoft services, enter it here.)

Email address

Sign up for a new email address

This person can sign in to easily get their online email, photos, files, and settings (like browser history and favorites) on all of their devices. They can manage their synced settings at any time.

FIGURE 5.14

Creating a new user account.

7. If the email address you entered is not for a Microsoft account, you'll be prompted to set up a Microsoft account. Enter the desired password into the New Password and Reenter Password boxes.

8. Enter the person's name into the First Name and Last Name boxes, enter the ZIP Code into the ZIP Code box, and then click Next.

9. When prompted to add security information, enter this person's birthdate, phone number, and alternate email address.

10. Choose a secret question and enter an answer for it, and then click the Next button.

11. Choose whether you want to let Microsoft Advertising use your account information and whether you want to receive promotional offers from Microsoft. (You probably don't want to do either.)

12. Enter the indicated characters into the bottom box, and then click the Next button.

13. When prompted, click the Finish button.

This new user is now able to sign in to Windows from the Lock screen.

TIP If you're adding an account for a child, check the Is This a Child's Account option to turn on Windows' Family Safety Monitoring. With Family Safety Monitoring, you can turn on web filtering (to block access to undesirable websites), limit when the kids can use the PC and what websites they can visit, set limits on games and Windows Store app purchases, and monitor the youngsters' PC activity.

Setting Up a New Local Account

The second type of account is a local account exclusive to your current computer. This is the only type of account you could create in older versions of Windows. In Windows 8.1, you can still use local accounts, even though online accounts are more versatile.

The chief advantage of a local account is privacy. With an online account, all your activities are linked to a central account, which Microsoft stores and manages. With a local account, your offline activities are not transmitted back to Microsoft.

Unfortunately, local accounts cannot provide personalized information for many Windows 8.1 apps. If you want to take full advantage of the News, Weather, Sports, and Stock apps, for example, you don't want to choose the local account option.

Follow these steps to create a new local account:

1. Follow the instructions in the previous section until you get through step 6.

2. Go to the bottom of the screen and click or tap Sign In Without a Microsoft Account.

3. Click or tap the Local Account button.

4. Enter the desired username into the User Name box.

5. Enter the desired password into the Password box and then type it into the Reenter Password box.

6. Enter some sort of hint about the password into the Password Hint box, and then click or tap the Next button.

7. Click or tap the Finish button on the final screen.

Switching Users

If other people are using your computer, they might want to log in with their own accounts. To switch users on a Windows 8.1 computer, follow these steps:

1. Click the Start button or press the Windows key to return to the Start screen.

2. Click or tap your username and picture in the top-right corner to display the pop-up menu.

3. Click or tap the desired user's name.

4. Enter the new user's password and then press Enter or click or tap the next arrow.

Logging Out

When you switch users, both accounts remain active; the original user account is just suspended in the background. If you'd rather log out completely from a given account and return to the Windows Lock screen, follow these steps:

1. Click the Start button or press the Windows key to return to the Start screen.

2. Click or tap your username and picture in the top-right corner to display the pop-up menu.

3. Click or tap Sign Out.

Logging In with Multiple Users

In Chapter 4, "Getting to Know Windows 8.1," you learned how to log into Windows when your computer first starts up. If you have more than one user assigned to Windows, however, the login process is slightly different. Follow these steps:

1. From the Windows Lock screen, press any key on your keyboard or gently tap the screen.

2. By default, the login screen lists the main user of this computer; click or tap the left arrow to display a list of all the users registered for this computer, as shown in Figure 5.15.

3. Click or tap your username.

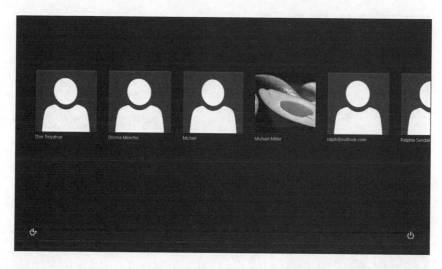

FIGURE 5.15

Logging into Windows with multiple users.

4. Your personal login screen displays. Enter your password, and then press the Enter key or click or tap the right arrow button.

Windows now displays your personal Start screen.

Configuring Other Windows Settings

There are many other Windows system settings that you can configure. In most cases, the default settings work fine, and you don't need to change a thing. However, you *can* change these settings, if you want to or need to.

Configuring Settings from the PC Settings Screen

You configure the most common Windows 8.1 settings from the PC Settings screen. This screen consists of a series of tabs, accessible from the left side of the screen, that present different types of settings.

1. From the Start screen, display the Charms bar, and then click or tap Settings to display the Settings panel.

2. Click or tap Change PC Settings to display the PC Settings screen, shown in Figure 5.16.

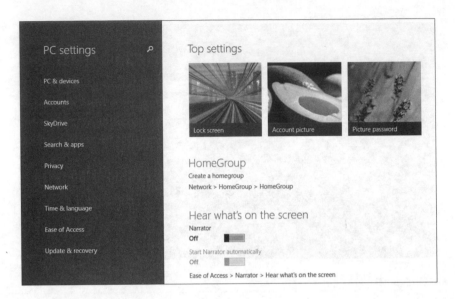

FIGURE 5.16

Configuring Windows from the PC Settings screen.

3. Select PC & Devices from the left column to configure the Windows Lock screen, determine your computer's display settings, add and remove devices from your system, configure your mouse and keyboard, turn on and off autocorrect and highlighting for misspelled words, enable and disable edge and corner functionality, configure your PC's screen and sleep settings, determine how AutoPlay responds when you attach certain types of devices, and display information about your PC.

4. Select the Accounts tab to change your account sign-in options and add new users to your computer.

5. Select the SkyDrive tab to manage your cloud-based storage space on Microsoft's SkyDrive service.

6. Select the Search & Apps tab to manage Windows' search functionality, determine which apps can be shared with other users, configure Windows' system notifications, view installed apps by file size, and choose which apps open which types of files by default.

7. Select the Privacy tab to configure various privacy options, including which apps can use your location information, webcam, and microphone.

8. Select the Network tab to configure various settings for your home network, HomeGroup, and workplace network.

9. Select the Time & Language tab to change your computer's date, time, region, and language settings.

10. Select the Ease of Access tab to configure accessibility options.

11. Select the Update & Recovery tab to configure automatic downloading of necessary system updates, enable or disable File History backup, and access Windows' Refresh and Restore functions.

Configuring Settings from the Traditional Control Panel

You can find even more configuration settings in the Windows Control Panel. The Control Panel is a holdover from older versions of Windows and operates from the Windows desktop. It's a good way to access a more complete set of system settings—even if most of those settings duplicate those found on the Windows PC Settings page.

1. Right-click on the Start button to display the Quick Access menu, and then click Control Panel.

2. This opens the Control Panel on the Windows desktop, as shown in Figure 5.17. Click the link for the type of setting you want to configure.

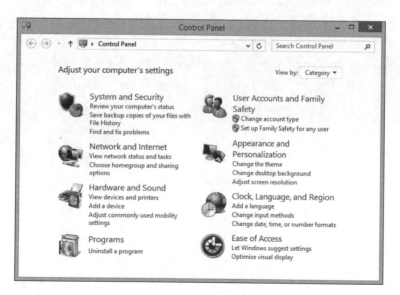

FIGURE 5.17

Configuring Windows from the desktop Control Panel.

THE ABSOLUTE MINIMUM

This chapter showed you pretty much everything you need to know to use Windows 8.1's Start screen and Modern operating environment. Here are the key points to remember:

- The most popular apps and accessories on your system are displayed as clickable tiles on the Start screen. You can display the Start screen at any time by clicking the Start button or pressing the Windows key on your computer keyboard.

- You access key system functions via the Charms bar, which you display by pressing Windows+C on your keyboard.

- You can personalize the Start screen with different colors and background patterns or by displaying the desktop background on the Start screen. You can also change the size of Start screen tiles, organize tiles into groups, and display the Apps screen instead of the Start screen if you like.

- You can customize the Lock screen with a selected image or display a photo slide show instead.

- If you have multiple people using your computer, you can create separate user accounts for each person.

- You can configure additional Windows settings from the PC Settings screen or from the desktop Control Panel.

6

USING THE TRADITIONAL WINDOWS DESKTOP

Not everything in Windows 8.1 is Modern. Yes, you have to use the Start screen or Apps screen to launch your favorite programs, but you're not stuck in the new Modern environment; you can still run traditional software programs on the tried-and-true Windows desktop.

Displaying the Desktop

If you've used a version of Windows prior to Windows 8 (or use a different version of Windows at work), you might wonder what happened to the Windows desktop. Well, it's still there in Windows 8.1; you just have to know where to look.

The desktop used to be the control center of Windows; it was where you launched all your programs and managed all your documents and files. That changed with Windows 8; everything now is done from the new tile-based Start screen. But if you're a more experienced user, you might be more comfortable using the old-style desktop, which is why it's still there in Windows 8.1—just not displayed as prominently as it used to be.

To display the traditional Windows desktop, all you have to do is click or tap the Desktop tile on the Start screen. This displays the Windows 8.1 version of the traditional desktop, shown in Figure 6.1.

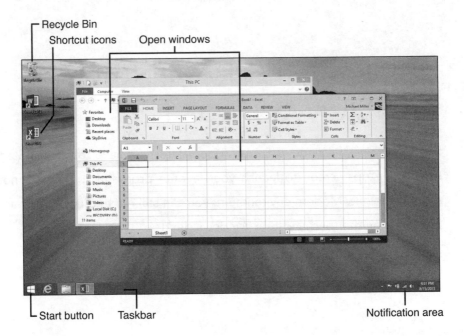

FIGURE 6.1

The Windows 8.1 desktop.

What's on the Windows 8.1 desktop? You'll see the following elements:

- **Taskbar**—Displays icons for your favorite applications and documents, as well as for any open window. By default, you'll see icons for Internet Explorer (the web browser for Windows) and File Explorer (the file management tool for Windows). Right-click an icon to see a "jump list" of recent open documents and other operations for that application.

- **Start button**—Missing in Windows 8 but returned to its rightful place in Windows 8.1, clicking the Start button takes you back to the Start screen. (Unless you're already on the Start screen, in which case it switches back to the desktop or to the last-used app.)

- **Notification area**—Previously known as the system tray, this part of the taskbar displays icons for a handful of key system functions, including the Action Center, power (on notebook PCs), networking/Internet, and audio (volume).

- **Shortcut icons**—These are links to software programs you can place on your desktop; a "clean" desktop includes just one icon—the one for the Windows Recycle Bin.

- **Recycle Bin**—This is where you dump any files you want to delete.

Again, if you're an experienced Windows user, you'll notice that even though the Start button is back, the Start menu is still missing. If you want to open a program, you need to click the Start button to return to the Start screen and launch it from there. (Unless, that is, you've created a desktop shortcut for that item or "pinned" it to the taskbar.)

Opening Desktop Applications

The Windows 8.1 desktop looks and works much the same as the traditional desktop in Windows 7 or Windows Vista, as do traditional desktop applications. All non-Modern programs you launch open in separate windows that can be resized and moved around the desktop. And you can still "pin" application shortcuts directly to the desktop or to the taskbar that appears at the bottom of the desktop.

Creating a Shortcut on the Desktop

If you frequently use a particular desktop program or file, you don't want to exit to the Start screen every time you want to launch that item. Instead, you can create a shortcut to that program or file on the desktop. Here's how:

1. Display the Windows Start or Apps screen and right-click the tile for the particular program to select the tile and open the Options bar for that program.

2. Click Open File Location to open File Explorer with the file selected.

3. Right-click the file and select Create Shortcut.

4. Close the File Explorer window.

Pinning a Program to the Taskbar

You can also pin a shortcut to any desktop program to the taskbar—that strip of icons that appears at the bottom of the desktop screen. Follow these steps:

1. Display the Windows Start or Apps screen and right-click the tile for the particular program to select the tile and open the Options bar for that program.

2. Click Pin to Taskbar.

Opening Desktop Applications

How you open a desktop program depends on where the shortcut to that program is. Here's what you need to know:

- From the Windows Start or Apps screen, click or tap the tile for the program.

- From the Windows Desktop, double-click the shortcut for the program.

- From the taskbar, click the icon for the program.

Working with Windows on the Desktop

Most traditional desktop software programs have different onscreen elements than do newer Modern-style apps. Let's examine how to use those traditional programs.

Moving and Resizing Windows

In Windows 8.1, most newer apps launch full screen. However, traditional software programs operate within the traditional Windows desktop and display in individual onscreen windows. When you open more than one program in this fashion, you get more than one window—and your desktop can quickly become cluttered.

 TIP The cursor changes shape—to a double-ended arrow—when it's positioned over the edge of a window.

There are many ways to deal with this sort of multiple-window desktop clutter. One way is to move a window to a new position. You do this by positioning your cursor over a blank area at the top of the window frame and then clicking and holding down the left button on your mouse. As long as this button is depressed, you can use your mouse to drag the window around the screen. When you release the mouse button, the window stays where you put it.

With Windows 8.1, you can quickly "snap" a window to the left or right side of the desktop. Just drag the window to the left side of the screen to dock it there and resize it to the left half of the desktop; drag the window to the right side of the screen to dock it on that side.

You also can change the size of most windows. You do this by positioning the cursor over the edge of the window—any edge. If you position the cursor on either side of the window, you can resize the width. If you position the cursor on the top or bottom edge, you can resize the height. Finally, if you position the cursor on a corner, you can resize the width and height at the same time.

After the cursor is positioned over the window's edge, press and hold down the left mouse button; then drag the window border to its new size. Release the mouse button to lock in the newly sized window.

Maximizing, Minimizing, and Closing Windows

Another way to manage a window on the Windows desktop is to make it display full screen. You do this by maximizing the window. All you have to do is click the Maximize button in the upper-right corner of the window, as shown in Figure 6.2.

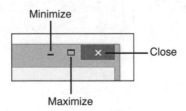

FIGURE 6.2

Use the Minimize, Maximize, and Close buttons to manage your desktop windows.

 TIP You can also "snap" a window full screen by using your mouse to drag the window to the top of the desktop. This automatically maximizes the window.

If the window is already maximized, the Maximize button changes to a Restore Down button. When you click the Restore Down button, the window resumes its previous (premaximized) dimensions.

If you would rather hide the window so that it doesn't clutter your desktop, click the Minimize button. This shoves the window off the desktop, onto the taskbar. The program in the window is still running, however—it's just not on the desktop. To restore a minimized window, all you have to do is click the window's icon on the Windows taskbar (at the bottom of the screen).

If what you really want to do is close the window (and close any program running within the window), just click the window's Close button.

 CAUTION   If you try to close a window that contains a document you haven't saved, you're prompted to save the changes to the document. Because you probably don't want to lose any of your work, click Yes to save the document, and then close the program.

Scrolling Through a Window

Many windows, whether full screen or otherwise, contain more information than can be displayed at once. When you have a long document or web page, only the first part of the document or page is displayed in the window. To view the rest of the document or page, you have to scroll down through the window using the various parts of the scrollbar (shown in Figure 6.3).

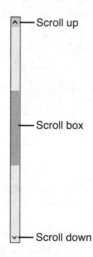

FIGURE 6.3

Use the scrollbar to scroll through long pages.

There are several ways to scroll through a window. To scroll up or down a line at a time, click the up or down arrow on the window's scrollbar. To move to a specific place in a long document, use your mouse to grab the scroll box (between the up and down arrows) and drag it to a new position. You can also click on the scrollbar between the scroll box and the end arrow, so that you scroll one screen at a time.

If your mouse has a scroll wheel, you can use it to scroll through a long document. Just roll the wheel backward or forward to scroll down or up through a window. Likewise, some notebook touchpads let you drag your finger up or down to scroll through a window. And, of course, if you're using a touchscreen display, you can simply swipe your finger downward in the document to scroll down, or swipe upward to scroll up.

Using Dialog Boxes, Tabs, and Buttons

When Windows or a specific app requires a complex set of inputs, you are often presented with a *dialog box*. A dialog box is similar to a form in which you can input various parameters and make various choices—and then register those inputs and choices when you click OK. (Figure 6.4 shows the Save As dialog box, found in many Windows apps.)

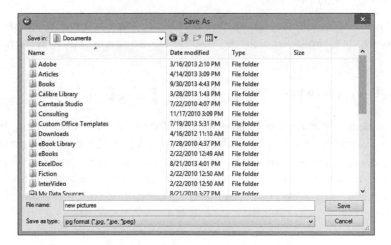

FIGURE 6.4

Use dialog boxes to control various aspects of your Windows applications.

Windows has several types of dialog boxes, each one customized to the task at hand. However, most dialog boxes share a set of common features, which include the following:

- **Buttons**—Most buttons either register your inputs or open an auxiliary dialog box. The most common buttons are OK (to register your inputs and close the dialog box), Cancel (to close the dialog box without registering your inputs), and Apply (to register your inputs without closing the dialog box). Click a button once to activate it.

- **Tabs**—These allow a single dialog box to display multiple "pages" of information. Think of each tab, arranged across the top of the dialog box, as a "thumbtab" to the individual page in the dialog box below it. Click the top of a tab to change to that particular page of information.

- **Text boxes**—These are empty boxes where you type a response. Position your cursor over the empty input box, click your left mouse button, and begin typing.

- **Lists**—These are lists of available choices; lists can either scroll or drop down from what looks like an input box. Select an item from the list with your mouse; you can select multiple items in some lists by holding down the Ctrl key while clicking with your mouse.

- **Check boxes**—These are boxes that let you select (or deselect) various standalone options.

- **Sliders**—These are sliding bars that let you select increments between two extremes, similar to a sliding volume control on an audio system.

Personalizing the Windows Desktop

As I said, the Windows 8.1 desktop is pretty much like the desktop that you might be familiar with from Windows 7 or Windows Vista. (Or even Windows XP!) As with previous versions of Windows, you can personalize the new Windows 8.1 desktop in a number of ways. You can change the color scheme and the desktop background and even "pin" your favorite programs to the taskbar or directly to the desktop.

Changing the Desktop Background

One of the most popular ways to personalize the desktop is to use a favorite picture or color as the desktop background. Follow these steps:

1. Right-click in any open area of the desktop and select Personalize from the pop-up menu.

2. This displays the Personalization window, shown in Figure 6.5. Click Desktop Background to display the Choose Your Desktop Background page.

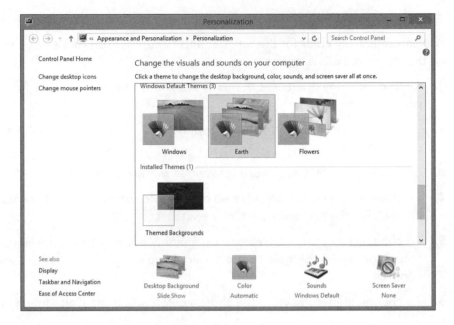

FIGURE 6.5

Personalizing the Windows desktop.

3. Pull down the Picture Location list and select the type of background image
   you want—Windows Desktop Backgrounds (stock background images that
   come with Windows), Pictures Library (your own pictures stored on your PC),
   Top Rated Photos (your favorite photos on your PC), Solid Colors (to display
   a solid-color background with no image), or Computer (to browse your entire
   hard drive for pictures).

4. Browse for and then check the image or color you want to use for the desktop
   background.

5. If the image is a different size from your Windows desktop, pull down the
   Picture Position list and select a display option—Fill (zooms into the picture to
   fill the screen), Fit (fits the image to fill the screen horizontally—but might leave
   black bars above and below the image), Stretch (distorts the picture to fill the
   screen), Tile (displays multiple instances of a smaller image), or Center (displays
   a smaller image in the center of the screen, with black space around it).

6. To display more than one image in a changing desktop slideshow, check more
   than one image. Pull down the Change Picture Every list to determine how quickly
   images change; check the Shuffle box to display images in a random order.

7. Click the Save Changes button when done.

Changing the Color Scheme

You can select any color for the title bar and frame that surrounds open windows on the desktop. Follow these steps:

1. Right-click in any open area of the desktop and select Personalize from the pop-up menu.

2. When the Personalization window displays, click Color to display the available color schemes.

3. Click the color you want to use for various window elements.

4. To change the window color based on the color of the current background image, click the first color tile (color swatch icon).

5. To choose a custom color, click Show Color Mixer and adjust the Hue, Saturation, and Brightness controls. Click Hide Color Mixer to hide these controls.

6. To change the saturation of the chosen color, adjust the Color Intensity slider.

7. Click the Save Changes button when done.

Choosing a Screen Saver

You can opt to display a screen saver when your computer is inactive for a set amount of time. Although this isn't necessary, some people find it entertaining.

 NOTE On older computers with old-fashioned tube-type monitors, a screen saver was necessary to prevent "burn-in" of static screen elements. With newer liquid crystal display (LCD) monitors (which are just like the LCD screen on your living room television set), burn-in isn't an issue—which means you don't have to use a screen saver if you don't want to.

1. Right-click in any open area of the desktop and select Personalize from the pop-up menu.

2. When the Personalization window opens, click Screen Saver to display the Screen Saver Settings window, shown in Figure 6.6.

FIGURE 6.6

Activating the Windows screen saver.

3. Pull down the Screen Saver list to select the type of screen saver to use—3D Text, Blank, Bubbles, Mystify, Photos, Ribbons, or None. (Your computer manufacturer might have installed additional screen savers, as well.)

4. Click the Settings button to adjust the settings for the selected screen saver; each screen saver has its own unique settings.

5. Use the Wait control to select how long your computer must remain inactive before displaying the screen saver.

6. If you want Windows to display the Lock screen when you resume work from screen saver mode, check the On Resume, Display Logon Screen option.

7. To preview the selected screen saver, click the Preview button.

8. Click OK when done.

TIP   Windows also offers several predesigned *themes* that combine background images, color schemes, system sounds, and a screen saver to present a unified look and feel. Some themes even change the color scheme to match the current background picture. To select a theme, right-click the desktop and select Personalize to open the Personalization window. All available themes are now displayed; click a theme to begin using it.

THE ABSOLUTE MINIMUM

This chapter walked you through how to use the traditional Windows desktop in Windows 8.1. Here are the key points to remember:

- All traditional (non-Modern) software programs still run in Windows 8.1, on the traditional desktop.

- You open the desktop by clicking the Desktop tile on the Start screen.

- You get back to the Start screen (to launch desktop apps) by clicking the Start button on the desktop taskbar.

- You can personalize how the desktop looks by choosing custom colors, background images, screen savers, and the like.

WORKING WITH FILES, FOLDERS, AND OTHER STORAGE

Managing the data stored on your computer is vital. After you've saved a file, you might need to copy it to another computer, move it to a new location on your hard drive, rename it, or even delete it. You have to know how to perform all these operations—which means learning how to work with files, folders, and disks in Windows.

Understanding Files and Folders

All the information on your computer is stored in *files*. A file is nothing more than a collection of digital data. The contents of a file can be a document (such as a Word memo or an Excel spreadsheet), a digital photo or music track, or the executable code for a software program.

Every file has its own given name. A defined structure exists for naming files, and you must follow the naming conventions for Windows to understand exactly what file you want when you try to access one. Each filename must consist of two parts, separated by a period—the *name* (to the left of the period) and the *extension* (to the right of the period). A filename can consist of letters, numbers, spaces, and characters and looks something like this: filename.ext.

Windows stores files in *folders*. A folder is like a master file; each folder can contain both files and additional folders. The exact location of a file is called its *path* and contains all the folders leading to the file. For example, a file named filename.doc that exists in the system folder, that is itself contained in the windows folder on your C: drive, has a path that looks like this: C:\windows\system\ filename.doc.

Learning how to use files and folders is a necessary skill for all computer users. You might need to copy files from one folder to another or from your hard disk to a floppy disk. You certainly need to delete files every now and then.

 TIP By default, Windows hides the extensions when it displays filenames. To display extensions in Windows 8.1, right-click the Start button and select Control Panel, select Appearance and Personalization, and then select Folder Options. When the Folder Options dialog box appears, select the View tab; then, in the Advanced Settings list, *uncheck* the Hide Extensions for Known File Types option. Click OK when you're finished.

Using File Explorer

In Windows 8.1, all the items stored on your computer—including programs, documents, and configuration settings—are accessible from *File Explorer*. This is a window on the traditional desktop that displays all the disk drives, folders, subfolders, and files on your computer system. You use File Explorer to find, copy, delete, and launch programs and documents.

NOTE What Microsoft now calls File Explorer used to be called (prior to Windows 8) Windows Explorer. Users may also know File Explorer/Windows Explorer as the My Computer or My Documents folder.

Launching File Explorer

You launch File Explorer from the traditional desktop. Follow these steps:

1. From the Start screen, click or tap the desktop tile to open the desktop.

2. Click the File Explorer icon on the taskbar, as shown in Figure 7.1.

File Explorer

FIGURE 7.1

Launching File Explorer from the desktop taskbar.

 TIP You can also launch File Explorer from the Start screen. Right-click the Start button to display the Quick Access menu, and then select File Explorer.

Exploring the File Explorer Window

When you open File Explorer, you see a Navigation pane on the left and a Contents pane on the right. The Navigation pane is divided into several sections.

The top section, Favorites, lists your most-used folders—Desktop, Downloads, Recent Places, and the like. Next is a SkyDrive section, which lists your folders stored on Microsoft's SkyDrive Internet-based storage service. Below that is a Homegroup section, which lets you access other computers on your network HomeGroup. Next is This PC, which provides access to all the disk drives and devices connected to your computer. Finally, the Network section lets you access all your networked computers.

Click any icon in the Navigation pane to view the contents of that item. For example, when you click This PC, you see the six main folders shown in Figure 7.2—Desktop, Documents, Downloads, Music, Pictures, and Videos. Double-click or tap a folder to view its contents.

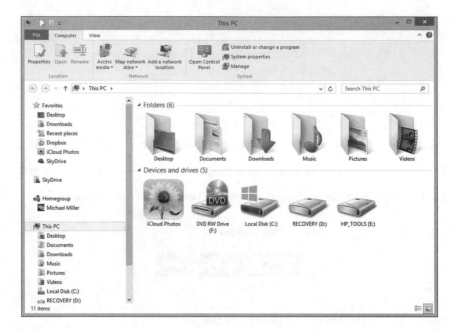

FIGURE 7.2

Navigating through your folders and subfolders with File Explorer.

Working with Ribbons and Tabs

The Windows 8/8.1 version of File Explorer displays what is called a *ribbon* at the top of the window. This ribbon contains all the operations and commands you need to manage your files and folders, organized into three tabs—File, Computer, and View. The available tabs change depending on what you're viewing in File Explorer; for example, when you're viewing the contents of a folder, you see the File, Home, Share, and View tabs.

If the ribbon is minimized, you'll see only the names of the tabs. To view the commands on a given tab, click or tap that tab to expand the tab downward and make visible the tab's commands. You can maximize the entire ribbon (expand it downward) by clicking or tapping the down arrow at the right side of the ribbon bar.

From time to time, you see additional tabs on the ribbon, beyond the basic four. That's because Windows displays additional commands relevant to the task at hand. For example, if you select one of the four library icons, you see a Manage tab that includes commands for managing the library.

Navigating the Folders on Your PC

After you've launched File Explorer, you can navigate through all your folders and subfolders in several ways:

 NOTE A *subfolder* is a folder that is contained within another folder. Multiple subfolders can be nested in this fashion.

- To view the contents of a disk or folder, double-click or tap the selected item.

- To move back to the disk or folder previously selected, click or tap the Back button (left arrow) on the toolbar beneath the ribbon.

- To choose from the history of disks and folders previously viewed, click or tap the down arrow in the Address bar at the top of the File Explorer window and select a disk or folder.

- If you've moved back through multiple disks or folders, you can move forward to the next folder by clicking or tapping the Forward button (right arrow) on the toolbar.

- Go directly to any disk or folder by entering the path in the Address bar (in the format x:\folder\subfolder) and pressing Enter.

- Move backward through the "bread crumb" path in the Address bar. Click or tap any previous folder location (separated by arrows) to display that particular folder.

 TIP Click or tap any arrow between locations in the Address bar to view additional paths from that location.

Viewing Files and Folders

There's no set way to view the files and folders stored on your computer. In fact, File Explorer has several options to change the way your files and folders are displayed.

Changing the Way Files Are Displayed

You can choose to view the contents of a folder in a variety of ways. To change the file view, select the View tab in the ribbon bar, shown in Figure 7.3. From here you can select from eight available views:

- Extra large icons
- Large icons
- Medium icons
- Small icons

- List
- Details
- Tiles
- Content

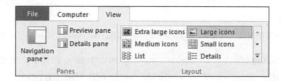

FIGURE 7.3

Use the View tab to change how files are displayed.

 TIP Any of the Icon views are good for working with graphics files or for getting a quick thumbnail glance at a file's contents. The Details view is better if you're looking for files by date or size.

Sorting Files and Folders

When viewing files in File Explorer, you can sort your files and folders in a number of ways. To do this, select the Views tab in the ribbon bar and then click or tap the Sort By button. You can then choose to sort by Name, Date Modified, Type, Size, Date Created, Folder Path, Authors, Categories, Tags, or Title. You can also choose to sort the items in either ascending or descending order.

If you want to view your files in alphabetical order, choose to sort by Name. If you want to see all similar files grouped together, choose to sort by Type. If you want to sort your files by the date and time you last edited them, choose the Date Modified option. And if you want to sort by a user-applied file tag (assuming you've done this in the file's host program), choose the Tags option.

Grouping Files and Folders

You can also configure File Explorer to group the files in your folder, which can make it easier to identify particular files. For example, if you sort your files by time and date modified, they're grouped by date (Today, Yesterday, Last Week, and so on). If you sort your files by type, they're grouped by file extension, and so on.

To turn on grouping, click or tap the Group By button on the View tab of the ribbon bar. You can then choose to group by any of the same parameters available for sorting. File Explorer groups your files and folders by the selected criteria.

Searching for Files

As organized as you might be, you might not always be able to find the specific files you want. Fortunately, Windows 8.1 offers an easy way to locate difficult-to-find files, via the Instant Search function. Instant Search indexes all the files stored on your hard disk (including email messages) by type, title, and contents. So you can search for a file by extension, filename, or keywords within the document.

To use the Instant Search feature, follow these steps:

1. From within File Explorer, locate the search box at the top right of the window.

2. Enter one or more keywords into the search box.

3. Press Enter.

Windows displays a list of files that match your search criteria. Double-click or double-tap any icon to open that file.

 TIP You can also search for files from anywhere in Windows. Press Win+S to display the Search pane, enter your query, and press Enter.

Performing Basic File and Folder Operations

In Windows 8.1, you accomplish most of the file and folder operations you want to do via the Home tab on the ribbon bar, shown in Figure 7.4. You use the buttons on this tab to move, copy, and delete items—as well as perform other key operations.

FIGURE 7.4

Use the Home tab to perform essential file and folder operations.

Creating New Folders

The more files you create, the harder it is to organize and find things on your hard disk. When the number of files you have becomes unmanageable, you need to create more folders—and subfolders—to better categorize your files.

To create a new folder, follow these steps:

1. Navigate to the drive or folder where you want to place the new folder.

2. Select the Home tab on the toolbar.

3. Click or tap the New Folder button.

4. A new, empty folder appears within the File Explorer window, with the filename New Folder highlighted.

5. Type a name for your folder (which overwrites the New Folder name), and press Enter.

 CAUTION Folder and filenames can include up to 255 characters—including many special characters. Some special characters, however, are "illegal," meaning that you *can't* use them in folder or filenames. Illegal characters include the following: \ / : * ? " < > |.

The one part of the filename you should never change is the extension—the part that comes after the "dot." That's because Windows and other software programs recognize different types of program files and documents by their extension. This is why, by default, Windows hides these file extensions—so you can't change them by mistake.

Renaming Files and Folders

When you create a new file or folder, it helps to give it a name that somehow describes its contents. Sometimes, however, you might need to change a file's name. Fortunately, Windows makes it relatively easy to rename an item.

To rename a file (or folder), follow these steps:

1. Click the file or folder you want to rename.

2. Select the Home tab on the ribbon bar.

3. Click or tap the Rename button to highlight the filename.

4. Type a new name for your file or folder (which overwrites the current name), and press Enter.

Copying Files

Copying a file lets you re-create that file in a different location, either on your computer's hard drive or on some sort of external media. Here's how to do it:

 NOTE   It's important to remember that copying is different from moving. When you *copy* an item, the item remains in its original location—plus you have the new copy. When you *move* an item, the file is no longer present in the original location—all you have is the item in the new location.

1. Select the item you want to copy.

2. Select the Home tab on the ribbon bar.

3. Click or tap the Copy To button; this displays a pull-down menu of popular and recently visited locations.

4. To copy directly to one of the listed locations, click or tap that location from the list.

5. To copy to another location, click or tap Choose Location from the pull-down menu to display the Copy Items dialog box. Navigate to the new location for the item, and then click or tap the Copy button.

That's it. You've just copied the file from one location to another.

Moving Files

Moving a file (or folder) is different from copying it. Moving cuts the item from its previous location and places it in a new location. Copying leaves the original item where it was *and* creates a copy of the item elsewhere.

In other words, when you copy something, you end up with two of it. When you move something, you have only the one instance.

To move a file, follow these steps:

1. Select the item you want to move.

2. Select the Home tab on the ribbon bar.

3. Click or tap the Move To button; this displays a list of popular and recently visited locations.

4. To move an item to one of the listed locations, click or tap that location from the list.

5. To move the item to another location, click or tap Choose Location on the pull-down menu to display the Move Items dialog box. Navigate to the new location for the item, and then click or tap the Move button.

Deleting Files

Too many files eat up too much hard disk space—which is a bad thing because you only have so much disk space. (Music and video files, in particular, can chew up big chunks of your hard drive.) Because you don't want to waste disk space, you should periodically delete the files (and folders) you no longer need.

Deleting a file is as easy as following these simple steps:

1. Select the file or files you want to delete.

2. Select the Home tab on the ribbon bar.

3. Click or tap the Delete button.

This simple operation sends the file to the Windows Recycle Bin, which is kind of a trash can for deleted files. (It's also a trash can that periodically needs to be dumped—as we discuss momentarily.)

 TIP You can also delete a file by selecting it and then pressing the Delete key on your computer keyboard.

Working with the Recycle Bin

As just discussed, all recently deleted files are stored in what Windows calls the Recycle Bin. This is a special folder on your hard disk that temporarily stores all deleted items—which is a good thing.

Restoring Deleted Files

Have you ever accidentally deleted the wrong file? If so, you're in luck, thanks to the Recycle Bin. As you now know, Windows stores all the files you delete in the Recycle Bin, at least temporarily. If you've recently deleted a file, it should still be in the Recycle Bin folder.

To "undelete" a file from the Recycle Bin, follow these steps:

1. From the Windows desktop, double-click or tap the Recycle Bin icon (shown in Figure 7.5) to open the Recycle Bin folder.

FIGURE 7.5

The Recycle Bin, where all your deleted files end up.

2. Click or tap the file(s) you want to restore.

3. Select the Manage tab on the ribbon bar, shown in Figure 7.6.

4. Click or tap the Restore the Selected Items button.

FIGURE 7.6

Managing deleted files in the Recycle Bin.

The deleted file is copied back to its original location, ready for continued use.

Managing the Recycle Bin

Deleted files do not stay in the Recycle Bin indefinitely. When you've deleted enough files to exceed the space allocated for these files, the oldest files in the Recycle Bin are automatically and permanently deleted from your hard disk.

If you'd rather dump the Recycle Bin manually (and thus free up some hard disk space), follow these steps:

1. Double-click or tap the Recycle Bin icon on your desktop to open the Recycle Bin folder.

2. Select the Manage tab on the ribbon bar.

3. Click or tap the Empty the Recycle Bin button.

4. When the confirmation dialog box appears, click or tap Yes to completely erase the files; click or tap No to continue storing the files in the Recycle Bin.

Working with Compressed Folders

Really big files can be difficult to move or copy. They're especially difficult to transfer to other users, whether by email or USB drive.

Fortunately, Windows includes a way to make big files smaller. *Compressed folders* (sometimes called *zip files*) take big files and compress their size, which makes them easier to copy or move. After you've transferred the file, you can uncompress the file to its original state.

Compressing a File

Compressing one or more files is a relatively easy task from within any Windows folder. Just follow these steps:

1. Select the file(s) you want to compress.

2. Select the Share tab on the ribbon bar, shown in Figure 7.7.

3. Click or tap the Zip button.

FIGURE 7.7

Use the Share tab to compress large files to a zip file.

Windows now creates a new folder that contains compressed versions of the file(s) you selected. (This folder is distinguished by a little zipper on the folder icon.) You can now copy, move, or email this folder, which is a lot smaller than the original file(s).

 NOTE The compressed folder is actually a file with a .ZIP extension, so you can use it with other compression/decompression programs, such as WinZip.

Extracting Files from a Compressed Folder

The process of decompressing a file is actually an *extraction* process. That's because you *extract* the original file(s) from the compressed folder. Follow these steps:

1. Select the compressed folder.

2. Select the Extract tab on the ribbon bar.

3. Pull down the Extract To list and select a location for the extracted files.

4. Click or tap the Extract All button.

Copying Files to Another Computer

Of course, you're not limited to copying and moving files from one location to another on a single PC. You can also copy files to other PCs via either a network connection or some sort of portable disk drive.

Copying Files over a Network

We talk more about network operations in Chapter 11, "Setting Up a Home Network." For now, it's important to know that if your PC is connected to a network and has file sharing activated, you can copy and move files from one network computer to another just as you can within folders on a single computer.

Copying Files with a Portable Drive

If you're not on a network, you can use a portable drive to transport files from one computer to another. The most popular type of portable drive today is the *USB drive* (sometimes called a *flash drive* or *thumb drive*), such as the one shown in Figure 7.8, which stores computer data in flash memory. You can find USB drives with capacities up to 32GB—more than big enough to hold even your biggest files.

FIGURE 7.8

Use a USB drive to transport files from one computer to another.

To use a USB drive, simply insert the device into an open USB port on your computer. After you've inserted it, the drive appears as a new drive in the This PC section of the File Explorer navigation pane. Double-click or double-tap the USB drive icon to view the contents of the drive; you can then copy and paste files from your hard drive to the USB drive and vice versa. When you're finished copying files, just remove the USB device. It's that simple.

Copying Files via Email

Another popular way to send files from one computer to another is via email. You can send any file as an email *attachment*; a file is literally attached to an email message. When the message is sent, the recipient can open or save the attached file when reading the message.

To learn how to send files as email attachments, turn to Chapter 16, "Sending and Receiving Email."

Working with Microsoft SkyDrive

In addition to the local storage found on your personal computer, Microsoft offers online storage for all your documents and data, via its SkyDrive service. When you store your files on SkyDrive, you can access them via any computer or mobile device connected to the Internet.

 NOTE Online file storage, such as that offered by SkyDrive, Apple's iCloud, and Google Drive, is called *cloud storage*. The advantage of cloud storage is that you can access files from any computer (work, home, or other) at any location. You're not limited to using a given file on one particular computer.

You use the Windows SkyDrive app, included with Windows 8.1, to manage all your online files. You can also use the SkyDrive app to manage your local files— although File Explorer is easier for that.

To use the SkyDrive app, follow these steps:

1. From the Windows Start screen, click or tap the SkyDrive tile to launch the SkyDrive app.

2. By default, SkyDrive displays your online files. To view and manage your local files, click the SkyDrive down arrow and select This PC.

3. As you can see in Figure 7.9, your SkyDrive files are stored in folders— Documents, Favorites, Photos, and so forth. Click a folder to view its contents.

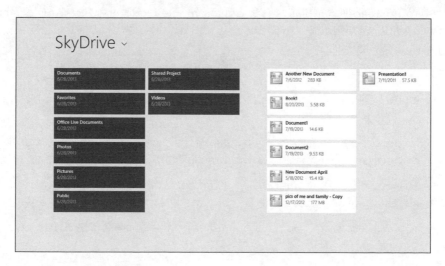

FIGURE 7.9

Viewing online folders and files in the SkyDrive app.

4. Click a file to view it or, in the case of an Office document, open it in its host application.

5. To copy, cut, or rename a file, right-click the file to display the Options bar, shown in Figure 7.10, and then select the action you want to perform.

FIGURE 7.10

Using the SkyDrive app to manage your files.

6. To download a file from SkyDrive to your local hard disk, click Make Offline in the Options bar.

 NOTE Microsoft gives you 7GB of storage in your free SkyDrive account, which is more than enough to store most users' documents, digital photos, and the like. If you need more storage, you can purchase an additional 20GB for $10/year.

THE ABSOLUTE MINIMUM

Here are the key points to remember from this chapter:

*   You manage your files and folders from File Explorer, which runs on the traditional Windows desktop.

*   Most common file and folder operations are found on the Home tab of the File Explorer ribbon bar.

*   If you accidentally delete a file, you might be able to recover it by opening the Recycle Bin window.

*   If you need to share a really big file, consider compressing it into a compressed folder (also known as a zip file).

*   To copy a file to another PC, you can copy the file over a network, send the file as an email attachment, or copy the file to a portable USB drive.

*   You can also store your files online, using the Microsoft SkyDrive app and service.

8

CONNECTING OTHER DEVICES TO YOUR PC— AND YOUR PC TO OTHER DEVICES

If you just purchased a brand-new, right-out-of-the-box personal computer, it probably came equipped with all the components you could ever want— or so you think. At some point in the future, however, you might want to expand your system by adding a printer, a scanner, an external hard drive, better speakers, a different mouse or keyboard, or something equally new and exciting.

Adding new hardware to your system is relatively easy if you know what you're doing. That's where this chapter comes in.

Getting to Know the Most Popular Peripherals

When it comes to adding stuff to your PC, what are the most popular peripherals? Here's a list of hardware you can add to or upgrade on your system:

- **Hard drive**—Adds more storage capacity to your system or performs periodic backups from your main hard disk. The easiest type of hard drive to add is an external unit, which typically connects via USB and costs under $100. If you have a traditional desktop PC, you might also be able to add a second internal drive inside your system unit, but that's a lot more work.

 NOTE Learn more about adding a hard drive to your system in Chapter 10, "Adding Storage and Backup."

- **Solid-state drive**—On many systems, a replacement for the traditional hard drive. A solid-state drive has less storage space than a hard drive but is much faster in terms of accessing that data. Some systems use a solid-state drive to store the Windows operating system (which makes everything run faster) and a separate hard drive to store files and other data.

- **Memory card reader**—Enables you to read data from devices (such as digital cameras) that use various types of flash memory cards.

- **USB memory device**—Provides gigabytes of removable storage; you can transport the USB memory device from one computer to another, connecting to each PC's USB port.

- **Monitor**—Replaces or supplements the built-in display on a notebook computer or replaces the existing monitor on a desktop system (typically with a larger screen).

- **Video card**—On traditional desktop PCs, upgrades your system's video playback and graphics, typically for video editing or playing visually demanding PC games.

- **Sound card**—On traditional desktop PCs, improves the audio capabilities of your systems; this is particularly important if you're playing state-of-the-art PC games, watching surround-sound DVD movies, or mixing and recording your own digital audio.

- **Speakers**—Upgrades the quality of your computer's sound system. (Surround-sound speaker systems with subwoofers are particularly popular, especially with PC gamers.)

- **Keyboard**—Supplements a notebook's built-in keyboard with a larger, more fully featured model, or upgrades the capabilities of a desktop's included keyboard.

- **Mouse**—Provides a more traditional input in place of a notebook PC's touchpad, or upgrades the capabilities of a desktop system's mouse. (For example, many users like to upgrade from wired to wireless mice.)

- **Joystick or other game controller**—Enables you to get better action with your favorite games.

- **CD/DVD drive (burner)**—Adds recordable/rewritable capabilities to a netbook or ultrabook that doesn't have a built-in CD/DVD drive. (Some CD/DVD drives also have Blu-ray capability.)

- **Printer**—Improves the quality of your printouts, adds color to your printouts, or adds photo-quality printing to your system.

 NOTE   Learn more about adding a printer or scanner to your system in Chapter 9, "Working with Printers."

- **Scanner**—Enables you to scan photographs and documents into a digital format to store on your computer's hard drive.

- **Webcam**—Enables you to send real-time video to friends and family.

- **Wireless router**—Enables you to create a wireless network in your home—and share your broadband Internet connection among multiple computers.

- **Wireless network adapter**—Enables you to connect a desktop computer to any wireless network.

Adding New Hardware to Your System

Everything that's hooked to your PC is connected via some type of *port*. A port is simply an interface between your PC and another device—either internally (inside your PC's system unit) or externally (via a connector on the back of the system unit).

Given the choice, the easiest way to add a new device to your system is to connect it externally. In fact, if you have an all-in-one desktop, notebook, or tablet computer, it's the *only* way to add new hardware; you can't get inside the case to add anything else. And even if you have a traditional desktop PC with a separate system unit, it's still a whole lot easier to add a new device via an external USB port than it is to open the case and add it that way.

NOTE No matter how you're connecting a new device, make sure to read the installation instructions for the new hardware and follow the manufacturer's instructions and advice.

The most common external connector today is the USB port, like the one shown in Figure 8.1. USB is a great concept (and truly "universal") in that virtually every type of new peripheral comes in a USB version. Want to add a second hard disk? Don't open the PC case; connect an external drive via USB. Want to add a new printer? Connect a USB printer. Want to connect to a home network? Don't bother with Ethernet cards; get a USB-compatible wireless adapter.

FIGURE 8.1

A USB port on a notebook PC. (Photograph courtesy Aidan C. Siegel via the Creative Commons Attribution-Share Alike 3.0 Unported license.)

Not that there aren't other types of ports that you might occasionally run into or need to use. For example, if you want to connect your PC to your TV (which we discuss later in this chapter), you'll probably connect a cable to your PC's HDMI port. (HDMI is a special kind of connection for transmitting high-definition audio/ video.) And some high-speed devices (such as really big and expensive hard drives) might connect via FireWire, which is kind of a faster version of USB. But for most purposes, USB is all you need to know about and use.

USB is popular because it's so easy to use. When you're connecting a USB device, not only do you not have to open your PC's case, but you don't even have to turn off your system when you add the new device. That's because USB devices are *hot swappable*. That means you can just plug the new device into the port, and Windows automatically recognizes it in real time.

 TIP   If you connect too many USB devices, it's possible to run out of USB connectors on your PC. If that happens to you, buy an add-on USB hub for $25 or so, which lets you plug multiple USB peripherals into a single USB port.

To connect a new USB device, follow these steps:

1. Find a free USB port on your system unit and connect the new peripheral.

2. Windows should automatically recognize the new peripheral and install the proper device driver automatically.

That's it! The only variation on this procedure is if the peripheral's manufacturer recommends using its own installation program, typically provided on an installation CD. If this is the case, follow the manufacturer's instructions to perform the installation and setup.

 NOTE   A *device driver* is a small software program that enables your PC to communicate with and control a specific device. Windows includes built-in device drivers for many popular peripherals. If Windows doesn't include a particular driver, you typically can find the driver on the peripheral's installation disk or on the peripheral manufacturer's website.

Connecting Portable Devices to Your PC

These days, a lot of the devices you connect to your PC really aren't computer peripherals. Instead, they are gadgets that you use on their own but plug into your PC to share files.

What kinds of portable devices are we talking about? Here's a short list:

• Portable music players, such as Apple's popular iPod and iPhone

• Smartphones, including iPhones, Android phones, and Windows phones

• Tablets, such as the Apple iPad or Kindle Fire

• Digital cameras

- Digital camcorders

- USB memory devices

All these devices connect to a USB port on your PC, which makes for an easy hookup. As mentioned earlier, USB ports are hot swappable, which means that all you have to do is connect the device to the proper port—no major configuration necessary. In some cases, the first time you connect your device to your PC, you need to run some sort of installation utility to install the device's software on your PC's hard drive. Each subsequent time you connect the device, your PC should recognize it automatically and launch the appropriate software program.

After your portable device is connected to your PC, what you do next is up to you. Most of the time, you'll be transferring files either from your PC to the portable device, or vice versa. Use the device's software program to perform these operations, or use File Explorer to copy files back and forth.

For example, you can use a USB memory device as a removable and portable memory storage system. One of these USB drives is smaller than a pack of chewing gum and can hold several gigabytes' worth of data in electronic flash memory. Plug a USB memory device into your PC's USB port, and your PC recognizes it just as if it were another disk drive. You can then copy files from your PC to the USB drive to take your work (or your digital music or photo files) with you.

For more detailed information, see the instructions that came with your portable device.

Connecting Your PC to Your Living Room TV

As you'll no doubt soon discover, there are a lot of good movies and TV shows on the Internet that you can watch on your PC—often for free. Although you can watch this programming on your computer screen, that might be a little small for those of us more familiar with the large screen experience.

 NOTE Learn more about finding movies and TV shows on the Internet in Chapter 28, "Watching Movies, TV Shows, and Other Videos."

Fortunately, there might be a way to connect your computer to your living room TV and watch your Internet-based programming in full big-screen glory. It's all a matter of which ports you have on the back (or side) of your PC and whether you have similar connectors on your flat-screen television.

The most common way to connect a computer to a flat-screen TV is via HDMI. You might already be familiar with HDMI, which is used to connect many Blu-ray players, cable boxes, and the like to high-definition television sets. (Figure 8.2 shows an HDMI port on a typical notebook PC.) HDMI is nice because it feeds both video and audio via a single cable, in full 1080p high def.

FIGURE 8.2

An HDMI port on a notebook PC.

 NOTE Some PCs, especially tablets and notebooks, feature mini-HDMI connectors. In this instance, you need a special HDMI cable with a mini-connector on one end (to connect to your PC) and a standard-sized connector on the other (to connect to your TV). You should be able to find such cables at your local electronics store.

If your computer has an HDMI connector, it's easy to connect an HDMI cable between your PC and an HDMI input on your TV. Connect that single cable, and the picture and sound (in full 5.1-channel surround!) from whatever you're watching on your computer is fed to your flat-screen TV.

If your PC doesn't have an HDMI port, you might still be able to connect it to your TV. Here's what to look for:

- Some TVs have a standard VGA connector (typically labeled "PC") that can connect (via a standard VGA cable) to the VGA or monitor output found on almost all PCs.

- If your computer has a DVI output, you can connect a DVI-to-HDMI adapter to this port and then use an HDMI cable to connect to your TV. Because DVI is video only, you also need to run an audio cable from your PC's audio output to your TV's audio inputs.

 NOTE DVI (short for *digital video interface*) is a digital connection for transmitting video signals and is often used to connect computers to LCD monitors. Both DVI and HDMI are digital formats, which is why you can convert DVI to HDMI.

- If your computer has an S-Video or single composite video output, you can connect a cable from this port to the similar input on your TV. (Know, however, that S-Video and composite video are standard resolution only; they do not transmit a high-definition video signal.)

After you've connected your computer to your TV, you can see and hear everything your PC is doing through your TV. Just connect to the movie or TV website of choice, switch your TV to the appropriate video input, and get out the popcorn!

 TIP Windows 8.1 includes support for Miracast technology, which lets you beam your PC's screen contents wirelessly to a Miracast-compatible TV or streaming media box. With Miracast, you can queue up your TV or movie programming on your computer and then watch it on your big-screen TV. As of this writing, however, there aren't a lot of TVs with Miracast built in; that may change over time.

THE ABSOLUTE MINIMUM

Here's what you need to know if you're adding new equipment to your computer system:

- The easiest way to connect a new peripheral is via an external USB connection.

- In most cases, Windows automatically recognizes your new hardware and automatically installs all the necessary drivers.

- Connecting a portable device, such as a portable music player or digital camera, is also done via an external USB port.

- You can connect your PC to your TV, typically via HDMI, to watch web-based programming on the bigger display.

WORKING WITH PRINTERS

Your computer monitor displays images in real time, but they're fleeting. To conveniently create permanent visual records of your work, you need to add a printer to your system. Printers create hard copy output from your software programs—or just make prints of your favorite pictures.

Selecting the Right Printer for Your Needs

You can choose from various types of printers for your system, depending on your exact printing needs. The two main types of printers today are inkjet and laser printers. Both are suitable for home use.

Understanding Inkjet Printers

The most popular type of printer for home use is the *inkjet* printer, like the one shown in Figure 9.1. An inkjet printer works by shooting jets of ink to the paper's surface to create the printed image.

FIGURE 9.1

A typical color inkjet printer. (Photo courtesy HP.)

To work, an inkjet printer needs to be filled with one or more replaceable ink cartridges. The typical inkjet printer has two cartridges—one that contains red, yellow, and blue ink (for color printing) and another with just black ink. You'll likely use up the black ink cartridge first because you'll probably print more single-color text documents than full-color pictures. Your printer should display a message on its front panel when a cartridge is running low; replacement ink cartridges are available at most home office stores.

Inkjet printers are typically lower priced than laser printers. That's because they're not quite as heavy duty as laser printers, which are more suited for larger print jobs. An inkjet printer is fine for typical home use, but it might not hold up as well in a busy office environment.

Understanding Laser Printers

Laser printers work a little differently than inkjet models. Instead of shooting liquid ink at the paper, a laser printer works much like a traditional copying machine, applying powdered ink (toner) to paper by using a small laser.

As such, laser printers (like the one in Figure 9.2) typically work a little faster than similar inkjets, and they produce slightly sharper results. This makes laser printers better suited for heavy-duty use, such as what you might get in an office environment.

FIGURE 9.2

A typical laser printer. (Photo courtesy HP.)

Of course, everything comes at a cost, and laser printers tend to be a little bigger and more expensive than comparable inkjet models. In addition, where most ink-jets offer full-color printing, not all laser printers do; you can find both black-and-white and color laser printers for home and office use.

Black and White or Color?

Especially when considering a laser printer, you'll have your choice of either black-and-white or color printers. (Almost all consumer inkjet printers today are full color.) Black-and-white printers are faster than color printers and better if you're printing memos, letters, and other single-color documents. Color printers, however, are great if you have kids, and they're essential if you want to print pictures taken with a digital camera.

As such, most home users tend to choose color printers—they're just more versatile.

Understanding Multifunction Printers

You also have the option of purchasing what is called a "multifunction" printer. This combines a traditional desktop printer with a scanner, a fax machine, and a copier—all in one multifunction unit. As you can see in Figure 9.3, multifunction printers are slightly larger than single-function printers. You can find multifunction printers of both the inkjet and laser varieties; these printers can be either black and white or color.

FIGURE 9.3

A *multifunction color laser printer. (Photo courtesy Brother.)*

If you need all these functions, by all means consider such a multifunction printer. Know, however, that you'll pay extra to get all this functionality; single-function printers are going to be more affordable than multifunction units.

Adding a Printer to Your System

Most printers connect directly to your computer, typically via USB. Some printers, however, can connect to your home network, typically via Wi-Fi, without being connected to a single PC.

Connecting a Printer Directly to Your Computer

In most instances, connecting a USB printer to your computer is a simple process:

1. Connect one end of a USB cable to the USB port on your printer.

2. Connect the other end of the USB cable to a USB port on your computer.

3. Connect the printer to a power outlet.

4. Turn on the printer.

Windows should automatically recognize the new printer and install the proper device driver automatically. Follow the onscreen instructions to finish the installation.

 NOTE It's possible that your printer might offer additional functionality, such as scanning, which is common in multifunction units. If so, you might need to install the printer and any necessary software from the accompanying installation CD or DVD. As always, follow the manufacturer's instructions for best results.

Connecting a Printer to Your Network

If you're sharing a printer between multiple computers on your home network, you might want to go with a network printer—one that connects to your wireless network but doesn't physically connect to any single computer. The primary benefit of a network printer is that you can place it anywhere in your home; because it's not tethered to a given PC, it doesn't have to sit next to any computer. In fact, most network printers can connect to your network wirelessly or via Ethernet.

In general, the setup goes something like this:

1. Turn on your printer.

2. Connect the printer to your wireless router, either via Wi-Fi or Ethernet. In most instances, the printer automatically detects and connects to your network.

3. If your wireless network has a security password (and it should), enter that password on your printer's keypad.

Follow any additional instructions in your printer's installation manual. When the printer is properly configured, it should appear as a printing option for all computers connected to your network.

Printing to Your System's Printer

Printing from a given app is typically as easy as clicking or tapping the Print button. In some instances, the print function might be contained within a pull-down File or Print menu.

In any case, one-click printing is the norm. That is, you click the Print button, and printing ensues. In most programs, however, you can fine-tune your printing options by selecting the File menu and clicking Print. This typically displays a Print Options dialog box or page, like the one shown in Figure 9.4. From here you can select which printer to print to, which pages to print, how many copies to print, whether to print in portrait (vertical paper) or landscape (horizontal paper) modes, and so forth.

FIGURE 9.4

The print options page in Microsoft Word.

Know, however, that print functionality does differ from program to program. Make sure you consult a given app's help files if you need assistance in configuring various print options.

THE ABSOLUTE MINIMUM

Here are the key points to remember when connecting and configuring your new computer:

- There are two types of consumer printers in use today: inkjet and laser.

- An inkjet printer is typically the lowest cost option; it works by shooting liquid ink onto sheets of paper.

- Laser printers are typically faster, more durable, and more expensive than inkjet models; laser printers work by applying solid ink (toner) to sheets of paper via laser.

- Both inkjet and laser printers are available in black-and-white and color models.

- Multifunction printers add scanning, copying, and faxing functionality to a basic printer.

- A printer can connect directly to a PC via USB or (in some models) wirelessly to your home network.

10

ADDING STORAGE AND BACKUP

Most desktop and traditional notebook computers these days come with a fairly large amount of internal storage, anywhere from 320GB (for a basic notebook) up to 4TB (that's four *terabytes*—one of which is equivalent to one thousand gigabytes) or even more. That's plenty of storage for most people, even if you download a lot of music and videos or store a ton of digital photos.

However, today's ultrabook and tablet PCs don't have that much internal storage because they don't have hard drives. (These lightweight computers use solid-state flash storage that typically provides no more than 128GB to 256GB storage capacity.) And tablet PCs have even less onboard storage.

What do you do, then, if you need more storage space for your valuable files? The solution is to add more capacity with an external hard drive. (And you can use that same external drive to back up your data.)

Understanding External Storage

Most traditional computers use internal hard drives to store digital data—software applications, documents, photos, music, and so forth. This same hard disk technology is available in external drives that connect to your computer via USB.

When it has been connected, an external hard disk appears as another drive in the Computer section of File Explorer. You can access it just like your internal hard drive, and you can use it to store files or software programs.

You can find external hard drives in a variety of capacities, starting at 500GB or so and going all the way up to 4TB. Most manufacturers offer traditional desktop hard drives, like the one in Figure 10.1, as well as smaller portable drives, like the one in Figure 10.2. As you might suspect, the portable drives are designed to work better with portable notebook PCs.

FIGURE 10.1

A typical desktop external hard drive. (Photo courtesy Seagate.)

FIGURE 10.2

A small portable external drive. (Photo courtesy Western Digital.)

Connecting an External Hard Drive

In most instances, connecting an external hard drive is a simple two-step process:

1. Connect the external hard drive to a power source.

2. Use a USB cable to connect the external hard drive to a USB port on your computer.

Some desktop hard drives have power switches. If yours does, you need to turn it on, as well.

When the hard drive is powered up and connected to your computer, it should appear in the This PC section of File Explorer as a new drive. It should take the next available letter; for example, if your internal hard drive is drive C: and your CD/DVD drive is drive D: then the new external drive should be labeled as drive E:.

Backing Up Your Important Files

Protecting your valuable data—including all your music and personal photos—is something you need to do. After all, what would you do if your computer crashed or your hard disk died? Do you really want to lose all your valuable documents and files?

Of course you don't—which is why you need to back up your key files on a regular basis.

Backing Up to an External Hard Drive

The easiest way to back up your files is with an external hard drive. Get a big enough external drive (about the same size as your main hard disk), and you can copy your entire hard disk to the external drive. Then, if your system ever crashes, you can restore your backed-up files from the external drive to your computer's system unit.

Most external hard drives come with some sort of backup software installed, or you can use a third-party backup program. The backup process can be automated, so that it occurs once a day or once a week and only backs up those new or changed files since your last backup.

Whichever program you use, you should back up your data at least weekly—if not daily. That way you won't lose much fresh data if the worst happens.

 TIP Given the affordability of external hard drives and how easy most backup programs make the process, there's no excuse not to back up your data on a regular basis. It's cheap protection in case something bad happens to your computer.

Using the Windows File History Utility

In Windows 8.1, you can back up all your important files with the File History utility. By default, File History saves copies of files every hour, and it keeps all saved versions forever.

To activate File History on your computer, follow these steps:

1. From the Start screen, display the Charms bar and click or tap Settings.

2. From the Settings pane, select Change PC Settings.

3. On the PC Settings page, select the Update & Recovery tab.

4. Select the File History tab to display the File History page, shown in Figure 10.3.

5. Click "on" the File History control.

6. File History automatically uses the first external drive on your system for its backup. If you want to use a different backup drive, click Select a Different Drive and, when the drive pane appears, select a different drive or network location.

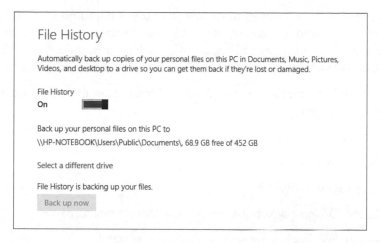

File History

Automatically back up copies of your personal files on this PC in Documents, Music, Pictures, Videos, and desktop to a drive so you can get them back if they're lost or damaged.

File History
On

Back up your personal files on this PC to
\\HP-NOTEBOOK\Users\Public\Documents\, 68.9 GB free of 452 GB

Select a different drive

File History is backing up your files.

Back up now

FIGURE 10.3

Backing up important files with the Windows File History utility.

To restore any or all files you've backed up, press Windows+S to display the search panel, enter **restore your files** into the search box, and press Enter. From the search results screen, click or tap Restore Your Files with File History to launch the File History desktop app. You can now navigate to and select those files or folders you want to restore; click the green Restore button to restore these files to their original locations.

 TIP You can also use File History to restore a given file to an earlier state. This is useful if you're editing a document, for example, and want to use an earlier version of the document before more recent editing.

Backing Up Online

The newest way to back up your data is to do it over the Internet, using an online backup service. This type of service copies your important files from your computer to the service's own servers, over the Internet. This way, if your local data is lost or damaged, you can then restore the files from the online backup service's servers.

The benefit of using an online backup service is that the backup copy of your library is stored offsite, so you're protected in case of any local physical catastrophe, such as fire or flood. Most online backup services also work in the background, so they're constantly backing up new and changed files in real time.

The downside of an online backup service comes if you need to restore your files. It takes a long time to transfer lots of big files to your computer over an Internet connection. Plus, you have to pay for the backup service—on an ongoing basis. Most online backup services run $50 or more per year, per computer.

If online backup appeals to you, check out these popular online backup services designed for home users:

- Carbonite (www.carbonite.com)

- IDrive (www.idrive.com)

- Mozy (www.mozy.com)

- Norton Online Backup (us.norton.com/online-backup/)

- SOS Online Backup (www.sosonlinebackup.com)

THE ABSOLUTE MINIMUM

Here are the key points to remember when connecting and configuring your new computer:

- External hard drives let you add extra storage capacity to your system—up to 4TB extra.

- You can find both desktop-type external drives and smaller, portable drives for use with notebook PCs.

- Connecting an external drive is typically as easy as connecting it to one of your PC's USB ports.

- An external drive shows up in File Explorer as just another drive on your system.

- You can also use an external hard drive to back up valuable data from your main hard drive.

- Windows 8.1 includes a File History utility that automates the backup process for files on your computer.

- Also available are online backup services, which back up your data over the Internet.

11

SETTING UP A HOME NETWORK

When you need to connect two or more computers, you need to create a computer *network*.

Why would you want to connect two computers? Maybe you want to transfer files or digital photos from one computer to another. Maybe you want to share an expensive piece of hardware (such as a printer) instead of buying one for each PC. Maybe you want to connect all your computers to the same Internet connection. Or maybe you want to play networked computer games with another player in your household. Whatever your reasons, it's easy to set up and configure a simple home network. Read on to learn how!

How Networks Work

When it comes to physically connecting your network, you have two ways to go—wired or wireless. A wireless network is more convenient (no wires to run), but a wired network is faster. Which you choose depends on how you use the computers you network.

If you use your network primarily to share an Internet connection or a printer or to transfer the occasional word processing file, wireless should work just fine. However, if you plan on transferring a lot of big files from one PC to another or using your network for multiplayer gaming, you should to stick to a faster wired network. (For that matter, if you watch a lot of streaming video over the network, wired can be more reliable than wireless.)

Wired Networks

A *wired network* is the kind that requires you to run a bunch of cables from each PC to a central hub or router. In a wired network, all your PCs are connected through a central *network router*, via an Ethernet cable. (Most new PCs come with built-in Ethernet capability, so you don't have to purchase anything additional—other than the router, that is.) Although this type of network is fast and easy enough to set up, you still have to deal with all those cables—which can be a hassle if your computers are in different areas of your house.

The speed you get from a wired network depends on the type of Ethernet technology used by each piece of equipment. The oldest Ethernet technology transfers data at just 10Mbps; Fast Ethernet transfers data at 100Mbps; and the newer Gigabit Ethernet transfers data at 1 *gigabit* per second (that's 1,000Mbps). Either Fast Ethernet or Gigabit Ethernet is fine for transferring really big files between computers or for playing real-time PC games.

 NOTE How quickly data is transferred across a network is measured in megabits per second, or Mbps. The bigger the Mbps number, the faster the network—and faster is always better than slower.

Wireless Networks

The alternative to a wired network is a *wireless network*. Wireless networks use radio frequency (RF) signals to connect one computer to another. The advantage of wireless, of course, is that you don't have to run cables. This is a big plus if you have a large house with computers on either end or on different floors.

Most home networks today are wireless, using Wi-Fi technology. The original Wi-Fi standard, known as 802.11b, transferred data at 11Mbps—slower than Fast Ethernet, but fast enough for most practical purposes. Next up was 802.11g, which transferred data at 54Mbps—more than fast enough for most home-networking needs.

 NOTE   Wi-Fi is short for *wireless fidelity.*

Even faster is the 802.11n standard, which delivers a blazing 600Mbps data transmission with a substantially longer range than older equipment. Current 802.11b and g equipment has a range of about 100 feet between transmitter and receiver; 802.11n gives you a 160-foot range, with less interference from other wireless household devices.

 NOTE   The 600Mbps rate for 802.11n networks is the theoretical maximum. In practice, expect rates between 200Mbps and 300Mbps.

Then there's the latest version of Wi-Fi, dubbed 802.11ac. Equipment running 802.11ac Wi-Fi is roughly twice as fast as 802.11n equipment, with a theoretical maximum speed of 1.3Gbps. (That's *gigabits* per second.) Naturally, 802.11ac routers will be more expensive than older models—but better suited for streaming high-definition video, if you do that.

In addition, you can combine wired and wireless technologies into a single network. Some PCs can connect directly to a wireless router via Ethernet, whereas others can connect via wireless Wi-Fi signals. This type of mixed network is quite common.

Connecting and Configuring

Whether you're going wired or wireless, the setup is surprisingly easy. You have to assemble the appropriate cables, along with a network router, and then install and connect it all. After everything is hooked up properly, you then have to configure all the PCs on your network. The configuration can be made from within Windows or via the configuration utility provided with your network router or wireless adapter. You run this utility on each computer you connect to your network and then configure the network within Windows.

Setting Up a Wireless Network in Your Home

Connecting multiple computers in a home network is fairly simple. Just make sure that you do the proper planning beforehand and buy the appropriate hardware and cables; everything else is a matter of connecting and configuration.

 NOTE For the purposes of this chapter, the assumption is that you're setting up a wireless network, as that's what most people today use. Connecting a wired network is equally easy; the big difference is that you have to connect Ethernet cables between your router and each computer instead of making a wireless connection.

How It Works

A wireless network revolves around a device called a *wireless router*. This device functions like the hub of a wheel and serves as the central point in your network; each computer on your network connects through the wireless router.

 NOTE Most wireless routers can make both wireless and wired connections. A typical wireless router includes four or more Ethernet ports in addition to wireless capabilities.

Every computer in a wireless network can connect to the router wirelessly— assuming, that is, that each computer contains wireless functionality. Almost all notebook and tablet PCs have built-in wireless connectivity, but many desktop PCs don't. (Although some do, of course.) You can add wireless functionality to a desktop PC via a wireless adapter, which is a small device that connects to your PC via USB.

When complete, your network should look something like the one in Figure 11.1.

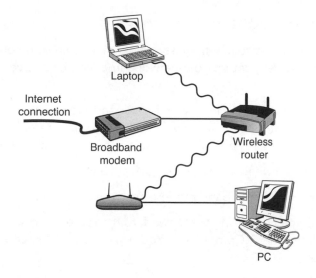

FIGURE 11.1

A typical wireless network.

What You Need

Here's the specific hardware you need to set up your network:

- Wireless router (one for the entire network)

- Broadband modem (typically supplied by your Internet service provider, or ISP; either cable modem or DSL modem, depending on your service)

 NOTE Some ISPs supply combination broadband modem/ wireless router boxes. If you have one of these devices, you don't need a separate wireless router.

- Wireless network adapters (one for each desktop PC; these are already built into notebook and tablet PCs, and they are sometimes built into desktops)

If you're connecting only notebook or tablet PCs to your network, you don't need wireless adapters (they're built into all portable computers)—you only need the wireless router and broadband modem. In addition, some desktop PCs have built-in wireless connectivity; if your desktops are so enabled, you don't need wireless adapters for them, either.

Making the Connections

Naturally, you should follow the instructions that come with your networking hardware to properly set up your network. In general, however, here are the steps to take:

1. Run an Ethernet cable from your broadband modem to your wireless router and connect it to the port on your router labeled Internet or WAN. (If your router doesn't have a dedicated Internet port, you can connect it to any port.)

2. Connect your wireless router to a power source.

3. Power on your broadband modem and wireless router.

4. Connect the first PC in your network to the router, as discussed in the "Connecting Your Computer to Your New Network" section, later in this chapter.

5. Follow the instructions provided by the router's manufacturer to create and configure a new wireless network. Make sure you configure your network to use wireless security, which requires a password (sometimes called a *network key*) before a device can connect to the network.

6. Configure the first PC for your new network.

7. Connect and configure all your remaining PCs for your new network.

 TIP When you first connect a new router to your network, you should configure the router using the software that came with the device. Follow the manufacturer's directions to configure the network and wireless security.

After you've connected all the computers on your network, you can proceed to configure any devices (such as printers) you want to share over the network. For example, if you want to share a single printer over the network, you can connect it to one of the network PCs and then share it through that PC. (You can also install network printers that connect directly to your wireless router, not to any specific PC.)

Connecting Your Computer to Your New Network

After your network hardware is all set up, you have to configure Windows to recognize and work with your new network. With Windows 8.1, this is a relatively painless and practically transparent step.

Connecting via Ethernet

If you're connecting to your network via Ethernet, you don't have to do a thing. After you connect an Ethernet cable between your PC and your router, Windows recognizes your new network and starts using it automatically.

Connecting Wirelessly

If you're connecting via a wireless connection, configuration is only slightly more involved. All you have to do is select which wireless network to connect to. Follow these steps:

1. Display the Charms bar and click or tap Settings to display the Settings panel, shown in Figure 11.2.

FIGURE 11.2

Click or tap the Wi-Fi icon to display available wireless networks.

2. Click or tap the Wi-Fi icon (typically labeled "Available" if you're not yet connected to a network) to display a list of available networks, as shown in Figure 11.3.

3. Click or tap your wireless network; the panel for this network expands.

4. Check the Connect Automatically box to connect automatically to this network in the future.

5. Click Connect.

FIGURE 11.3

Select your wireless network from the list.

6. When prompted, enter the password (called the *network security key*) for your network. You should have created this password when you first set up your wireless router. Click Next to continue.

7. When the next screen appears, click Yes to connect with other PCs and devices on your home network. (This lets you share pictures, music, and other files with other computers connected to your home network.) You're now connected to your wireless router and should have access to the Internet.

 NOTE If the wireless router on your network supports "one-button wireless setup" (based on the Wi-Fi Protected Setup technology), you might be prompted to press the "Connect" button on the router to connect. This is much faster than going through the entire process outlined here.

Adding Your Computer to a HomeGroup

The easiest way to network multiple home computers is to create a HomeGroup for your network. A HomeGroup is kind of a simplified network that enables you to automatically share files and printers between connected computers.

 NOTE   Only PCs running Windows 7, 8, or 8.1 can be part of a HomeGroup. PCs running older versions of Windows do not have the HomeGroup feature and must use the normal networking functions instead.

To create a new HomeGroup, follow these steps:

1. Display the Charms bar and click or tap Settings to display the Settings panel.

2. Click or tap Change PC Settings to display the PC Settings screen.

3. Scroll down the list on the left and select Network.

4. Click or tap HomeGroup on the left, and then click or tap the Create button to display the HomeGroup screen, shown in Figure 11.4.

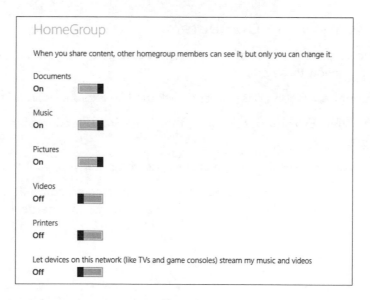

FIGURE 11.4

Setting up a HomeGroup on your network.

5. Click or tap "on" those items you want to share with other computers—Documents, Music, Pictures, Videos, and Printers.

6. If you want non-PC devices, such as network-connected TVs or videogame consoles, to be able to access the content on this computer, click or tap "on" the option for Let Devices on This Network (Like TVs and Game Consoles) Stream My Music and Videos.

7. Go to the Password section and write down the password that Windows generated. You'll need to provide this to users of other computers on your network who want to join your HomeGroup.

 NOTE You'll need to configure each computer on your network to join your new HomeGroup. Enter the original HomeGroup password as instructed.

Accessing Computers on Your Network

After you have your home network set up, you can access shared content stored on other computers on your network. How you do so depends on whether the other computer is part of your HomeGroup or not.

Accessing HomeGroup Computers

You access the content of other computers connected to your HomeGroup via File Explorer. Follow these steps:

1. Open the Windows desktop and click the File Explorer icon on the taskbar.

2. When File Explorer opens, go to the HomeGroup section of the Navigation pane.

3. Click or tap the name of the user whose computer you want to access.

4. Windows displays the shared folders on the selected computer, as shown in Figure 11.5; double-click or tap a library to access that particular content.

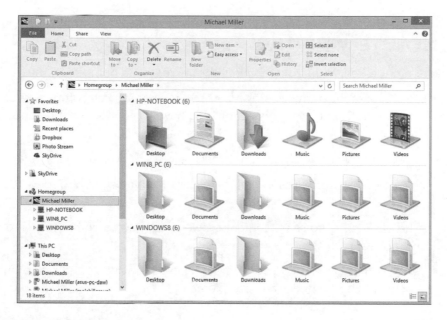

FIGURE 11.5

Viewing shared folders on a HomeGroup computer.

Accessing Other Computers on Your Network

A computer doesn't have to be connected to your HomeGroup for you to access its content. Windows enables you to access any computer connected to your home network—although you can only share content the computer's owner has configured as sharable.

To access other computers on your network, follow these steps:

1. Open the Windows desktop and click the File Explorer icon on the taskbar.

2. Go to the Network section of the Navigation pane.

3. Click or tap the computer you want to access.

4. Windows displays the shared folders on the selected computer; double-click or tap a folder to view that folder's content.

 TIP On most older computers, shared files are stored in the Public folder. Look in this folder first for the files you want.

THE ABSOLUTE MINIMUM

Here are the key things to remember about creating a home network:

- To share information or hardware between two or more computers, as well as to share an Internet connection, you have to connect your computers in a network.

- There are two basic types of networks: wired and wireless (Wi-Fi).

- A wireless network uses a wireless router to serve as the hub for all connected devices.

- The easiest way to share content between connected computers is to create a HomeGroup.

- After you've connected your computers in a network, you access other connected computers via File Explorer.

12

CONNECTING TO THE INTERNET—AT HOME AND ON THE ROAD

It used to be that most people bought personal computers to do serious work—word processing, spreadsheets, databases, the sort of programs that still make up the core of Microsoft Office. But today, people also buy PCs to access the Internet—to send and receive email, surf the Web, watch movies and listen to music, and socialize with other users.

To do this, of course, you first have to connect your computer to the Internet. Fortunately, Windows makes this easy to do.

Different Types of Connections in the Home

The first step in going online is establishing a connection between your computer and the Internet. When you're connecting from home, you need to sign up with an Internet service provider (ISP). This is a company that, as the name implies, provides your home with a connection to the Internet.

Most ISPs today offer some form of *broadband* access. Broadband is the fastest type of Internet connection available to homes today, and it comes in many flavors—cable, digital subscriber line (DSL), Fiber Optic Service (FiOS), and even satellite. Whichever type of broadband connection you choose, the Internet comes into your home via a wire or cable and connects to a device called a *modem*, which then connects either directly to your computer or to a wireless modem, so you can share the connection with all the computers and wireless devices in your home.

NOTE   In some rural areas, broadband access might not be available. If you don't have access to broadband Internet, you may have to connect via a much slower *dial-up connection*—that is, by dialing in through your normal telephone line. There's also the option of using a satellite-based Internet service, such as HughesNet, which is faster than dial-up but still not as fast as cable or DSL.

Broadband DSL

DSL is a phone line–based technology that operates at broadband speeds. DSL service piggybacks onto the existing telephone line, turning it into a high-speed digital connection (384Kbps to 10Mbps, depending on your ISP). With DSL, you don't have to surrender your normal phone line when you want to surf, as you do with traditional dial-up service; DSL connections are "always on." Most providers offer DSL service for $30–$50 per month. Look for package deals that offer a discount when you subscribe to both Internet and phone services.

CAUTION   Many ISPs provide slower speeds for data uploaded from your computer. So you may see, for example, an offer of 50Mbps downstream but just 8Mbps upstream. In addition, some ISPs employ "speed caps" for customers who download too much data, effectively throttling their use or charging extra for excessive data usage. It pays to check the fine print on these items before you sign up.

Broadband Cable

Another popular type of broadband connection is available from your local cable company. Broadband cable Internet piggybacks on your normal cable television line, providing speeds in the 500Kbps to 100Mbps range, depending on the provider. Most cable companies offer broadband cable Internet for $30–$50 per month, which is about the same as you pay for a similar DSL connection. As with DSL, look for package deals from your cable company, offering some sort of discount on a combination of Internet, cable, and (sometimes) digital phone service.

FiOS Broadband

The newest type of broadband connection is FiOS. As the name implies, this type of service delivers an Internet connection over a fiber optic network.

FiOS connection speeds are similar to those of broadband cable, with different speeds available at different pricing tiers. Most ISPs offer download speeds between 3Mbps and 50Mbps. Pricing is also similar to broadband cable, in the $30/month to $50/month range.

In the home, the FiOS line connects to a modem-like device called an optical network terminal (ONT) that can split the signal to provide a combination of Internet, television, and telephone services. You typically connect the ONT to your wireless router or PC via Ethernet. In the United States, FiOS Internet service is available in limited areas through AT&T and Verizon.

Broadband Satellite

If you can't get DSL, cable, or FiOS Internet in your area, you have another option—connecting to the Internet via satellite. Any household or business with a clear line of sight to the southern sky can receive digital data signals from a geosynchronous satellite at speeds between 1Mbps and 52Mbps.

The largest provider of satellite Internet access is HughesNet. (Hughes also developed and markets the popular DIRECTV digital satellite system.) The HughesNet system (www.hughesnet.com) enables you to receive Internet signals via a small dish that you mount outside your house or on your roof. Fees range from $50 to $110 per month.

Sharing an Internet Connection

If you have more than one PC in your home, you can connect them to share a single high-speed Internet connection. That is, you don't have to bring in separate lines and modems for each of your PCs, nor do you have to pay for more than one connection.

You share an Internet connection by connecting your broadband modem to your home network. It doesn't matter whether you have a wired or a wireless network; the connection is similar in both instances. All you have to do is run an Ethernet cable from your broadband modem to your network router, and then Windows does the rest, connecting your modem to the network so that all your computers can access the connection.

To work through all the details of this type of connection, turn to Chapter 11, "Setting Up a Home Network." It's really quite easy!

Connecting to a Public Wi-Fi Hotspot

If you have a notebook or tablet PC, you also have the option to connect to the Internet when you're away from home. Many coffeehouses, restaurants, hotels, and public spaces offer wireless Wi-Fi Internet service, either free or for an hourly or daily fee. Assuming that your notebook has a built-in Wi-Fi adapter (which almost all do), connecting to a public Wi-Fi hotspot is a snap.

 NOTE A *hotspot* is a public place that offers wireless access to the Internet using Wi-Fi technology. Some hotspots are free for all to access; others require some sort of payment.

When you're near a Wi-Fi hotspot, your PC should automatically pick up the Wi-Fi signal. Make sure that your PC's Wi-Fi adapter is turned on (some notebooks have a switch for this, either on the front or on the side of the unit), and then follow these steps:

1. From the Windows Start screen, display the Charms bar and click or tap Settings to display the Settings panel, shown in Figure 12.1.

2. If there's a hotspot nearby, the Wi-Fi icon should be labeled "Available." Click or tap this icon to display a list of available networks, as shown in Figure 12.2.

 TIP Most public networks do *not* have wireless security engaged. They'll display on the Settings panel with a little warning shield next to the wireless icon.

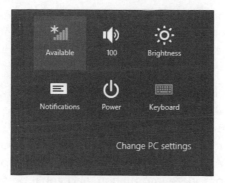

FIGURE 12.1

Click or tap the Wi-Fi icon to display available wireless networks.

FIGURE 12.2

Select your wireless network from the list.

3. Click or tap the wireless hotspot to which you want to connect; this expands the panel.

4. Click Connect to connect to the selected hotspot.

After Windows connects to the selected hotspot, you can log on to the wireless network. Windows may do this automatically, prompting you that further input is required and displaying the hotspot's logon screen. You may also have to do this manually.

Just open Internet Explorer or another web browser and try to go to a website—any website. If the hotspot has free public access without any logon necessary, you'll see the website and be able to surf normally. If the hotspot requires a password, payment, or other logon procedure, it intercepts the request for your normal home page and instead displays its own login page, like the one in Figure 12.3. Enter the appropriate information, and you'll be surfing in no time!

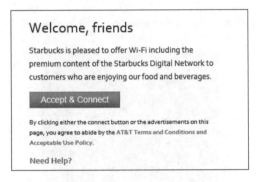

Welcome, friends

Starbucks is pleased to offer Wi-Fi including the premium content of the Starbucks Digital Network to customers who are enjoying our food and beverages.

Accept & Connect

By clicking either the connect button or the advertisements on this page, you agree to abide by the AT&T Terms and Conditions and Acceptable Use Policy.

Need Help?

FIGURE 12.3

Logging onto the Internet from a Starbucks coffee shop.

TIP If your notebook or tablet is configured to connect to your mobile phone carrier's data network, you see additional mobile broadband connection options within Windows. By default, Windows connects to available Wi-Fi networks first, as they're typically free or lower cost; if no Wi-Fi networks are available, then it connects to the data network you select.

Activating Airplane Mode

If you're using your notebook or tablet computer on an airplane, you can switch to Window's special Airplane Mode, which suspends all your PC's signal transmitting and receiving functions. It's just like the Airplane Mode you find on many smartphones, and it enables you to use your computer while you're in the air without fear of interfering with the plane's electronics.

To switch into Airplane Mode, follow these steps:

1. Display the Charms bar and click or tap Settings to display the Settings panel.

2. Click or tap the Wi-Fi icon to display the Networks page.

3. Click or tap "off" the Airplane Mode option.

You can switch off Airplane Mode when your plane lands.

Of course, if your flight offers onboard Wi-Fi service (many now do), you don't have to bother with Airplane Mode. Instead, just connect to the plane's wireless network as you would to any Wi-Fi hotspot. You might have to pay for it, but it enables you to use the Internet while you're en route—which is a great way to spend long trips!

THE ABSOLUTE MINIMUM

When you're configuring your new PC system to connect to the Internet, remember these important points:

- You connect to the Internet through an Internet service provider, or ISP; you need to set up an account with an ISP before you can connect.

- There are three common types of broadband service available today: DSL, cable, and FiOS, and the more expensive satellite service is an option for rural areas.

- If you have more than one computer at home, you can share your Internet connection by connecting your broadband modem to your home network.

- If you have a notebook PC, you can connect to the Internet wirelessly at any public Wi-Fi hotspot, such as those offered by Starbucks, Caribou Coffee, and similar establishments.

13

USING INTERNET EXPLORER TO SURF THE WEB

Now that you've connected to the Internet, either at home or via a public wireless hotspot, it's time to get surfing. The World Wide Web is a particular part of the Internet with all sorts of cool content and useful services, and you surf the Web with a piece of software called a *web browser*.

The most popular web browser today is Microsoft's Internet Explorer (IE). There's a new version of IE in Windows 8.1 that's fully integrated into the full-screen touch-enabled experience, which makes it fun and cool to use. That's in addition to the traditional desktop version of IE that many users are familiar with.

Whichever version of IE you prefer, this chapter helps you use the browser to navigate the Web. It's as easy as clicking your mouse!

Understanding the Web

Before you can surf the Web, you need to understand a little bit about how it works.

Information on the World Wide Web is presented in *pages*. A web page is similar to a page in a book, made up of text and graphics. A web page differs from a book page, however, in that it can include other elements, such as audio and video, and links to other web pages.

It's this linking to other web pages that makes the Web such a dynamic way to present information. A *link* on a web page can point to another web page on the same site or to another site. Most links are included as part of a web page's text and are called *hypertext links*, or just *hyperlinks*. (If a link is part of a graphic, it's called a *graphic link*.) These links are usually in a different color from the rest of the text and often are underlined; when you click a link, you're taken directly to the linked page.

Web pages reside at a *website*. A website is nothing more than a collection of web pages (each in its own computer file) residing on a host computer. The host computer is connected full time to the Internet so that you can access the site—and its web pages—anytime you access the Internet. The main page at a website is called the *home page*, and it often serves as an opening screen that provides a brief overview and menu of everything you can find at that site. The address of a web page is called a *URL*, which stands for *uniform resource locator*. Most URLs start with http://, add a www., continue with the name of the site, and end with a .com, .org, or .net.

 TIP You can normally leave off the http:// when you enter an address into your web browser. In most cases, you can even leave off the www. and just start with the domain part of the address.

Using Internet Explorer (Modern Version)

The web browser included in Microsoft Windows is Internet Explorer (IE). In Windows 8.1, there are actually two versions of IE. There's a full-screen version, accessible from the Start screen, that's designed to take full advantage of Windows 8.1's Modern interface. Then there's another, more traditional, windowed version of IE that runs on the Windows desktop.

NOTE Windows 8.1 includes Internet Explorer version 11 (IE11), which is vastly improved over the previous version 10—especially in the Modern, full-screen version. New to the Modern version of IE11 are the abilities to save Favorite sites and easily display different tabs.

Launching Internet Explorer from the Start Screen

As you can see in Figure 13.1, the Modern version of IE lets you view web pages on your full computer screen. It's obviously the version you want to use if you primarily work within the Modern Windows environment.

FIGURE 13.1

IE with Address bar and Tab bar displayed.

You launch the Modern version of IE from the Start screen, like this:

1. Click the Start button or press the Windows key to return to the Windows Start screen.

2. Click or tap the Internet Explorer tile.

Browsing the Web

You can go directly to any page on the Web by entering its web address. Many web pages include links to other web pages; click a link to jump to the linked-to page.

1. When you first launch the Modern version of IE, the Address bar should be displayed at the bottom of the screen, as shown in Figure 13.2. If you don't see the Address bar, right-click anywhere on the screen to display it.

FIGURE 13.2

Enter the address for a web page into the Address box.

2. Type the address for the page you want to go to into the Address box and then press Enter.

3. Click any underlined or bold link or picture on a web page to open the linked-to page. This lets you jump from one web page to another, via these page links.

4. To return to the last-viewed web page, click the Back button on the Address bar, or press the Backspace key on your keyboard.

5. If you've backed up several pages and want to return to the page you were on last, click the Forward button.

Opening Multiple Pages in Tabs

If you're visiting more than one web page during a single session, you can display each page as a separate *tab* in the web browser. This use of tabs enables you to keep multiple web pages open simultaneously—which is great when you want to reference different pages or want to run web-based applications in the background.

Here's how to work with tabs in IE:

1. Right-click within the browser to open the Address bar at the bottom of the screen, and then right-click again to display the row of tabs above the Address box, as shown in Figure 13.3.

FIGURE 13.3

Displaying tabs in the browser.

2. Click another open tab to switch to it.

3. Click or tap the X by the tab to close it.

4. To open a new tab, click or tap the New Tab (+) button to display the Frequent bar.

5. Either click a tile on this screen or enter a new web page address in the Address box.

Saving Your Favorite Web Pages

When you find a web page you like, you can save it in your Favorites list. Returning to a favorite page is as easy as clicking or tapping it in this list, as detailed here:

1. Navigate to the web page you want to pin, and then right-click the page to display the Address bar.

2. If the Favorites list is not displayed, click or tap the Favorites (star) button.

3. Click or tap the Add to Favorites button, shown in Figure 13.4, to display the Pin panel.

FIGURE 13.4

Working with favorite pages.

4. Confirm or edit the name of the page.

5. Click or tap the Add button.

NOTE You can also pin a favorite page to the Windows Start screen. Display the Favorites list in the Address bar, and then click or tap the Pin Site button on the far right.

Returning to a Saved Page

To return to a page you've saved as a favorite, click or tap that page's tile in the Favorites list. Follow these steps:

1. Right-click the current page in IE to display the Address bar.

2. Click or tap within the Address box to display the Favorites bar.

3. Click or tap the page you want to revisit.

 TIP You can organize favorite pages into folders in the Favorites list. To view favorites in a folder, click or tap the folder name. To return to the master Favorites list, click or tap All by the Favorites title.

Browsing in Private

Sometimes you might want to visit websites that you don't want friends or family members to know about. Fortunately, IE offers an InPrivate Browsing mode that lets you visit web pages anonymously, without traces of your history recorded. Here's how to do it:

1. Right-click the current page in IE to display the Address bar.

2. Click the "three dot" (...) button to display a pop-up menu of options.

3. Click New InPrivate Tab.

A new tab opens, with a blue InPrivate box next to the normal Address box. Enter the URL you want to browse to, and then press Enter. Any browsing you do on this screen is not recorded.

Using the Desktop Version of Internet Explorer

The Modern version of IE is easy to use and more than sufficient for most users. If you've used an older version of Windows, however, you might prefer the more traditional browsing experience of the desktop version of IE.

Figure 13.5 shows the desktop version of IE. This version of IE looks and acts more like a traditional web browser.

FIGURE 13.5

The traditional desktop version of the IE web browser.

Launching Internet Explorer from the Desktop

To launch the desktop version of IE, follow these steps:

1. From the Windows Start screen, click or tap the Desktop icon.

2. When the Windows desktop appears, as shown in Figure 13.6, click or tap the Internet Explorer icon on the taskbar at the bottom of the screen.

FIGURE 13.6

Click the Internet Explorer icon to launch the desktop version of IE.

Browsing the Web

Browsing the Web with the desktop version of IE is similar to using the Modern version. The big difference is that all the navigational elements are always visible in the browser.

1. To go to a specific web page, enter that page's address into the Address box and then press Enter.

2. To return to the previous web page, click the Back (left arrow) button beside the Address box.

3. To reload or refresh the current page, click the Refresh button.

4. To jump to a linked-to page, click the hyperlink on the current page.

 NOTE If you've backed up several pages and want to return to the page you were on last, click the Forward button.

Revisiting History

What do you do if you remember visiting a page earlier in the day, or even in the past few days, but can't get there by clicking the Back button? There are actually a few different ways to revisit your browsing history in IE.

The first thing to do is to click and hold the Back button. This displays a list of pages you've recently visited. Click a page to revisit it.

To see even older pages, click and hold the Back button and then click History. This displays a full history list of pages you've visited.

 TIP If you want to delete your browsing history—say you've visited a web page you don't want anyone to know you visited—you can do that, too. Click the Tools (gear) button in the IE browser and select Internet Options. When the Internet Options dialog box appears, select the General tab, go the Browsing History section, and then click the Delete button. Click Delete when prompted to delete your browsing history, and all the pages you've visited will be purged from the history list.

Opening Multiple Pages in Tabs

Just as the Modern version of IE features tabbed browsing, so does the desktop version. You can display web pages as separate tabs in the browser, and thus easily switch between web pages—which is great when you want to reference different pages or want to run web-based applications in the background.

Here's how to work with tabs in the desktop version of IE:

1. To switch to another open tab, click that tab.

2. To close an open tab, click the X on that tab.

3. To open a new tab, click the New Tab tab next to the last open tab.

4. Click a tile on the new tab page, shown in Figure 13.7, or...

5. ...enter a new web page address into the Address box.

FIGURE 13.7

The new tab page in IE.

Saving Your Favorite Pages

The desktop version of IE also lets you save your favorite pages in the Favorites list. Follow these steps:

1. Navigate to the web page you want to pin, and then click or tap the Favorites (star) button on the toolbar.

2. Click the Add to Favorites button to display the Add a Favorite dialog box, shown in Figure 13.8.

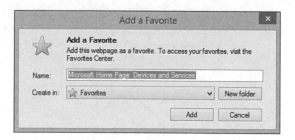

FIGURE 13.8

Adding a new web page to your Favorites list.

3. Confirm or enter a name for this page.

4. Click the Add button.

TIP You can organize your favorite pages into separate folders in the Favorites list. When the Add a Favorite dialog box appears, select a folder from the Create In list or click the New Folder button to create a new folder.

Returning to a Favorite Page

To return to a page you've saved as a favorite, follow these steps:

1. Click the Favorites (star) button to display the Favorites list, shown in Figure 13.9.

2. Click or tap the page you want to revisit.

FIGURE 13.9

Revisiting favorite pages in the Favorites list.

 TIP For even faster access to your favorite pages, display the Favorites bar at the top of the browser window, beneath the Address bar. Right-click any open area at the top of the browser and then select Favorites Bar from the pop-up menu.

Browsing in Private

Just as with the Modern version of IE, the desktop browser lets you browse anonymously via the InPrivate Browsing mode. Here's how to activate it:

1. Click the Tools (gear) button to display the menu of options.

2. Select Safety and then InPrivate Browsing.

This opens a new browser window with InPrivate Browsing turned on. You can now browse anonymously, to your heart's content.

Setting Your Home Page

The desktop version of IE lets you set a *home page* that automatically opens whenever you launch the browser. Here's how to do it:

1. Navigate to the page you want to use as your home page.

2. Click the Tools (gear) button, and then select Internet Options to display the Internet Options dialog box.

3. Select the General tab.

4. Go to the Home Page section and click the Use Current button.

5. Click OK.

 TIP   You're not limited to using just IE on the Windows desktop. There are several other third-party web browsers available, and some users prefer them for their simplicity and speed. The most popular of these non-Microsoft web browsers include Google Chrome (www.google.com/chrome/), Mozilla Firefox (www.mozilla.org/firefox/), and Apple Safari (www.apple.com/safari/).

THE ABSOLUTE MINIMUM

Here are the key things to remember about surfing the Web:

- You surf the Web with the Internet Explorer web browser.

- Windows 8.1 includes two versions of Internet Explorer—a full-screen Modern version and a traditional desktop version.

- To display the Address bar in the Modern version, right-click within a web page or swipe up from the bottom of the page (on a touchscreen display).

- To go to a particular web page in either version of IE, enter the page's address in the Address box and then press Enter. (You can also click or tap a hyperlink on a web page to jump to the linked page.)

- Internet Explorer offers tabbed browsing, where you can open new web pages in additional tabs; click or tap a tab to switch to that web page.

14

SEARCHING AND RESEARCHING ONLINE

Now that you know how to surf the Web, how do you find the precise information you're looking for? Fortunately, there are numerous sites that help you search the Web for the specific information you want. Not surprisingly, these are among the most popular sites on the Internet.

This chapter is all about searching the Web and using the Internet for research. It covers the best places to search and research the information you need. I even help you cheat a little by listing some of the most popular sites for different types of information.

So pull up a chair, launch Internet Explorer, and loosen up those fingers—it's time to start searching!

How to Search the Web

Internet *search engines* are sites that employ special software programs (called *spiders* or *crawlers*) to roam the Web automatically, feeding what they find back to a massive bank of computers. These computers then build giant *indexes* of the Web.

When you perform a search at a search engine site, your query is sent to the search engine's index. (You never actually search the Web itself; you only search the index that was created by the spiders crawling the Web.) The search engine then creates a list of pages in its index that match, to one degree or another, the query you entered.

Constructing a Query

Almost every search site on the Web contains two basic components—a *search box* and a *Search button*. You enter your query—one or more *keywords* that describe what you're looking for—into the search box and then click the Search button (or press the Enter key) to start the search. The search site then returns a list of web pages that match your query; click any link to go directly to one of the pages.

How you construct your query determines how relevant the results you receive will be. It's important to focus on the keywords you use because the search sites look for these words when they process your query. Your keywords are compared to the web pages the search site knows about; the more keywords found on a web page, the better the match.

Choose keywords that best describe the information you're looking for—using as many keywords as you need. Don't be afraid of using too many keywords; in fact, using too *few* keywords is a common fault of many novice searchers. The more words you use, the better idea the search engine has of what you're looking for.

Searching for an Exact Phrase

Normally, a multiple-word query searches for web pages that include all the words in the query, in any order. There is a way, however, to search for an exact phrase. All you have to do is enclose the phrase in quotation marks.

For example, to search for Monty Python, you could enter **Monty Python** as your query, and you might get decent results. However, you'll bet *better* results by entering **"Monty Python"**—with the two keywords surrounded by quotation marks. This tells the search engine to search for an exact phrase, not two separate words. In our example, surrounding the phrase with quotation marks returns results about the comedy troupe, whereas entering the words individually also returns pages about snakes and guys named Monty.

Where to Search

Now that you know *how* to search, *where* should you search? There's one obvious choice and a few alternatives.

Google—The Most Popular Search Site on the Web

The most popular search engine today is Google (www.google.com). Google is easy to use, extremely fast, and returns highly relevant results. That's because it indexes more pages than any other site—billions and billions of pages, if you're counting.

Most users search Google several times a week, if not several times a day. The Google home page, shown in Figure 14.1, is a marvel of simplicity and elegant web page design. All you have to do to start a search is enter one or more keywords into the search box and then click the Google Search button. This returns a list of results ranked in order of relevance, such as the one shown in Figure 14.2. Click a results link to view that page.

FIGURE 14.1

Searching the Web with Google.

Google also offers a variety of advanced search options to help you fine-tune your search. Click Search Tools at the top of the search results page to see these options, which are fine-tuned for specific types of searches. For example, you may have the option to filter your search results by time (Past 24 Hours, Past Week, and so on), reading level, and location (show nearby results only).

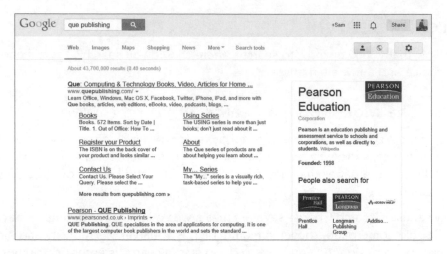

FIGURE 14.2

The results of a Google search.

Additional options are found on the Advanced Search page, which you get to by clicking the Options (gear) button on any search results page and then selecting Advanced Search. To narrow your search results, all you have to do is make the appropriate selections from the options present.

TIP You can also use Google to display stock quotes (enter the stock ticker), answers to mathematical calculations (enter the equation), and measurement conversions (enter what you want to convert). Google can also track USPS, UPS, and FedEx packages (enter the tracking number), as well as the progress of airline flights (enter the airline and flight number).

Bing—Microsoft's Answer to Google

Google's a great search site, but it has serious competition in the form of Bing (www.bing.com). Bing is Microsoft's search site; not surprisingly, it's designed to integrate well with Windows 8 and 8.1.

As you can see in Figure 14.3, Bing looks and feels a little like a Modern-style Windows app. Its design fits in well with Windows 8.1's full-screen approach. And, also not surprisingly, it's the default search engine when you enter a query into Internet Explorer's Address box.

FIGURE 14.3

Searching the Web with Bing.

You search Bing the same way you search Google. Enter your query into the search box and press Enter on your keyboard. Bing displays its results on a separate page, like the one shown in Figure 14.4; click a result to see that web page.

FIGURE 14.4

The results of a Bing search.

Other Search Sites

Although Google and Bing are far and away the most popular search engines today, many other search engines provide excellent (and sometimes different) results. These search engines include

- Ask.com (www.ask.com)
- Open Directory (www.dmoz.org)
- Yahoo! (www.yahoo.com)

Smart Searching from Within Windows

Windows 8.1, like previous versions of Windows, lets you search your computer for files and apps. New to Windows 8.1, however, is the ability to expand this internal search to the Web and use Bing to provide integrated web-based search results. This new global search is dubbed *Smart Search*, and it can make your searching more effective and efficient.

To use Windows Smart Search, follow these steps:

1. Display the Charms bar and click or tap Search (or press Win+S) to display the Search pane.

2. Enter your query into the search box; then press Enter.

3. You now see a list of files and apps on your computer that match your query, as shown in Figure 14.5. Click or tap an item to open it.

FIGURE 14.5

Smart Search results from within Windows.

Depending on your query, you may also see web results from Bing. Scroll to the right to see additional results; then click an item to view that web page.

Some web-based Smart Searches return what Microsoft calls "hero" results, where information about the subject is preassembled from data on the Web. For example, if you search for **Seattle**, Windows displays the city's current weather conditions, population, and attractions, as well as a dining guide, images, current news, and more—along with traditional web search results. It's pretty neat, actually.

Searching for People and Businesses

As good as Google and other search sites are for finding specific web pages, they're not always that great for finding people. When there's a person (or an address or a phone number) you want to find, you need to use a site that specializes in people searches.

People listings on the Web go by the common name of *white pages directories*, the same as traditional white pages phone books. These directories typically enable you to enter all or part of a person's name and then search for his address and phone number. Many of these sites also let you search for personal email addresses and business addresses and phone numbers.

The best of these directories include

- AnyWho (www.anywho.com)
- InfoSpace (www.infospace.com)
- Switchboard (www.switchboard.com)
- WhitePages.com (www.whitepages.com)

 TIP   All these white pages directories also serve as yellow pages directories for looking up businesses. They're one-stop search sites for any individual or business you want to look up!

Using Wikipedia for Research

Although many people use Google or Bing for research, searching the Web for just the right information can sometimes be like looking for a needle in a haystack; the information you get is totally unfiltered and not always accurate. A better way to research is to use a site designed primarily for research.

Such a site is Wikipedia (www.wikipedia.com), which is fast becoming the primary information site on the Web.

Understanding Wikipedia

Wikipedia is like a giant online encyclopedia—but with a twist. Unlike a traditional encyclopedia, Wikipedia's content is created solely by the site's users, resulting in the world's largest online collaboration.

At present, Wikipedia hosts more than 4 million English-language articles, with at least that many articles available in more than 250 different languages. The articles are written and revised by tens of thousands of individual contributors. These users volunteer their time and knowledge at no charge, for the good of the Wikipedia project.

You don't have to be an academic type to contribute to Wikipedia, and you don't have to be a student to use it. Anyone with specialized knowledge can write an article, and regular people like you and me can read them.

 CAUTION Since Wikipedia content is provided by users, not professional editors, it may not always be 100% accurate. Use it at your own discretion.

Searching Wikipedia

Information on the Wikipedia site is compiled into a series of articles. You search Wikipedia to find the exact articles you need.

To find an article on a given topic, go to the Wikipedia home page, shown in Figure 14.6, enter your query into the search box, and then click the right arrow button. If an article directly matches your query, Wikipedia now displays that article. If a number of articles might match your query, Wikipedia displays the list of articles, organized by type or topic. Click the article name to display the specific article.

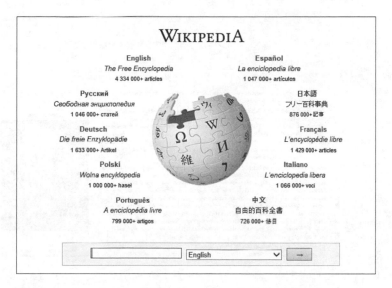

FIGURE 14.6

The Wikipedia home page.

For example, if you search Wikipedia for **john adams**, it displays the article on founding father John Adams. If, instead, you search only for **adams**, it displays a disambiguation page with sections for matching people and places bearing the name of "Adams." From there you can find the article on the second president, as well as lots of other articles.

Reading Wikipedia Articles

As you can see in Figure 14.7, each Wikipedia article is organized into a summary and subsidiary sections. Longer articles have a table of contents, located beneath the summary. Key information is sometimes presented in a sidebar at the top right of the article.

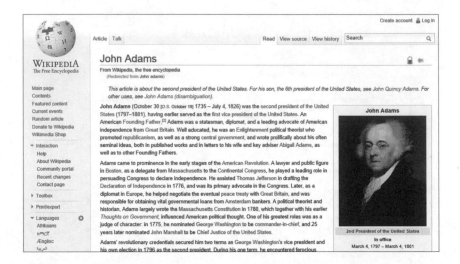

FIGURE 14.7

A typical Wikipedia article.

One of the things I liked about reading the encyclopedia when I was a kid was jumping around from article to article. This is easier than ever in Wikipedia, as the text of each article contains blue hypertext that links to related articles in the Wikipedia database. Click one of these links to jump to that article.

If you want to know the source for the information in an article, scroll to the bottom of the page, where the sources for key facts within the article are footnoted. Additional references and information about the topic also appear at the bottom of the page.

And, because Wikipedia articles are continually updated by users, it's often useful to view the history of an article's updates. This way you can see how an article looked before its most recent revisions. Click the View History tab to see a list of edits and who made those edits. You can also use the View History tab to read previous versions of an article.

 TIP Some articles feature discussions from users, which can sometimes provide additional insight. Click the Talk tab to read and participate in ongoing discussions.

THE ABSOLUTE MINIMUM

Here are the key points to remember from this chapter:

- When you need to search for specific information on the Internet, you can use one of the Web's many search engine sites.

- The most popular Internet search engine is Google, which indexes billions of individual web pages.

- Also popular is Microsoft's search engine, Bing.

- Windows 8.1 offers a built-in Smart Search that combines a search of your computer system with Bing web search. Some Smart Searches display so-called hero results, which contain essential information about the subject in addition to web links.

- It's better to search for people (and their phone numbers and addresses) at specific people-search sites, such as InfoSpace and Switchboard.

- When you need to research specific topics, Wikipedia is a good source; it contains information written and edited by its large user base.

15

SHOPPING AND SELLING ONLINE

Many users have discovered that the Internet is a great place to buy things—all kinds of things. All manner of online merchants make it easy to buy books, CDs, and other merchandise with the click of a mouse.

The Web isn't just for shopping, however. You can also use sites such as eBay and craigslist to sell your own stuff online. It's a great way to get rid of all that old stuff cluttering your attic—or a few unwanted Christmas presents!

How to Shop Online

If you've never shopped online before, you're probably wondering just what to expect. Shopping over the Web is actually easy; all you need is your computer and a credit card—and a fast connection to the Internet!

Online shopping is pretty much the same, no matter which retailer website you visit. You proceed through a multiple-step process that goes like this:

1. **Find an online store** that sells the item you're shopping for.

2. **Find a product**, either by browsing or searching through the retailer's site.

3. **Examine the product** by viewing the photos and information on a product listing page.

4. **Order the product** by clicking a "buy it now" button on the product listing page that puts the item in your online shopping cart.

5. **Check out** by entering your payment (credit card) and shipping information.

6. **Confirm the order** and wait for the merchant to ship your merchandise.

Let's look at each of these steps separately.

Step 1: Find an Online Store

The first step in online shopping is finding where you want to shop. Most major retailers, such as Target and Walmart, have their own websites you can use to shop online, as do most catalog merchants. In addition, there are online-only retailers that offer a variety of merchandise, such as Amazon.com. You should find no shortage of places to shop online.

You can also use a price comparison site to help find the best merchandise and pricing online. These sites let you search for specific products and then sort and filter the results in a number of different ways. Many of these sites include customer reviews of both the products and the available merchants; some even let you perform side-by-side comparisons of multiple products, which is great if you haven't yet made up your mind as to what you want to buy.

The most popular (and useful) of these price comparison sites include

- BizRate (www.bizrate.com)
- Google Shopping (www.google.com/shopping)
- mySimon (www.mysimon.com)
- NexTag (www.nextag.com)

- PriceGrabber (www.pricegrabber.com)

- Shopping.com (www.shopping.com), shown in Figure 15.1

- Yahoo! Shopping (shopping.yahoo.com)

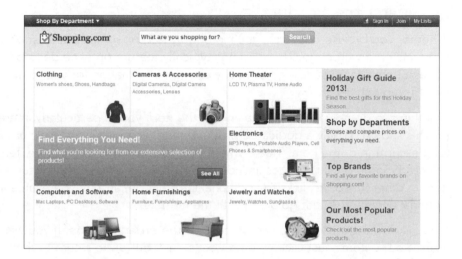

FIGURE 15.1

Comparing prices at Shopping.com.

Step 2: Find a Product

After you've determined where to shop, you need to browse through different product categories on that site or use the site's search feature to find a specific product.

Browsing product categories online is similar to browsing through the departments of a retail store. You typically click a link to access a major product category, and then click further links to view subcategories within the main category. For example, the main category might be Clothing; the subcategories might be Men's, Women's, and Children's clothing. If you click the Men's link, you might see a list of further subcategories: outerwear, shirts, pants, and the like. Just keep clicking until you reach the type of item that you're looking for.

Searching for products is often a faster way to find what you're looking for if you have something specific in mind. For example, if you're looking for a men's silk jacket, you can enter the words **men's silk jacket** into the site's search box and get a list of specific items that match those criteria. The only problem with searching is that you might not know exactly what it is you're looking for; if this describes your situation, you're probably better off browsing. But if you *do* know what you want—and you don't want to deal with lots of irrelevant items—then searching is the faster option.

TIP When searching for items at an online retailer, you can use the same general search guidelines I discussed in Chapter 14, "Searching and Researching Online."

Step 3: Examine the Product

Whether you browse or search, you'll probably end up looking at a list of different products on a web page. These listings typically feature one-line descriptions of each item—in most cases, not nearly enough information for you to make an informed purchase.

The thing to do now is to click the link for the item you're particularly interested in. This should display a dedicated product page, complete with a picture and full description of the item. This is where you can read more about the item you selected. Some product pages include different views of the item, pictures of the item in different colors, links to additional information, and maybe even a list of optional accessories that go along with the item.

If you like what you see, you can proceed to the ordering stage. If you want to look at other items, just click your browser's Back button to return to the larger product listing.

Step 4: Order the Product

Somewhere on each product description page should be a button labeled Purchase, Buy Now, Add to Cart, or something similar. This is how you make the actual purchase: by clicking that "buy" button. You don't order the product just by looking at the product description; you have to manually click the "buy" button to place your order. (Figure 15.2 shows a product page on Amazon.com; click the Add to Cart button to purchase this item.)

When you click the "buy" button, that particular item is added to your *shopping cart*. That's right, the online retailer provides you with a virtual shopping cart that functions just like a real-world shopping cart. Each item you choose to purchase is added to your virtual shopping cart.

After you've ordered a product and placed it in your shopping cart, you can choose to shop for other products on that site or proceed to the site's checkout. It's important to note that when you place an item in your shopping cart, you haven't actually completed the purchase yet. You can keep shopping (and adding more items to your shopping cart) as long as you want.

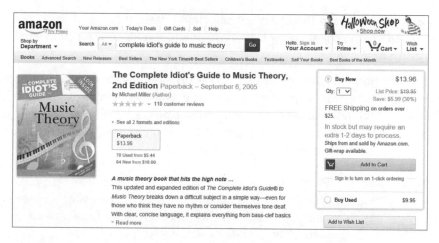

FIGURE 15.2

Getting ready to purchase a book on Amazon.com.

You can even decide to abandon your shopping cart and not purchase anything at this time. All you have to do is leave the website, and you won't be charged for anything. It's the equivalent of leaving your shopping cart at a real-world retailer and walking out the front door; you don't actually buy anything until you walk through the checkout line. (Although, with some sites, the items remain in your shopping cart—so they'll be there waiting for you the next time you shop!)

Step 5: Check Out

To finalize your purchase, you have to visit the store's *checkout*. This is like the checkout line at a traditional retail store; you take your virtual shopping cart through the checkout, get your purchases totaled, and then pay for what you're buying.

The checkout at an online retailer typically consists of one or more web pages with forms you have to fill out. If you've visited the retailer before, the site might remember some of your personal information from your previous visit. Otherwise, you have to enter your name, address, and phone number, as well as the address you want to ship the merchandise to (if that's different from your billing address). You also have to pay for the merchandise, typically by entering a credit card number.

The checkout provides one last opportunity for you to change your order. You can delete items you decide not to buy or change quantities on any item. At some merchants you can even opt to have your items gift-wrapped and sent to someone as a present. You should be able to find all these options somewhere in the checkout process.

You might also have the option of selecting different types of shipping for your order. Many merchants offer both regular and expedited shipping—the latter for an additional charge.

Another option at some retailers is to group all items for reduced shipping cost. (The alternative is to ship items individually as they become available.) Grouping items is attractive cost-wise, but you can get burned if one of the items is out of stock or not yet available; you could end up waiting weeks or months for those items that could have been shipped immediately.

 TIP The better online retailers tell you either on the product description page or during the checkout process whether or not an item is in stock. Look for this information to help you decide how to group your items for shipment.

Step 6: Confirm the Order

After you've entered all the appropriate information, you're asked to place your order. This typically means clicking a button that says Place Your Order or something similar. You might even see a second screen asking you whether you *really* want to place your order, just in case you had second thoughts.

After you place your order, you see a confirmation screen, typically displaying your order number. Write down this number or print this page; you need to refer to this number if you have to contact customer service. Most online merchants also send you a confirmation message, including this same information, via email.

That's all there is to it. You shop, examine the product, place an order, proceed to checkout, and then confirm your purchase. It's that easy!

How to Shop Safely

Shopping online is every bit as safe as shopping at a traditional brick-and-mortar retailer. The big online retailers are just as reputable as traditional retailers, offering safe payment, fast shipping, and responsive service.

How do you know that you're shopping at a reputable online retailer? Simple—look for the following features:

- **Payment by major credit card**—Smaller merchants might accept credit cards via PayPal or a similar online payment service; this is also acceptable.

- **A *secure server* that encrypts your credit card information—and keeps online thieves from stealing your credit card numbers**—You know that you're using a secure site when the little lock icon appears in the lower-right corner of your web browser.

- **Good contact information—email address, street address, phone number, fax number, and so on**—You want to be able to physically contact the retailer if something goes wrong.

- **A stated returns policy and satisfaction guarantee**—You want to be assured that you'll be taken care of if you don't like whatever you ordered.

- **A stated privacy policy that protects your personal information**—You don't want the online retailer sharing your email address and purchasing information with other merchants—and potential spammers.

- **Information *before you finalize your order* that tells you whether the item is in stock and how long it will take to ship**—More feedback is better.

 TIP Credit card purchases are protected by Federal law. In essence, you have the right to dispute certain charges, and your liability for unauthorized transactions is limited to $50. In addition, some card issuers offer a supplemental guarantee that says you're not responsible for *any* unauthorized charges made online. (Make sure that you read your card's statement of terms to determine the company's exact liability policy.)

Buying and Selling on eBay

Some of the best bargains on the Web come from other consumers, just like you, selling their own items online. The most popular website for individual sales is eBay, which is an online marketplace that facilitates transactions between people and businesses that have things to sell and customers who want to buy those things.

The sellers on eBay can opt to sell their products via traditional fixed-priced transactions, or via *online auctions*. An online auction is, quite simply, a Web-based version of a traditional auction. You find an item you'd like to own and then place a bid on it. Other users also place bids, and at the end of the auction—typically a seven-day period—the highest bidder wins.

How Does an eBay Auction Work?

If you've never used eBay before, you might be a little curious about what might be involved. Never fear; participating in an online auction is a piece of cake—something hundreds of millions of other users have done before you. That means you don't have to reinvent any wheels; the procedures you follow are well established and well documented.

An eBay auction is an Internet-based version of a traditional auction—you know, the type where a fast-talking auctioneer stands in the front of the room, trying to coax potential buyers into bidding *just a little bit more* for the piece of merchandise up for bid. The only difference is that there's no fast-talking auctioneer online (the bidding process is executed by special auction software on the auction site), and your fellow bidders aren't in the same room with you—in fact, they might be located anywhere in the world. Anyone who has Internet access and is registered with eBay can be a bidder. You do this from eBay's home page (www.ebay.com), shown in Figure 15.3.

FIGURE 15.3

Where all the auction action starts—eBay's home page.

NOTE There is no cost to register with eBay, although if you want to sell items, you have to provide your credit card and checking account numbers. (eBay uses this information to help weed out potential scammers and to provide a billing option for the seller's eBay fees.)

When a buyer has something to sell, she creates an item listing. This is essentially a sale page for the item, with photos and a description and all that, as shown in Figure 15.4. In the case of an auction listing, the page includes a form for interested buyers to enter their bids.

FIGURE 15.4

A typical eBay auction listing.

A potential buyer reads the item listing and makes a bid, specifying the maximum amount he will pay; this amount has to be equal to or greater than the seller's minimum bid, or higher than any other existing bids.

At this point, eBay's built-in bidding software automatically places a bid for the bidder that bests the current bid by a specified amount—but doesn't reveal the bidder's maximum bid. For example, the current bid on an item might be $25. A bidder is willing to pay up to $40 for the item and enters a maximum bid of $40. eBay's "proxy" software places a bid for the new bidder in the amount of $26— higher than the current bid, but less than the specified maximum bid. If there are no other bids, this bidder wins the auction with a $26 bid. Other potential buyers, however, can place additional bids; unless their maximum bids are more than the current bidder's $40 maximum, they are informed (by email) that they have been outbid—and the first bidder's current bid is automatically raised to match the new bids (up to the specified maximum bid price).

At the conclusion of an auction, eBay informs the high bidder of his winning bid. When the seller receives the buyer's payment (typically via PayPal), the seller then ships the merchandise directly to the buyer. eBay also bills the seller 10% of the final bid price as a final value fee.

Buying Fixed-Price Items

Tired of waiting around for the end of an auction, only to find out you didn't have the winning bid? Well, there's a way to actually *buy* some items you see for auction without going through the bidding process. All you have to do is look for those item listings that have a Buy It Now option.

Buy It Now is an option that some (but not all) sellers add to their auctions. With Buy It Now, the item is sold (and the auction ended) if the first bidder places a bid for a specified price. (For this reason, some refer to Buy It Now auctions as "fixed-price" auctions—even though they're slightly different from eBay's *real* fixed-priced listings.)

Other eBay sellers choose to skip the auction process entirely and sell their items at a fixed price. These listings also display the Buy It Now button but without a bidding option. Fixed-priced listings are also common in eBay Stores, where larger sellers offer a constant supply of fixed-priced merchandise for sale all year round.

Buying a fixed-price item on eBay is really simple. If you see an item identified with a Buy It Now price, just click the Buy It Now button. You are immediately notified that you've purchased the item and are instructed to pay—typically via PayPal.

Protecting Yourself Against Fraudulent Sellers

When you're bidding for and buying items on eBay, you're pretty much in "buyer beware" territory. You agree to buy an item, almost sight unseen, from someone whom you know practically nothing about. You send that person a check and hope and pray that you get something shipped back in return—and that the thing that's shipped is the thing you thought you were buying, in good condition. If you don't like what you got—or if you received nothing at all—the seller has your money. And what recourse do you have?

The first line of defense against frauds and cheats is to intelligently choose the people you deal with. On eBay, the best way to do this is via the Feedback system.

Next to every seller's name is a number and percentage, which represents that seller's Feedback rating. You should always check a seller's Feedback rating before you bid. If the number is high with an overwhelmingly positive percentage, you can feel safer than if the seller has a lot of negative feedback. For even better protection, click the seller's name in the item listing to view his Member Profile, where you can read individual feedback comments. Be smart and avoid those sellers who have a history of delivering less than what was promised.

 TIP If you're new to eBay, you can build up your feedback fast by purchasing a few low-cost items—preferably using the Buy It Now feature, so you get the transaction over quickly. It's good to have a Feedback rating of 20 or better before you start selling!

What do you do if you follow all this advice and still end up receiving unacceptable merchandise—or no merchandise at all? Fortunately, eBay offers a Buyer Protection plan for any auction transaction gone bad.

To file for a claim under the Buyer Protection plan, go to eBay's Resolution Center (resolutioncenter.ebay.com). Follow the onscreen instructions from there. (You have 45 days to file a claim after you've paid for the item.)

eBay Selling, Step-by-Step

Have some old stuff in your garage or attic that you want to get rid of? Consider selling it on eBay. Selling on eBay is a little more involved than bidding but can generate big bucks if you do it right.

 NOTE   eBay makes its money by charging sellers two types of fees. (Buyers don't pay fees to eBay.) *Insertion fees* are based on the minimum bid or reserve price of the item listed. *Final value fees* are charged when you sell an item, based on the item's final selling price. Fees are typically charged directly to the seller's credit card account.

Here's how selling works:

1. If you haven't registered for an eBay seller account yet, do so now. You need to provide eBay with your credit card and checking account number, for verification and billing purposes.

2. Before you list your first item, you need to do a little homework. That means determining what you're going to sell and for how much, as well as how you're going to describe the item. You need to prepare the information you need to write a full item description, as well as take a few digital photos of the item to include with the listing.

3. Homework out of the way, it's time to create the item listing. Start by clicking the Sell button on eBay's home page. As you can see in Figure 15.5, eBay displays a series of forms for you to complete; the information you enter into these forms is used to create your item listing. You need to select a category for your item; enter a title and description; insert a photo of the item, if you have one; and determine whether you want to sell at a fixed price or via auction. You'll also need to enter the item's price (or, in the case of an auction, the minimum bid price).

4. After you enter all the information, eBay creates and displays a preliminary version of your listing. If you like what you see, click OK to go live or start the auction.

5. When the auction is over or the item is sold, eBay notifies you (via email) and provides the email address of the winning bidder.

6. Most buyers pay via credit card (using the PayPal service). Once you receive notice of payment, pack the item and ship it out.

FIGURE 15.5

Creating a new eBay item listing.

TIP You can monitor the progress of all your current eBay activity from the My eBay page. Just click the My eBay link at the top of eBay's home page.

That's it—you've just become a successful eBay seller!

Buying and Selling on Craigslist

eBay isn't the only place to buy and sell items on the Web. When you want to buy or sell something locally, craigslist is the place.

Craigslist is a network of local online classifieds sites. On craigslist you pick your local site and then create a classified ad for what you're selling; potential buyers browse the ads, contact the seller, and pay for and pick up the items locally.

Understanding Online Classifieds

Like eBay, craigslist is just a middleman, facilitating sales between individual buyers and sellers. Unlike eBay, all craigslist sales are at a fixed cost; there's no bidding involved. Of course, as with traditional print-based classified ads, some sellers might accept lower prices than listed if you make an offer, or they might list an item at a fixed price "or best offer." All negotiations are between the seller and the buyer. Most sales are paid for with cash.

Another big difference between eBay and craigslist is that eBay is a fairly full-featured marketplace; eBay offers a number of tools for both buyers and sellers that help to automate and take the guesswork out of the process. Not so with craigslist, which resembles what eBay was like about 10 years ago, before it became more sophisticated. Creating an ad is pretty much filling in a blank text box, with little help from craigslist on how to do it. Craigslist doesn't even get involved in the selling process; buyers pay sellers directly, often in cash. There's no PayPal to deal with, and no way to pay via credit card.

For that matter, craigslist doesn't offer the buyer and seller protection plans that you find on eBay—which makes buying via classified ad that much more risky. If a buyer pays with a bad check, there's not much the seller can do about it; if a seller gets an item home and finds out it doesn't work as promised, *caveat emptor*.

Browsing the Listings

As noted previously, craigslist is actually a network of individual local sites. In fact, the craigslist home page is nothing more than a listing of these local sites. So to use craigslist, you first have to navigate to your specific local site; you do this by going to the national craigslist home page and then clicking your city or state from the list.

After you're on your local craigslist site, you see links to all the product and service categories offered by craigslist in your area, as shown in Figure 15.6. The categories available mirror those in a typical newspaper classifieds section, including Housing, Jobs, Personals, and the like.

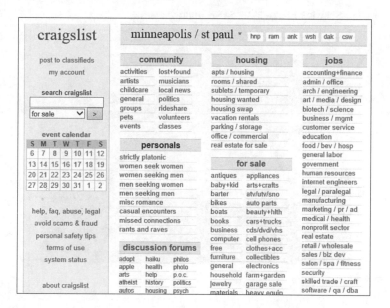

FIGURE 15.6

A local craigslist site.

If you're looking for an item for sale, it's probably going to be in the For Sale category. If you're looking for something else, however, then the other categories might hold interest. It might surprise you to know that in many cities craigslist is the largest marketplace for job wanted ads; it's also a big site for home and apartment listings. For that matter, craigslist has a thriving personals section, in case that's what you're looking for.

Buying on Craigslist

If you want to buy a specific type of item, you need to browse craigslist's For Sale listings. Within this major category there are additional subcategories, such as Computers, Furniture, Musical Instruments, Electronics, Tools, and the like. Click through to a subcategory to view the ads within that category.

As you can see in Figure 15.7, a typical craigslist ad includes a title, a description of the item being sold, and one or more pictures of the item. Unlike with eBay, craigslist offers no direct mechanism for contacting the seller or for purchasing directly from the listing page. Although some ads include the seller's phone number, most don't. Instead, you contact the seller by clicking the email link included in the ad.

FIGURE 15.7

A typical craigslist For Sale ad.

So if you're interested in the item, contact the seller via email and express your interest. You can then arrange a time to view the item; if you like what you see, you can pay for it then and take it with you.

Listing an Item for Sale

If you're a seller, the big difference between eBay and craigslist is that most listings on craigslist are free. The site charges nothing to list most items for sale, and it charges no final value or commission fees. This makes craigslist quite attractive to sellers; you can list anything you want and don't have to pay if it doesn't sell.

 NOTE Although the vast majority of craigslist ads are free, not all are. In particular, craigslist charges for job listings in some major cities, brokered apartment listings in New York City, and all listings in the adult services category.

Listing an item for sale on craigslist is similar to listing a fixed-price item on eBay. The differences are more in what you *don't* have to do; there are fewer "blanks" to fill in—and fewer options for your listing.

 TIP Selling on craigslist is better than eBay when you have a big or bulky item that might be difficult to ship long distances. Local buyers can pick up the items they purchase.

To list an item for sale on the craigslist site, follow these steps:

1. Navigate to the home page for your local craigslist community.

2. Click the Post to Classifieds link on the left side of the page.

3. When the next page appears, click the category in which you want to list— probably the For Sale category. When prompted, select an appropriate subcategory.

4. You now see the listing creation page, as shown in Figure 15.8. Enter information into the appropriate fields: Posting Title, Price, Specific Location, Posting Description, and Reply To (your email address). Click Continue to proceed.

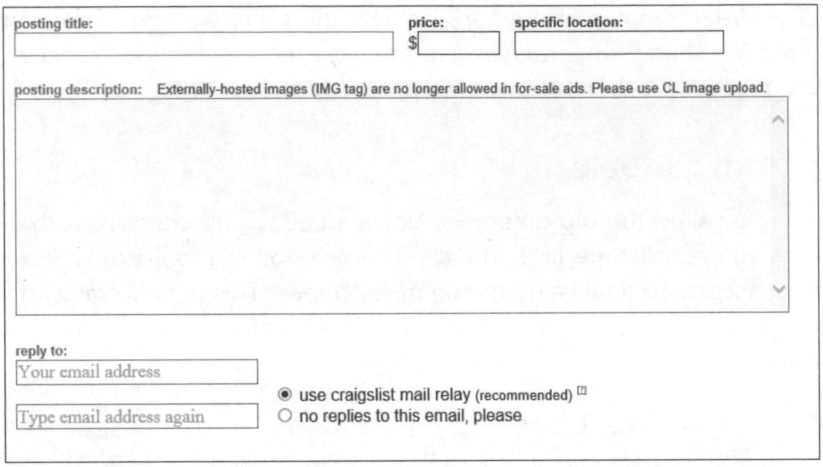

posting title:	price:	specific location:

posting description: Externally-hosted images (IMG tag) are no longer allowed in for-sale ads. Please use CL image upload.

reply to:

Your email address

Type email address again

⦿ use craigslist mail relay (recommended) [1]
◯ no replies to this email, please

FIGURE 15.8

Creating a new craigslist classified listing.

5. When the next page appears, click the Choose Files button to select any digital photos you want to include with the item. Click the Done with Images button when you're ready to proceed.

6. Craigslist now displays a preview of your listing. If you like what you see, click the Publish button. (If you don't like what you see, click the Edit Text or Edit Images button to make changes.) Your listing appears on the Craigslist site within the next 15 minutes or so.

For your protection, craigslist displays an anonymized email address in your item listing. Buyers email this anonymous address, and the emails are forwarded to your real email address. That way you won't get email stalkers from your craigslist ads—in fact, no one will know exactly who is doing the posting!

Making the Sale

When someone replies to your listing, craigslist forwards you that message via email. You can then reply to the potential buyer directly; in most instances, that means arranging a time for that person to come to your house to either view or purchase the item of interest.

Unlike eBay, where you have to ship the item to the buyer, craigslist buyers more often than not pick up the items they purchase. That means you have to be at home for the buyer to visit, and you have to be comfortable with strangers visiting. You also have to be prepared to help the buyer load up whatever it is you're selling into her vehicle for the trip home—which can be a major issue if you're selling big stuff and you're a small person.

 CAUTION If you're not comfortable with strangers visiting your house and you're selling something portable, arrange to meet at a neutral location. If you're selling a larger item, make sure another family member or friend is home when the buyer is supposed to visit.

As to payment, the vast majority of craigslist purchases are made with cash. You might want to keep some ones and fives on hand to make change in case the buyer pays with larger bills.

For higher priced items, you might want to accept payment via cashier's check or money order. Just be sure that the check or money order is made out for the exact amount of the purchase; you don't want to give back cash as change for a money order purchase.

 CAUTION Under no circumstances should you accept payment via personal check. It's far too easy for a shady buyer to write you a check and take off with the merchandise, only for you to discover a few days later that the check bounced. If you *must* accept a personal check, hold onto the merchandise for a full 10 working days to make sure the check clears; it's probably easier for all involved for the buyer to just get the cash.

THE ABSOLUTE MINIMUM

Here are the key points to remember from this chapter:

- You can find just about any type of item you want for sale somewhere on the Internet.

- Shopping online is a lot like shopping in a traditional store; you find the product you want, go through the checkout system, and make your payment.

- Internet shopping is very safe, especially if you buy from a major merchant that offers a secure server and a good returns policy.

- If you want to sell your own items online, try eBay, which lets you list items either at a fixed price or via online auction format.

- Another good place to sell items you own is craigslist, which functions like a local classified advertising site.

16

SENDING AND RECEIVING EMAIL

Email is a modern way to communicate with friends, family, and colleagues. An email message is like a regular letter, except that it's composed electronically and delivered almost immediately via the Internet.

You can use a dedicated email program, such as Microsoft Outlook or Windows 8.1's Mail app, to send and receive email from your personal computer. If you prefer, you can use a web mail service such as Gmail or Yahoo! Mail to manage all your email from any web browser on any computer. Either approach is good and enables you to create, send, and read email messages from all your friends, family, and colleagues.

How Email Works

Email—short for "electronic mail"—is like traditional postal mail, except that you compose messages that are delivered electronically, via the Internet. When you send an email message to another Internet user, that message travels from your PC to your recipient's PC through a series of Internet connections and servers, almost instantaneously. Email messages can be of any length and can include file attachments of various types.

To make sure your message goes to the right recipient, you have to use your recipient's *email address.* Every Internet user has a unique email address, composed of three parts:

- The user's name
- The **@** sign
- The user's domain name (usually the name of the Internet service provider, or ISP)

As an example, if you use Comcast as your Internet provider (with the domain name comcast.net) and your login name is jimbo, your email address is jimbo@comcast.net.

POP Email Versus Web Mail

There are actually two different ways to send and receive email via the Internet.

The traditional way to send and receive email uses a protocol called the Post Office Protocol (POP). POP email requires use of a dedicated email software program and—at the ISP level—separate email servers to send and receive messages.

 NOTE   Many POP email providers also offer web-based access from any web browser.

The other way to send and receive email is via Web-based email services, also known as *web mail.* Unlike straight POP email, you can access web mail from any computer, using any web browser; no special software is required.

POP Email

POP email is the standard type of email account you receive when you sign up with an ISP. You're assigned an email account, given an email address, and provided with the necessary information to configure your email program to access this account.

To use POP email, you have to use a special POP email program, such as Microsoft Outlook (part of the Microsoft Office suite) or the Mail app included with Windows 8.1. That email program has to be configured to send email to your ISP's outgoing mail server (called an *SMTP server*) and to receive email from your ISP's incoming mail server (called a *POP3* or *IMAP server*). If you want to access your email account from another computer, you have to use a similar email program and go through the entire configuration process all over again on the second computer.

Web Mail

You're not limited to using the "hard-wired" POP email offered by your ISP; you can also send and receive email from web mail services, such as Google's Gmail and Yahoo! Mail. These web mail services enable you to access your email from any computer, using any web browser.

If you use a PC in multiple locations—in the office, at home, or on the road—this is a convenient way to check your email at any time of day, no matter where you are. You don't have to go through the same sort of complicated configuration routine that you use with POP email. All you have to do is go to the email service's website, enter your user ID and password, and you're ready to send and receive messages.

 TIP Your ISP might offer web-based access to its traditional POP email, which is convenient when you're away from home and need to check your email.

Most web mail services are completely free to use. Some services offer both free versions and paid versions, with paid subscriptions offering additional message storage and functionality.

The largest web mail services include the following:

- AOL Mail (webmail.aol.com)
- Gmail (mail.google.com)
- Lycos Mail (mail.lycos.com)
- Mail.com (www.mail.com)
- Outlook.com (www.outlook.com)
- Yahoo! Mail (mail.yahoo.com)

Using Gmail

One of the largest web mail services today is Google's Gmail. It's the web mail service I use, and one I definitely recommend.

Navigating Gmail

You access the Gmail home page at mail.google.com. If you don't yet have a Google account, you're prompted to sign up for one. Do so now; signing up is free.

After you activate your Gmail account, you're assigned an email address (in the form of *name*@gmail.com), and you get access to the Gmail Inbox page.

The default view of the Gmail page is the Inbox, shown in Figure 16.1, which contains all your received messages. You can switch to other views by clicking the appropriate links on the left side of the page. For example, to view all your sent mail, simply click the Sent Mail link on the left.

FIGURE 16.1

The Gmail Inbox.

Gmail attempts to organize your incoming mail by type and display each type of message on a separate tab. The Primary tab displays standard correspondence; the Social tab displays messages from Facebook, Google+, and other social networks; the Promotions tab displays advertising email; and the Updates tab displays messages from your bank, credit card company, and similar services you use on a regular basis. Click a tab to read all messages of a given type.

Each message is listed with the message's sender, the message's subject, a snippet from the message, and the date or time the message was sent. (The snippet typically is the first line of the message text.) Unread messages are listed in bold; after a message has been read, it's displayed in normal, nonbold text with a shaded background. And if you've assigned a label to a message, the label appears before the message subject.

To perform an action on a message or group of messages, put a check mark by the message(s), and then click one of the buttons at the top of the list. Alternatively, you can click the More button to display a list of additional actions to perform.

Reading Messages

To read a message, all you have to do is click the message title in the Inbox. This displays the full text of the message on a new page.

If you want to display this message in a new window, click the In New Window icon. To print the message, click the Print All icon. To return to the Inbox, click the Back to Inbox button.

Viewing Conversations

One of the unique things about Gmail is that all related email messages are grouped in what Google calls *conversations*. A conversation might be an initial message and all its replies (and replies to replies). A conversation might also be all the daily emails from a single source with a common subject, such as messages you receive from subscribed-to mailing lists.

A conversation is noted in the Inbox list by a number in parentheses after the sender name(s). If a conversation has replies from more than one person, more than one name is listed.

To view a conversation, simply click the message title; the most recent message displays in full. To view the text of any individual message in a conversation, click that message's subject. To expand *all* the messages in a conversation, click the Expand All link. All the messages in the conversation are stacked on top of each other, with the text of the newest message fully displayed.

Replying to a Message

Whether you're reading a single message or a conversation, it's easy enough to send a reply. In the original message, click the Reply button to expand the message to include a reply box. Or, if a conversation has multiple participants, you can reply to all of them by clicking the down arrow next to the Reply button and then selecting Reply to All.

The text of the original message is already quoted in the reply. Add your new text above the original text. Because the original sender's address is automatically added to the To line, all you have to do to send the message is click the Send button.

Composing a New Message

To compose and send a new message, follow these steps:

1. Click the Compose button at the top of the left column on any Gmail page.

2. When the Compose Mail pane opens, as shown in Figure 16.2, enter the recipient's email address in the To box. Separate multiple recipients with commas.

FIGURE 16.2

Composing a new Gmail message.

3. Enter a subject for the message into the Subject box.

4. Enter the text of your message in the large text box. Click the Formatting Options button at the bottom of the pane to enhance your text with bold, italic, and other formats.

5. When you're done composing your message, click the Send button.

TIP You can also carbon copy and blind carbon copy additional recipients by clicking the Cc and Bcc links. This expands the message to include Cc or Bcc boxes, into which you enter the recipients' addresses.

Sending Files via Gmail

When you need to send a digital photo or other file to a friend or colleague, you can do so via email. To send a file via email, you attach that file to a standard email message. When the message is sent, the *file attachment* travels along with it; when the message is received, the file is right there, waiting to be opened.

Dangers of File Attachments

It's an unfortunate fact that email file attachments are the biggest sources of computer virus and spyware infection. Malicious users attach viruses and spyware to email messages, oftentimes disguised as legitimate files; when a user clicks to open the file, his computer is infected with the virus or spyware.

 NOTE Learn more about computer viruses and spyware in Chapter 29, "Protecting Your PC from Computer Attacks, Malware, and Spam."

This doesn't mean that all file attachments are dangerous, simply that opening file attachments—especially those you weren't expecting—is risky. As such, you should avoid opening any file sent to you from a user you don't know. You should also avoid opening files that you weren't expecting from friends and colleagues.

The only relatively safe file attachments are those that come from people you know who previously told you they were being sent. So if your boss previously emailed you to tell you he'd be sending you an important Excel file, and you later get an email from him containing an .XLS-format file, that file is probably safe to open. On the other hand, if you receive an email from a complete stranger with an unknown file attached, that's almost definitely a malicious file that you shouldn't open.

What should you do when you receive an unexpected or unwanted file attachment? Fortunately, just receiving an email attachment doesn't activate it; you have to open the file to launch the virus or spyware. What you should do then is delete the entire message. Don't open the file attachment; just delete the whole thing—message and attachment together. What's deleted can't harm you or your computer.

Attaching a File in Gmail

It's easy to send file attachments in Gmail. Just follow these steps:

1. Compose a new message and then click the Attach Files (paperclip) button at the bottom of the pane.

2. When the Files screen or Open dialog box appears, navigate to and select the file you want to attach, and then click the Open button.

3. The file you selected now appears under the Subject box on the new message page. Continue to compose, and then send your message as normal.

 CAUTION Gmail blocks the transmittal of all executable program files (with an .EXE extension) in an attempt to prevent potential computer viruses.

Opening an Attachment in Gmail

When you receive a Gmail message with an attachment, you see a paper clip icon next to the message subject/snippet. To view or save an attachment, click the message to open it, and then scroll to the bottom of the message.

If the attachment is a picture, you'll see the picture in the message, as shown in Figure 16.3. If the attachment is another type of file, you'll see a View link; click this link to view the file in your web browser.

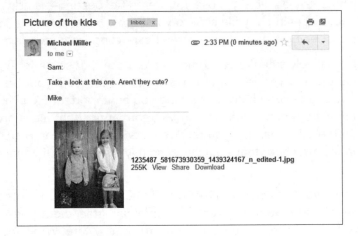

FIGURE 16.3

Viewing and downloading attachments to an email message.

To save the file to your hard disk, click the Download link. When you're asked if you want to open or save the file, click or tap the Save button. After a quick security scan, Windows saves the file and asks if you want to open it. Click the Open button to do so.

Managing Your Email with the Windows Mail App

Windows 8.1 includes a built-in Mail app for sending and receiving email messages. You open the Mail app by clicking or tapping its tile on the Windows Start screen. This is a "live" tile; your most recent unread messages scroll across the face of the tile, and the number at the bottom left indicates how many unread messages you have.

By default, the Mail app manages email from the Outlook.com or Hotmail account linked to your Microsoft Account. This means you see Outlook.com and Hotmail messages in your Mail Inbox, and you can easily send emails from your Outlook. com account.

 NOTE Microsoft's web-based email service used to be called Hotmail but recently was renamed to Outlook.com. All older accounts retain the @hotmail.com part of the email address; newer accounts have an @outlook.com address.

Checking Your Inbox

As you can see in Figure 16.4, the left panel of the app displays all the folders from the selected email account. Select a folder, such as your Inbox, and all the messages from that folder are displayed in the center panel. To read a message, all you have to do is click or tap it; the message content is then displayed in the large right panel.

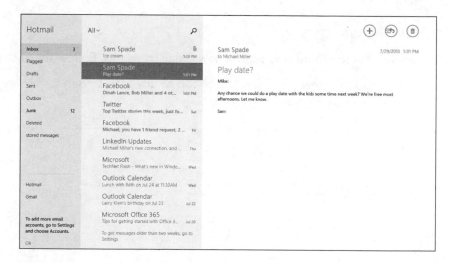

FIGURE 16.4

Viewing a message from your Inbox.

To reply to a message, follow these steps:

1. From an open message, click or tap the Respond button at the top of screen.

2. Select Reply from the pop-up menu to display the Reply screen, shown in Figure 16.5.

3. Enter your reply at the top of the message; the bottom of the message "quotes" the original message.

4. Click or tap the Send button at the top of the screen when you're ready to send the message.

FIGURE 16.5

Replying to a message.

Sending New Messages

It's equally easy to create and send a new email message. Follow these steps:

1. Click or tap the New (+) button at the top of any Mail screen to display the new message screen, shown in Figure 16.6.

FIGURE 16.6

Creating a new email message.

2. Click or tap within the To box and begin entering the name or email address of the message's recipient. Mail displays a list of matching names from your contact list; select the person you want to email.

3. Click or tap the Add a Subject area and type a subject for this message.

4. Click or tap within the main body of the message area and type your message. Use the Bold, Italic, Underline, Font, Font Color, and other buttons in the bottom bar to format your message.

5. To attach a file to this message, click or tap Attachments in the left column. When the Files screen appears, navigate to and select the file you want to attach, then click or tap the Attach button.

6. When you're ready to send the email, click or tap the Send button at the top of the message.

That's it. Windows now sends your message, using your default email account.

Adding Another Email Account

By default, the Mail app sends and receives messages from the email account associated with your Microsoft account. You can, however, configure Mail to work with other email accounts, if you have them. Follow these steps:

1. From within the Mail app, display the Charms bar and then click or tap Settings.

2. When the Settings pane appears, click or tap Accounts.

3. When the Accounts pane appears, click or tap Add an Account.

4. When the next pane appears, as shown in Figure 16.7, click the type of account you want to add.

5. When the Add Your Account pane appears, enter your email address and password, and then click the Connect button.

The Mail app lets you add Outlook.com, Gmail (Google), Yahoo! Mail, AOL Mail, and Microsoft Exchange email accounts. To view the Inbox of another email account, click the name of that account at the bottom of the navigation pane in the Mail app.

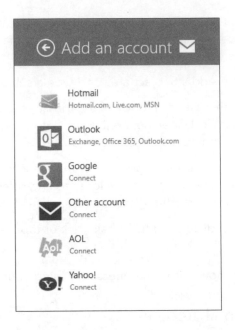

FIGURE 16.7

Attaching a new email account to the Mail app.

THE ABSOLUTE MINIMUM

Here are the key points to remember from this chapter:

- Email is a fast and easy way to send electronic letters over the Internet.

- There are two types of email: POP email, which requires a separate email program, and web mail, which can be sent and received from any web browser.

- The most popular web mail services include Google's Gmail, Microsoft Outlook.com, and Yahoo! Mail.

- You can use the Mail app in Windows 8.1 to send and receive email from your default email account; the app also consolidates messages from other services you've connected to your account.

- Don't open unexpected files attached to incoming email messages; they might contain computer viruses!

SOCIAL NETWORKING WITH FACEBOOK

Want to find out what your friends, family, and colleagues are up to? Want to let them know what you're doing today? Then you need to hop onboard the social networking train; it's how savvy online users are connecting today.

Social networking enables people to share experiences and opinions with each other via community-based websites; it's a great way to keep up-to-date on what your friends and family are doing. The biggest social network today is a site called Facebook. Chances are all your friends are already using it!

How Social Networking Works

In practice, a social network isn't a network at all; it's just a large website that aims to create a community of users. Your personal community consists of "friends" that you make on the site; these friends can be actual friends, family members, or just people you know online.

The process of finding new friends is called *friending*, and some specific rules are involved. First, it's important to be connected to all your real-world friends and acquaintances. Second, you want to be connected to people whom you might not personally know, but whom you've heard of and respect. Third, although it's important to have a lot of friends, the coolness of your friends matters more than the number of them. In other words, it's better to have ten good friends than 100 nobodies. (Although it's hard to convince some social butterflies of that last point...)

When you have something new or interesting to share, you post it as a *status update* to the social networking site. All your online friends read your posts, as well as posts from other friends, in a continuously updated *news feed*. The news feed is the one place where you can read updates from all your online friends and family; it's where you find out what's really happening.

In addition, you can use social networks to share family pictures and videos with your friends. All you have to do is upload a photo or video, and all your online friends can view it from your news feed. It's an efficient way to "pass around" your latest vacation photos!

Getting to Know Facebook

No question about it, the number-one social network today is Facebook (www.facebook.com). Facebook has more than a billion active users worldwide; chances are, most of your friends and family are already on Facebook, just waiting for you to join in the fun.

 NOTE Learn more about Facebook in my companion books *Easy Facebook*, *Facebook for Grown-Ups*, and *My Facebook for Seniors*, all published by Que.

Signing Up and Signing In with the Facebook App

You can access Facebook using Internet Explorer (or any web browser), at www.facebook.com. You can also access Facebook using the Facebook app for Windows 8.1. It's available for free from the Windows Store; just search for **facebook** and it should be the first app in the search results.

 CAUTION In addition to the official Facebook app, there are several unofficial Facebook apps in the Windows Store. Some of these unofficial apps are quite good, some aren't, but none are published by Facebook itself. When you open the app's page in the Store, make sure it's the one published by Facebook, Inc.

The Facebook app does almost everything you can do on the website and might be the preferred approach for many users. However, there are some things that you can't yet do from the Facebook app that you'll have to do from the website; I'll mention those as appropriate throughout this section.

When you first launch the Facebook app, you're prompted to sign in with your email address and password. If you're already a Facebook member, enter this information and click the Login button to get started.

If you're new to Facebook, however, you'll first need to sign up for your free account. Click Sign Up for Facebook at the bottom of the screen, and your web browser will launch and take you to Facebook's sign-up page on the Web. Click the New Account button, and then follow the onscreen instructions to create your account.

Getting to Know the Facebook App

You navigate the Facebook app (and the Facebook website) from the navigation sidebar on the left. The middle of the screen displays the selected page or content, and the right column displays your list of friends and any group chats you've participated in.

 NOTE Facebook is constantly upgrading its feature set, so what you see might differ somewhat from what is described here.

The default selection in the navigation sidebar is your News Feed, and for good reason; as you can see in Figure 17.1, this is where all the status updates from your friends are displayed. Scroll down the page to view more updates.

Search box   News Feed   Facebook toolbar

Friends sidebar

Navigation sidebar

FIGURE 17.1

The Facebook Home page—complete with News Feed of your friends' status updates.

You can also navigate the Facebook app (and website) from the toolbar at the top of the page. In addition to the big Search box, which you use to search for people and things on the Facebook site, the toolbar lets you click to see friend requests, private messages, and notifications.

Keeping Tabs on Friends

Social networking is all about keeping in touch with friends. To get the most out of Facebook, then, you need to find some—friends, that is.

Finding Friends

The easiest way to find friends on Facebook is to let Facebook find them for you—based on the information you provided for your personal profile. The more Facebook knows about you, especially in terms of where you've worked and gone to school, the more friends it can find.

The best way to find new Facebook friends is to use the Facebook website (www.facebook.com); the Facebook app doesn't have quite the friend-finding features that the website does. To find new friends on Facebook, then, follow these steps:

1. Use your web browser to go to and sign into the Facebook website, at www.facebook.com.

2. Click the Friends button on the toolbar to display the pull-down menu, shown in Figure 17.2. This menu lists any friend requests you've received and offers a number of friend suggestions from Facebook ("People You May Know"). To add one of these people to your friends list, click the Add Friend button.

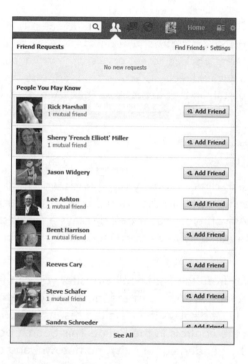

FIGURE 17.2

Finding friends on the Facebook website.

 NOTE The people Facebook suggests as friends are typically people who went to the same schools you did, worked at the same companies you did, or are friends of your current friends.

3. To continue searching for friends, click Find Friends at the top of the menu to display your Friends page.

4. Scroll down the page to view other suggested friends from Facebook in the People You May Know section. Click the Add Friend button for any person you'd like to add as a friend.

5. To find people in your email contacts list who are also members of Facebook, scroll to the top of the Friends page. Click the Find Friends link for the email service you use and then enter any requested information (typically your email address and password). Facebook lists all matching contacts.

6. Check the people you'd like to add as a friend and then click the Send Invites button.

 NOTE Facebook doesn't automatically add a person to your friends list. Instead, that person receives an invitation to be your friend; she can accept or reject the invitation. To accept or reject any friend requests you've received, click the Friend Request button on the Facebook toolbar. (And don't worry; if you reject a request, that person won't be notified.)

Searching for Friends

You can also search directly for any old friends who might be on Facebook by entering a person's name into the Search box on the Facebook website or in the Facebook app. As you type, Facebook displays a list of suggestions beneath the search box; if the person you want is listed, click that person's name to see her Timeline page.

If you're searching from the Facebook website, you can fine-tune your search by clicking See More at the bottom of the initial search suggestions. The next page, shown in Figure 17.3, displays the detailed results of your search. You can adjust the results using the controls in the Refine This Search box. For example, you can filter the results by gender, current city, hometown, and school. If your friend is listed, click the Add Friend button to send him a friend request.

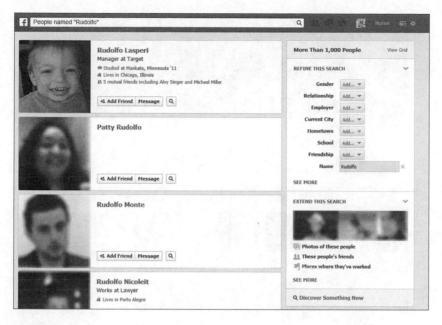

FIGURE 17.3

Searching for friends on the Facebook website.

Viewing a Friend's Timeline Page

After you've added some folks to your Facebook friends list, you can easily see what they've been up to by visiting their Timeline pages. A Facebook Timeline page is essentially a person's profile page on Facebook.

A Timeline page, like the one shown in Figure 17.4, displays all that person's status updates and activities on the Facebook site, in the form of a timeline. But that's not all that's there.

FIGURE 17.4

A typical Facebook Timeline page in the Facebook app.

To view detailed personal information about your friend, click the About box. To view the pictures this person has uploaded, click Photos, and to see a list of this person's friends, click Friends.

Keeping in Touch with Status Updates

We've talked a lot about Facebook being the perfect place to update your friends and family on what you're up to—things you're doing, thoughts you're thinking, accomplishments you're accomplishing, you name it. The easiest way to let people know what's what is to post what Facebook calls a *status update*.

Every status update you make is broadcast to everyone on your friends list, displayed in the News Feed on their Home pages. This way everyone who cares enough about you to make you a friend knows everything you post about. And that can be quite a lot—from simple text posts to photos and videos and even links to other web pages.

Posting Status Updates

Facebook makes it extremely easy to post a status update. Here's how you do it from within the Facebook app:

1. Click News Feed in the navigation sidebar to display the News Feed.

2. Click Status at the top of the News Feed to display the Update Status pane, shown in Figure 17.5.

3. Type a short message into the Update Status pane, where it says "What's on your mind?"

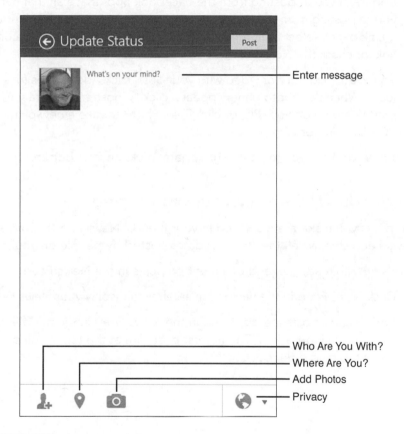

FIGURE 17.5

Posting a new status update.

4. If you're with someone else and want to mention them in the post, click the With? button to display the With? pane. You can then select a friend from the list or search for a specific friend, and then click the Save button.

5. If you want to include your current location in your post, click the Add Location button to display the Add Location pane. Choose a location from the list or search for a specific location, and then click the Save button.

6. To determine who can read this post, click the Audience (AKA Privacy) button to display the Audience pane. You can opt to make any post Public (meaning anyone can read it), visible to your Friends, visible to Friends of Friends, visible to Friends Except Acquaintances, or visible to Only Me (so that no one sees it except you).

7. To include a link to another web page, enter that page's URL in your status update. If you're posting from the Facebook app, that's all that happens. If you're posting from the Facebook website, however, Facebook now displays a Link panel; select a thumbnail image from the web page to accompany the link, or check the No Thumbnail box.

8. To include a picture or video with your post, click Add Photos (the camera icon). When the photo panel appears, click Choose from Library to select a picture stored on your PC, or click Take Photo to take a new picture with your PC's built-in webcam.

9. When you're ready to post your update, click the Post button.

Viewing Friends' Updates in Your News Feed

The posts you make are displayed in your friends' News Feeds. Conversely, your News Feed displays all the status updates posted by people on your friends list.

Here's how to read, like, and comment on posts in the News Feed:

1. Click News Feed in the navigation sidebar to display your News Feed.

2. Your friends' posts are displayed in the News Feed in the middle of the page, as shown in Figure 17.6. The newest posts are at the top; scroll down through the list to read older posts.

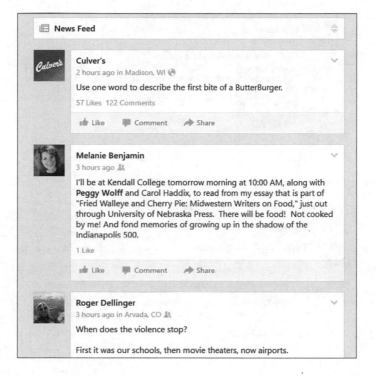

FIGURE 17.6

Viewing friends' posts in the News Feed.

3. To leave a comment about a post, click Comment and then enter your text into the resulting Write a Comment box.

4. To "like" a post, click Like.

5. If a post includes one or more photos, click the photo to view a larger version of that photo.

6. If a post includes a video (which is indicated by a Play icon in the middle of the thumbnail), click the video thumbnail to begin playback.

7. If a post includes a link to another web page, that link appears beneath the post, along with a brief description of the page, as shown in Figure 17.7. Click the link to open the other page in your web browser.

FIGURE 17.7

A status update with a link to a web page included.

TIP Facebook offers feeds other than the default News Feed. In the Facebook app, click the Feed List control above the News Feed to choose from other feeds such as All Friends, Most Recent, Following (pages you follow), Groups, Photos, and Games. (On the Facebook website, the Feed List is to the right of the News Feed.)

Sharing Photos

Facebook is a social network, and one of the ways we connect socially is through pictures. We track our progress through life as a series of pictures. We document events small and large, from picnics in the backyard to family vacations to births, graduations, weddings, and everything else that transpires.

Uploading Photos to Facebook

Facebook lets you upload and store photos in virtual photo albums. You can upload new photos to an existing album or create a new album for newly uploaded photos.

Unfortunately, the Facebook app doesn't let you upload photos to photo albums. (You can still include photos with a status update in the app, however.) To create photo albums and upload photos to those albums, you have to use the Facebook website. Just follow these steps:

1. Click Photos in the navigation sidebar or on your Timeline page to display your Photos page.

2. Click the Create Album button to display the Files page; then select the photos you want to upload.

3. You now see the Untitled Album page, with thumbnails of your photos displayed, as shown in Figure 17.8. You want to give this album a name, so click Untitled Album and enter the desired album name.

| Untitled Album | | ♀ Where were these taken? · | Add Date |
| Say something about this album... | | ⇌ Order by Date Taken ‚ | |

FIGURE 17.8

Uploading photos to a new photo album.

4. Click Say Something About This Album and enter an album description.

5. To enter a geographic location for all the photos in this album, go to the Where Were These Taken box and enter a location.

6. To add a date to all the photos in this album, click Add Date and select a date from the pop-up box.

 NOTE All the information you can add to a photo album is entirely optional; you can add as much or as little as you like. You don't even have to add a title. (If you don't, Facebook uses the title Untitled Album.)

7. To enter information about a specific picture, enter a description in the Say Something About This Photo box, shown in Figure 17.9.

FIGURE 17.9

Entering information about an uploaded photo.

8. To tag a person who appears in a given photo, click that person's face and enter his or her name when prompted.

NOTE You identify people in your photos by *tagging* them. That is, you click on a person in the photo and then assign a friend's name to that part of the photo. You can then find photos where a given person appears by searching for that person's tag.

9. To enter the date a photo was taken, click that photo's Date button and then select the year, month, and date.

10. To enter the place a photo was taken, click that photo's Location button and then enter a location into the Where Was This box.

11. To determine who can view the photos in this album, click the Privacy button and make a selection: Public, Friends, Friends Except Acquaintances, Only Me, or Custom.

12. Click the Post Photos button when done.

TIP To achieve the best possible picture quality for anyone downloading or printing your photos, check the High Quality option to upload and store your photos at their original resolution. Note, however, that it takes longer to upload high-quality photos than those in standard quality.

After you've created a photo album, you can easily upload more photos to that album; you don't have to create a new album every time you want to upload new photos.

To upload pictures to an existing album, go to your Photos page and click Albums to display your photo albums. Click to open the album to which you want to add new photos; then click the Add Photos button and select the photos to upload.

The photos you selected are now added to the album page. Add any information you want about a given photo—location, date, information, and the like. You can also tag people in each photo. Click the Post Photos button when you're done.

Viewing Photos

Viewing a friend's photos is as easy as going to that person's Timeline page and clicking Photos. This displays your friend's Photos page.

If you're using the Facebook website, you have to click Albums to view your friend's photo albums. In the Facebook app, you automatically see all his albums, like those shown in Figure 17.10.

FIGURE 17.10

Viewing a friend's Photos page in the Facebook app.

Click the thumbnail of the picture you want to view. If you're viewing on Facebook's website, you see the selected picture in a *lightbox* superimposed on top of the previous page. If you're viewing in the Facebook app, you see the photo full screen, as shown in Figure 17.11. You move to the next photo in the album by clicking the right arrow or pressing the right arrow on your keyboard; there's no need to close the photo before moving to the next one. Keep clicking the right arrow to move through all the photos in the album; click the left arrow to go back through the previously viewed photos. To close the viewer and get back to the photo album, just click the X (close) button at the top right of the lightbox (on the website) or click the back arrow button at the top left of the screen (in the app).

FIGURE 17.11

Viewing a photo in the Facebook app.

Managing Your Privacy on Facebook

Facebook is all about connecting users to one another. That's how the site functions, after all, by encouraging "friends" and all sorts of public sharing of information.

The problem is that Facebook, by default, shares all your information with just about everybody. Not just your friends or friends of your friends, but the entire membership of the site. And not just with Facebook members, either; Facebook also shares your information with third-party applications and games and with other sites on the Web.

Fortunately, you can configure Facebook to be much less public than it is by default. If you value your privacy, this might be worth doing.

Controlling Your Default Privacy

The first step to ensuring your Facebook privacy is to determine who, by default, can see the new posts you make. By default, Facebook makes your posts public, so that anyone can see them. This makes sense for Facebook, which believes that the more it knows about you, the more connections it can recommend and make.

Making your entire life totally public may not be your cup of tea, however. You may want to limit your posts just to your friends, or even a select group of friends. You may even want to configure things so that specific people *can't* see your posts.

With that in mind, here's how to configure Facebook's default privacy settings. You have to do this from Facebook's website; there's no way to do this from the Facebook app.

1. On the Facebook website, click the Privacy Shortcuts button on the Facebook toolbar to display the pull-down menu.

2. Click the down arrow next to Who Can See My Stuff to expand the menu, as shown in Figure 17.12.

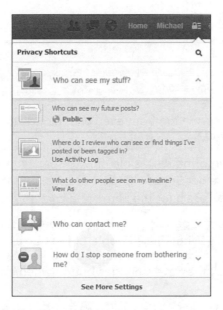

FIGURE 17.12

Configuring Facebook's default privacy options.

3. Go to the Who Can See My Future Posts? section, click the down arrow, and select one of the resulting options.

4. Click Public to let anyone on Facebook see your posts.

5. Click Friends to restrict viewing to only people on your Facebook friends list.

6. Click Only Me to keep your posts totally private—that is, to keep anyone from seeing them.

What if you want to create a custom list of people who can or can't see your posts? Then click the Custom option to open the Custom Privacy dialog box, shown in Figure 17.13. From here you can do the following:

FIGURE 17.13

Customizing your privacy settings.

- To hide your information from everyone, pull down the Share This With list and select Only Me.

- To make your information visible only to specific people, pull down the Share This With list, select Specific People or Lists, and then enter the names of those Facebook users (or the name of a custom friends list).

- To prevent specific people from viewing your posts, enter names into the Don't Share This With These People or Lists box.

Remember to check the Save Changes button when done.

Selecting Who Can See (or Not See) Individual Posts

Even after you set these global posting privacy settings, you can change the privacy setting for any individual post you make. That is, any given post can be sent to a specific list of people that overrides the global settings you made previously.

For example, you might have set your global privacy settings so that your friends can see your posts. But if you have a new post that you want only your immediate family to see, you can configure that single post to go only to your family members, not to everyone else on your friends list.

You can set the privacy setting for individual posts both from the Facebook website and in the Facebook app. Here's how to do it:

1. Start a new status update as normal.

2. Click the Post Privacy Setting button and select one of the following options, as shown in Figure 17.14: Public, Friends, Friends Except Acquaintances, Only Me, or Custom.

3. Post the status update as normal. Only those friends you selected will see this post.

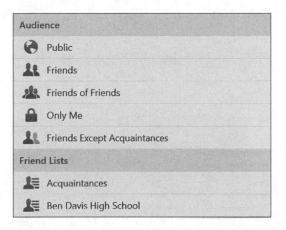

FIGURE 17.14

Setting privacy settings for an individual post in the Facebook app.

THE ABSOLUTE MINIMUM

Here are the key points to remember from this chapter:

- Social networking sites let you keep in touch with what your friends and family are doing.

- The largest social networking site today is Facebook, with more than one billion users.

- You can access Facebook from Facebook's Windows 8.1 app or from the Facebook website.

- You view your friends' activity in the News Feed.

- You let others know what you're doing by posting status updates, which appear in your friends' News Feeds.

- You can also use Facebook to share photos with your friends.

- Facebook enables you to control who sees specific things you post.

18

MORE SOCIAL NETWORKING WITH PINTEREST, LINKEDIN, AND TWITTER

Facebook might be the biggest social network on the Web today, but it's not the only one. There are several other social networks that help you keep in touch with friends and family—and, in some cases, focus on specific types of users or interests.

The most popular of these social networks are Pinterest, LinkedIn, and Twitter. We'll look at each in this chapter.

Using Pinterest

Pinterest is kind of a visual version of Facebook that's become increasingly popular among average, nontechnical users. The user base includes a fairly large number of women aged 30 and older who like to share pictures of clothing, DIY projects, and the like.

What Pinterest Is and What It Does

Unlike Facebook, which lets you post text-based status updates, Pinterest is all about images. The site consists of a collection of virtual online "pinboards" that people use to share pictures they find interesting. Users "pin" photos and other images to their personal message boards and then share their pins with online friends.

Here's how it works. You start by finding an image on a web page that you like and want to share. You then "pin" that image to one of your personal online pinboards, which are like old-fashioned corkboards, except online.

A pinboard becomes a place where you can create and share collections of those things you like or find interesting. You can have as many pinboards as you like, organized by category or topic.

Friends who follow you see the images you pin, and you see the ones they pin. You can also "like" other people's pins and repin their items to your pinboards, thus repeating the original pin. It's a visual way to share things you like online.

Joining Pinterest is free; in fact, you can sign up using your Facebook username and password. (Or with your email address, of course.) Go to www.pinterest.com to get started.

Navigating the Pinterest Site

Pinterest is a relatively easy website to get around. After you've logged on, it's a simple matter of displaying certain types of pins from certain users and then knowing how to get back to the main page.

The Pinterest home page, shown in Figure 18.1, consists of a toolbar of sorts at the top, with individual pins filling the bulk of the page beneath that. You use the toolbar to navigate the site.

To search for pins about a particular topic, enter your query into the search box and press Enter. To browse pins by category, click the Category (three line) button on the left side of the toolbar and select a category from the resulting list.

FIGURE 18.1

Pinterest's home page.

Viewing Pinboards and Pins

A user's presence on Pinterest is defined by her pinboards and the pins posted there. To view a friend's pinboards and the contents, all you have to do is click that friend's name anywhere on the Pinterest site. Your friend's personal Pinterest page displays with thumbnails of her pinboards, as shown in Figure 18.2.

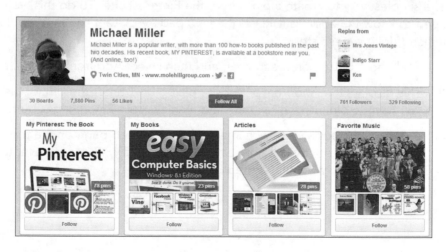

FIGURE 18.2

Viewing a Pinterest profile page.

To open a pinboard, click the board's thumbnail image. This displays all the pins for the selected board. Each pin consists of the pinned image, descriptive text (supplied by the user who pinned the item), and the URL for the website where this image was found. To view the web page where the image originally appeared, click the pin.

Following Other Users

When you find someone who posts a lot of things you're interested in, you can follow that person on Pinterest. When you follow a person, all that person's new pins display on your Pinterest home page.

You can find people to follow by using Pinterest's search box (in the toolbar) to search by name or interest. After you've located a person you want to follow, just go to that person's personal Pinterest page and click the Follow All button.

You can also opt to follow a specific board, rather than all of that person's pins. From the person's personal page, click the Follow Board button for the board you want to follow.

Pinning Items to a Pinboard

Pinterest is all about pinning items of interest—hence the name, a combination of "pin" and "interest." To fully participate in the Pinterest community, you have to learn how to pin items to your pinboards. There are several ways to do this.

The simplest way to create a pin is from the Pinterest site. To do this, you first need to know the address (URL) of the web page you want to pin. With that URL in hand, follow these steps:

1. Click the + button on the toolbar, and then select Add from a Website.

2. This displays the Add from a Website dialog box. Enter the URL of the page you want to pin into the text box and then click the Find Images button.

3. Pinterest displays a page with images from that web page on the top, and previously pinned items below, as shown in Figure 18.3. Mouse over the item you want to pin and click the red Pin It button.

FIGURE 18.3

Selecting an image to pin.

4. You now see the Create a Pin dialog box, shown in Figure 18.4. Pull down the Board list and select the board to which you'd like to pin this image.

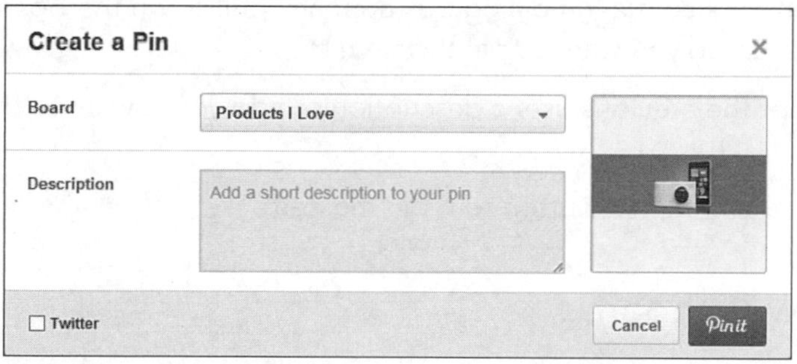

FIGURE 18.4

Creating a new pin.

5. Enter a short (500 characters or less) text description of or comment on this image into the Description box.

6. Click the red Pin It button when done.

Repinning Existing Items

You can also "repin" items that other users have previously pinned. This adds the pinned item to one of your pinboards. To repin an item from its thumbnail image, follow these steps:

1. Mouse over the item you want to repin and then click the Pin It button, as shown in Figure 18.5.

FIGURE 18.5

Repinning an item.

2. When the Repin a Pin dialog box appears, pull down the Board list and select which board you want to pin this item to.

3. Accept the previous user's description or add your own into the Description box.

4. Click the red Pin it button to repin the item.

Creating New Pinboards

You can create as many different pinboards as you like, each focusing on a specific topic. Create individual pinboards to match your own interests and hobbies.

To create a new pinboard, follow these steps:

1. Click the + button on the toolbar and select Create a Board.

2. When the Create a Board dialog box appears, as shown in Figure 18.6, enter a name for this board into the Name box.

3. Enter a short description of the board's contents into the Description box.

4. Pull down the Category list and select a category for this board.

5. Make sure the Secret option is turned off. (Turn it on if you want to create a private board that no one but you can see.)

6. Click the red Create Board button.

Pinterest creates the board and displays the page for this board. (It's currently empty.) You can now start pinning items to the board!

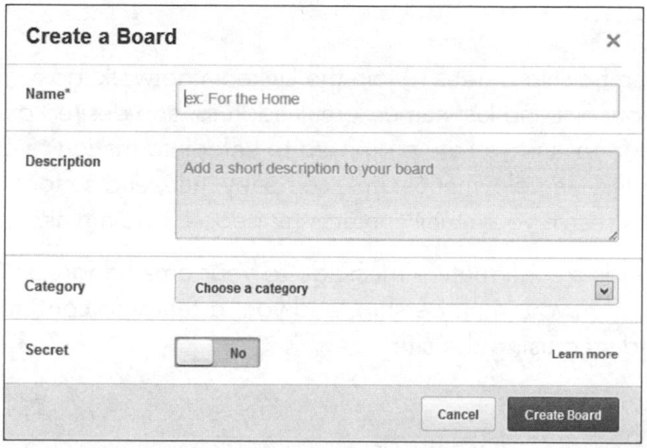

FIGURE 18.6

Creating a new pinboard.

Using LinkedIn

LinkedIn is a different kind of social network—not necessarily in how it works, but in whom it appeals to. Whereas Facebook and Pinterest are aimed at a general audience, LinkedIn is targeted at business professionals. As such, you can use LinkedIn to network with others in your industry or profession or even to hunt for a new position at another firm. (Figure 18.7 shows the LinkedIn home page—with a definite business slant.)

FIGURE 18.7

The LinkedIn home page.

Creating an Account

LinkedIn membership is free. To join the LinkedIn network, go to www.linkedin.com and enter your first and last names, email address, and desired password. Click the Join Now button, and you are prompted to enter information to complete your personal profile—employment status, company, title, and so forth. You also are prompted to search your email contacts for people who are already on LinkedIn.

LinkedIn sends a confirmation message to your email address. Click the link in the email to confirm your membership, and you're ready to continue building your network and start using the site.

 TIP Use the menu bar at the top of each page to find your way around the LinkedIn site. The menu bar contains links to the LinkedIn home page, your personal profile, your LinkedIn contacts, groups you belong to, LinkedIn's job search features, and your message Inbox.

Personalizing Your Profile

Each LinkedIn member has his own personal profile page. This profile page is what other LinkedIn users see when they search for you on the site; it's where you make your initial impression to potential employers and people with whom you want to make contact.

Because your profile page serves as your *de facto* resume on the LinkedIn site, you want to control the information you display to others. Presenting only selected information can help you present yourself in the best possible light.

Fortunately, your LinkedIn profile is fully customizable; you can select which content others see. This content can include a snapshot of your personal information (shown in Figure 18.8), your contact info, summaries of your professional experience and education, recommendations from other users, and more.

To edit your profile page, click Profile on the menu bar and then select Edit Profile. When the Edit My Profile page appears, click the Edit button for the section(s) you want to edit.

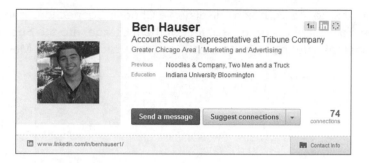

FIGURE 18.8

Snapshot information on a LinkedIn profile page.

Finding New Connections

LinkedIn's equivalent of Facebook friends is called *connections*. These are business or professional contacts you know and trust. Anyone on the LinkedIn site can become a connection; you can also invite people who are not yet LinkedIn members to join your connections list.

You can search for LinkedIn members in your email contacts list. (LinkedIn searches AOL Mail, Gmail, Outlook, Yahoo! Mail, and other email programs and services.) In addition, LinkedIn can search for members who've gone to the same schools or worked for the same employers that you have. You can also invite non-LinkedIn members to be new connections.

To add new connections, pull down the Network menu and select Add Connections. From there you can search for people you know, or you can invite others to join your LinkedIn network.

Contacting Other LinkedIn Members

Networking on LinkedIn involves a lot of personal contact, using LinkedIn's own internal email system. This system enables you to send messages to and receive messages from people on your connections list and anyone else who is a member of the LinkedIn site.

To send a new message, click the Messages button on the toolbar to display your Inbox page, and then click the Compose Message button. When the Message page appears, as shown in Figure 18.9, enter the recipient's name or email address into the To box. (Or, to email one of your connections, click the blue graphic next to the To box to display the Choose Connections panel and select a name from there.) Type the subject of the message into the Subject box, type your message into the large text box, and then click the Send Message button.

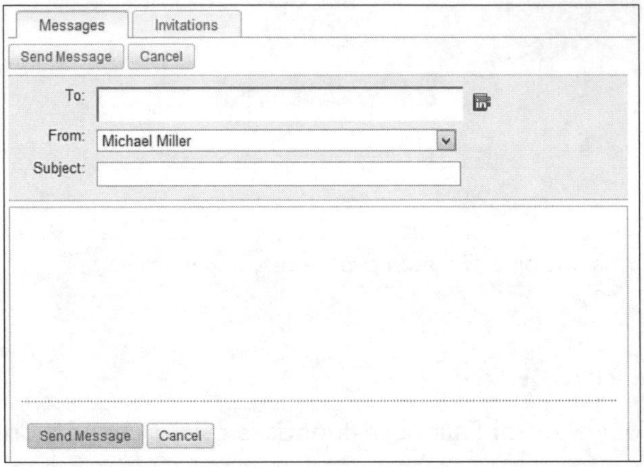

| Messages | Invitations |
| Send Message | Cancel |

To: _____
From: Michael Miller
Subject: _____

Send Message   Cancel

FIGURE 18.9

Sending a new message.

To view messages you've received, click the Messages button on the toolbar. This displays all messages you've received. The newest messages are listed first; unread messages are in bold. To read a message, all you have to do is click the message header.

CAUTION   LinkedIn sends out a lot of emails to its members—so much so that it verges on the spam category. You may want to adjust your LinkedIn preferences to minimize the number of emails you receive. Click your picture on the toolbar, and then click Review next to Privacy and Settings. When the next page appears, click the Communications tab, and then click Set the Frequency of Emails. Edit the settings on the following screen to determine which emails you see how often.

Using Twitter

Then there's Twitter. Unlike Facebook, Pinterest, and LinkedIn, Twitter isn't a fully featured social network per se. Instead, Twitter is a kind of microblogging service that lets you create short (up to 140 characters) text posts—called *tweets*—that your followers receive and read.

NOTE   Most people use Twitter to follow other users rather than to tweet themselves. The most popular tweeters include celebrities, companies and brands, and news organizations and reporters.

Joining and Using Twitter

You can access Twitter from the Twitter website (www.twitter.com), using Internet Explorer or another web browser, or from the Modern-style Twitter app for Windows 8.1. We'll focus our attention on the Twitter app, although the website is similar in operation.

 NOTE   Download the Twitter app for free from the Windows Store. Just search for **Twitter**; the official Twitter app should be the first thing you see in the search results.

When you first launch the Twitter app, you're prompted to either sign in or sign up. If you're already a Twitter user, click the Sign In button and enter your username and password. If you're new to Twitter, click the Sign Up button to create your free Twitter account. (You can also create a Twitter account from the www.twitter.com web page.)

After you've registered and signed in, you see the main screen of the Twitter app, shown in Figure 18.10. The left side of the page is the navigation pane; click Home at any point to return to the home page. The main part of the home page displays the most recent tweets from the users you're following, newest first. You can also click any links in a tweet to go to the mentioned web page or view an embedded photo.

The navigation sidebar enables you to navigate to other sections of the Twitter site. Click @Connect to view tweets that have mentioned you, click #Discover to view trending topics, or click Me to view your own personal Twitter info.

You can also search for specific topics in others' tweets. Click the search (magnifying glass) icon at the top right to display the Search pane, enter your query, and see the results.

FIGURE 18.10

Twitter's home page.

Tweeting with Twitter

To compose and send a tweet, start by clicking the New Tweet button at the top-right corner of any screen. This displays the New Tweet pane, shown in Figure 18.11. Enter your text at the blinking cursor, up to 140 characters long. (Spaces count as characters, by the way.) You can also include your location by clicking the Location button, or you can attach a photo by clicking the Photo button. When you're done, click the Tweet button to send your message on its way.

FIGURE 18.11

Composing a new tweet.

TIP Because space is limited, many tweeters use abbreviations in their tweets. You can mention a hot topic (and make the term searchable) by preceding it with a hashtag (#), like this: #hottopic. To mention a given user in a tweet, put an @ sign in front of his username, like this: @username.

Following Other Users

If friends or family members are on Twitter, you can follow their activities by "following" their tweets.

The easiest way to do this is to use Twitter's search function. As we've previously discussed, click the Search (magnifying glass) icon to display the Search pane, and then enter the person's name, Twitter username, or email address.

If the person you want is listed in the search results, click that person's name to display his, profile page, like the one shown in Figure 18.12. Click the Follow button, and all tweets from that user will start appearing on your Twitter home page.

FIGURE 18.12

A typical Twitter profile page; click Follow to follow this person.

 CAUTION Some users protect their profiles so that strangers can't follow them without their permission. When you click the Follow button for these users, they have to register their approval before you can follow them.

Customizing Your Profile

As you've just seen, every Twitter use has his own personal profile page on the site. To view your profile page, click Me in the navigation sidebar.

From there, right-click to display the Options bar, and then click the Edit Profile button to begin editing. You can edit any of the information on this page, and you can even change the profile picture that others see.

Using Social Networks—Smartly and Safely

Social networking puts your whole life out there in front of your friends and family—and, in some cases, just about anyone perusing a network's profiles. With so much personal information displayed publicly, how do you protect yourself against those who might want to do harm to you or your children?

Protecting Your Children

Given that social networks are so popular among teenagers and preteens, many parents worry about their children being cyberstalked on these sites. That worry is not ill founded, especially given the amount of personal information that most users post on their social networking profiles.

It's important to note that all social networking sites try to police themselves, typically by limiting access for younger users. In addition, sites such as Facebook work hard to keep known sex offenders off their sites by monitoring lists of known sex offenders and culling those users from their sites.

That said, the best way to protect your children on social networking sites is to monitor what they do on those sites. As such, it's important that you become "friends" with your children on Facebook, follow their Twitter feeds, and visit their profile pages on a regular basis. You might be surprised what you find there.

It's an unfortunate fact that not all teens and preteens are wise about what they put online. It's not unusual to find provocative pictures posted on their social networking profiles; you probably don't want your children exposing themselves in this fashion.

You also need to warn your kids that not everyone on Facebook or Twitter is truly a "friend." They should be circumspect about the information they make public and with whom they communicate. It's also worth noting that kids shouldn't arrange to meet in person strangers who they're "friends" with online; it's not unheard of for unsavory adults to use social networks as a stalking ground.

In other words, teach your kids to be careful. Hanging out on a site like Facebook is normally no more dangerous than hanging out at the mall, but even malls aren't completely safe. Caution and common sense are always called for.

Protecting Yourself

The advice you give to your children regarding social networks also applies to yourself. Think twice before posting personal information or incriminating photographs, and don't broadcast your every move on your profile page. Also, don't automatically accept friend requests from people you don't know.

Most important, don't view Facebook and similar sites as online dating services. Yes, you might meet new friends on these social networks, but use caution about transferring online friendships into the physical world. If you decide to meet an online friend offline, do so in a public place and perhaps with another friend along. Don't put yourself at risk when meeting strangers—and remember that until you get to know them in person, anyone you correspond with online remains a stranger.

THE ABSOLUTE MINIMUM

Here are the key points to remember from this chapter:

- Pinterest is a popular social network among regular users, a way to share interesting images with friends.

- LinkedIn is a social network for business professionals.

- Twitter is a way to broadcast short text messages to your followers—and to follow others who tweet.

- Whichever social networking sites you use, be smart about the information you post; some personal information is best not made public.

19

MANAGING YOUR SOCIAL ACTIVITY (AND CONTACTS) IN WINDOWS

If you follow a lot of friends on several social networks, it can be quite time consuming to everyone. Log into Facebook to view your News Feed there, then onto Twitter to view the latest tweets, then onto LinkedIn to see what your contacts are saying there. Wouldn't be nice if there was a way to follow all your friends' activity in one place?

Well, there is, thanks to the Windows People app. This app enables you to consolidate tweets and status updates and posts from the people you follow on Facebook, Twitter, LinkedIn, and other networks—as well as make new posts without having to visit each of those websites. Viewing all your friends' activity is just a click (or a tap) away!

Understanding the People App

The Windows 8.1 People app consolidates messages from several major social networks and your email accounts. You can view the latest updates from your friends in one place—as well as comment on and retweet those updates—without having to visit the social networking sites themselves. It's truly a single hub for all your social networking needs.

What social networks can you connect to from the People app? Here's the list:

- Facebook
- Twitter
- LinkedIn
- Google+ (via your Google Account)

You can also connect the People app to your Gmail, Outlook.com/Hotmail, Microsoft Exchange email accounts, and Skype account.

And here's something else: The People app manages and centralizes your contacts for all your Windows applications. So if there's a person who's in your Outlook.com contacts list, in your Facebook friends list, and whom you follow on Twitter, he appears as a single contact in the People app. When you want to contact that person, just open the People app, find his name, and email away.

Adding Accounts to the People App

By default, the People app connects to the Microsoft account you used to create your Windows account and the corresponding email account. You have to manually add all other email and social networking accounts.

To add a new account to the People app, follow these steps:

1. From the Windows Start screen, click or tap the People tile.

2. Click or press Connected To at the bottom-right corner of the screen to display the Accounts panel. All your current linked accounts are listed here.

3. Click Add an Account to display the Add an Account panel, shown in Figure 19.1.

4. Click the type of account you want to add, and then follow the onscreen instructions specific to that type of account.

FIGURE 19.1

Adding a new account to the People app.

Monitoring Social Networks with the People App

The People app is a convenient full-screen hub for most of your day-to-day social networking activity. While it isn't as full featured as using the Facebook or Twitter websites, it does let you consolidate all your social networking activity in a single place.

You launch the People app by clicking or tapping the People tile on the Windows Start screen. The People tile is a "live" tile that displays a changing selection of profile pictures from your friends, along with the latest status updates.

Viewing Your Friends' Social Activity

The People app displays the most recent posts from your social media friends, from all your connected social networks. (Well, not from Pinterest, but all the others can be linked.) You can then like or comment on any specific post.

Start by opening the People app and clicking What's New. The What's New screen, shown in Figure 19.2, displays status updates and tweets in their own panels. Scroll right to view additional posts.

FIGURE 19.2

Viewing status updates and tweets in the People app.

When you're viewing a Facebook post, you can like or comment on it if you wish. To like a Facebook post, click the Like link. To comment on a post, click the Comment link to display the Comments pane, and then start typing.

You can also favorite, retweet, or reply to a Twitter tweet. Click Favorite to "like" the tweet, Retweet to retweet it, or Reply to enter a direct reply to that person.

Posting to Facebook and Twitter

In addition to displaying the most recent posts from your Facebook (and other) friends, the People app lets you post new status updates to your Facebook and Twitter accounts. Follow these steps:

1. Open the People app and click the Me tile to display your personal People screen.

2. Go to the What's New section, shown in Figure 19.3, and click the down arrow to display a list of your linked social media accounts. Select which account you want to post to.

3. Enter your status update or tweet into the large text box, and then press Enter. Your message is now posted to your Facebook or Twitter feed.

FIGURE 19.3

Posting to Facebook from the People app.

Managing Contacts in the People App

As noted, the People app not only consolidates your social network feeds, but stores all the personal contacts on your computer. Use the People app to manage your contacts—and create new ones.

Viewing Contact Information

When you want to access all your contacts, open the People app and go to the All section. As you can see in Figure 19.4, all your contacts from all your accounts are listed here, in alphabetical order.

FIGURE 19.4

Viewing all your contacts in the People app.

Scroll right and left through the list by pressing the left and right arrow keys on your keyboard, dragging the scrollbar at the bottom of the window with your mouse, or swiping your finger left or right on a touchscreen display. You can also skip directly to names starting with a given letter by pressing that letter on your keyboard; for example, pressing "G" takes you right to those contacts that start with the letter G.

You can also search for a particular contact. Press Windows+Q to display the Search pane; then enter the name of the person you're looking for and press Enter. Windows returns a list of contacts that match your search criteria. Click or tap the contact you want to view.

 NOTE If a person is listed in multiple programs or services, the People app consolidates all that information into a single contact. So, for example, if a contact is listed in your Hotmail, Facebook, and Twitter accounts, information from all those accounts (Hotmail, Facebook, and Twitter) is listed in his single People contact page.

Click or tap a contact name to view full details about this person. There are three panels' worth of info for each contact. The first panel, shown in Figure 19.5, contains Contact Info. It shows the person's profile picture (typically the one used for his Facebook or Twitter profile) and contains links to send a message to that person (via whatever social networks and email accounts that person has), map the person's address, and view all info about that person.

The second panel, dubbed What's New, scrolls through this person's latest posts on Facebook, Twitter, or LinkedIn. You can also use this panel to send messages via social media to this person.

The third panel, Photos, shows photographs or photo albums uploaded by this person to the various social networks. Click an album to open it, and click a photo to display it full screen.

In short, the All screen tells you everything you want to know about everyone you know—and enables you to message them, too.

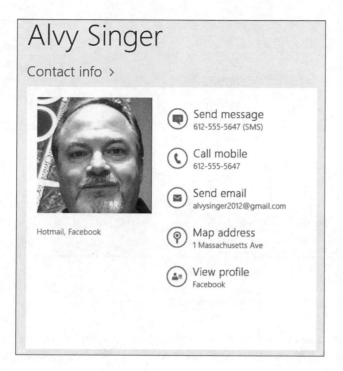

FIGURE 19.5

Viewing information about a contact.

Adding New Contacts

When you find someone you know online, you can add that person as a contact via the People app. Here's how to do it:

1. From within the People app, right-click anywhere on the screen to display the Options bar.

2. Click New Contact to display the New Contact screen, shown in Figure 19.6.

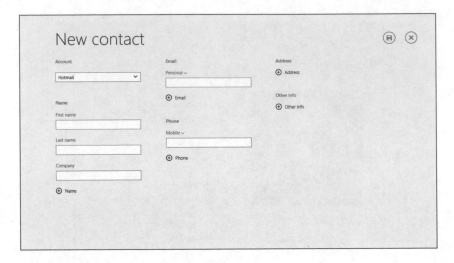

FIGURE 19.6

Adding a new contact to the People app.

3. If you have more than one email account connected to the People app, pull down the Account list and select which account you want to use to send email to this person.

4. Enter the person's name into the First Name and Last Name boxes.

5. Enter the person's employer into the Company box.

6. Enter the person's email address into the Email box.

7. Click the down arrow to select what type of email account this is (Personal, Work, or Other).

8. Enter the person's phone number into the Phone box.

9. Click the down arrow to select what type of phone this is (Home, Work, Mobile, and so forth).

10. Click + Address to enter the person's address.

11. Click + Other Info to enter other information about this person.

12. Click Save when done.

This person's contact is now listed within the People app.

THE ABSOLUTE MINIMUM

Here are the key points to remember from this chapter:

- The Windows People app consolidates contact information and posts from all your friends across all major social networks.

- You can use the People app to view and post status updates, tweets, and messages from and to Facebook, Twitter, and LinkedIn.

- The People app also functions as a universal contacts list for all your Windows apps, consolidating contact information from your email accounts and social networks.

20

VIDEO CHATTING WITH FRIENDS AND FAMILY

Not everyone lives close to family and friends. Even if you do have a close-knit local community, you may find yourself missing loved ones when you're traveling. Just because you're far away, however, doesn't mean that you can't stay in touch—on a face-to-face basis.

When you want to talk to your family members and other loved ones, nothing beats a video call. All you need is a webcam built into or connected to your PC and a service that lets you make face-to-face calls. When it comes to Windows 8.1, you can use either the built-in Skype app or Facebook's video calling function. Either one lets you talk via video to the people you love.

Video Calling with Skype

Skype is a service that enables subscribers to connect with one another over the Internet, in real time. You can use Skype to conduct one-on-one text chats, audio conversations, and video chats. You can even use Skype to make Internet-based phone calls from your PC to landlines or mobile phones (for a fee).

To use Skype for video calling, both you and the person you want to talk to must have webcams built into or connected to your PCs. In addition, you both must be connected to the Internet for the duration of the call.

 NOTE Most notebook PCs have webcams built in, which you can use to make video calls with Skype. If your PC doesn't have a built-in webcam, you can purchase and connect an external webcam to make Skype and Facebook video calls. Webcams are manufactured and sold by Logitech and other companies and connect to your PC via USB. They're inexpensive (as low as $30 or so) and sit on top of your monitor. After you've connected it, just smile into the webcam and start talking.

Windows 8.1 includes a Skype app that runs full screen on your computer. Although you can also use Skype's desktop application (available from www.skype.com), the full-screen app takes full advantage of Windows 8.1's Modern interface and works just fine for most folks.

To launch the Skype app, just go to the Windows Start screen and click or tap the Skype tile.

The Skype app automatically connects to and uses information from the Microsoft Account you use to log into Windows. You have the same username and password, and you can access your full list of contacts. (To log into Skype with a different user account, you must first switch to that user within Windows.)

 NOTE The basic Skype service is free and lets you make one-on-one voice and video calls to other Skype users. Skype also offers a Premium service, from $4.99/month, which offers the capability of group video chats with up to 10 participants. You can also use Skype to call landline and mobile (non-Skype) phones, for 2.3 cents/minute; monthly subscriptions are also available if you do a lot of non-Skype calling.

Configuring Your Skype Account

You can, at any time, configure the various details of your Skype account. This personal information is seen by those you chat with on Skype.

Follow these steps:

1. From within the Skype app, click the Available icon in the top-right corner to display the Options pane.

2. Click Account to launch Internet Explorer and open Skype's My Account page.

3. Scroll to the Account Details section and click Profile.

4. When the Profile page appears, as shown in Figure 20.1, scroll to the Personal Information section and click Edit to open all the fields for editing.

5. Enter the necessary information, as you deem fit.

6. Click the Save button when done.

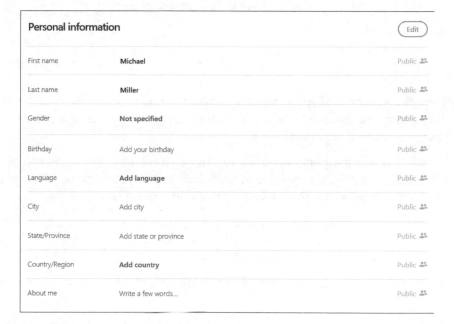

FIGURE 20.1

Editing your Skype profile information.

Adding a Contact

Before you call someone with Skype, you have to add that person to your Skype contacts list. Here's how to do it:

1. From within the Skype app, right-click anywhere on the screen to display the Options bar.

2. Click Add Contact to display the Search screen.

3. Enter into the search box the actual name or Skype username of the person you want to add, and then press Enter or click the Search (magnifying glass) button.

4. When the search results appear, click the name of the person you want to add.

5. Click the Add to Contacts button.

6. You now have to send a contact request to this person; if he accepts your request, you'll be added to each other's contact lists. Enter a short message into the text box, or accept the default message.

7. Click Send.

Making a Video Call

The whole point of Skype is to let you talk to friends and family. You can use Skype to make voice-only calls or to make video calls—which are great for seeing your loved ones, face to face.

If both you and the person you want to talk to have webcams built into or attached to your PCs, and if you're both online at the same time, it's easy to use Skype to initiate a one-to-one video call. Follow these steps:

1. From within the Skype app, scroll to the People section and click or tap the tile for the person you want to call. (People who are online and ready to chat have green dots next to their names.)

2. Click or tap the Camera button at the left side of the screen, as shown in Figure 20.2.

3. Skype now calls this person. When she answers the call, her live picture appears in the main part of the screen, as shown in Figure 20.3. (Your live picture appears smaller, in the lower-right corner.) Start talking!

4. When you're done talking, click the red "hang up" button to end the call.

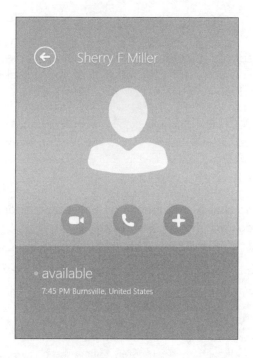

FIGURE 20.2

Click the Camera button to video call this person.

FIGURE 20.3

A Skype video call, in progress.

Video Calling in Facebook

If you're on Facebook, you also have video chat available to you through that social network. You can video chat with any of your Facebook friends, as long as they're online and have webcams.

 NOTE Interestingly, Facebook's video chat feature is powered by Skype. In fact, you can connect your Facebook and Skype accounts, so that your Facebook friends appear as Skype contacts.

When you want to chat with someone on Facebook, open your web browser, log into your Facebook account, and follow these steps:

1. Go to your friend's Timeline page and click the Call button. (If your friend doesn't have a working webcam or isn't online at the moment, you won't see a Call button.)

 NOTE The first time you use Facebook's video chat, you are prompted to download and install the necessary background chat applet on your computer. Follow the onscreen instructions to do so.

2. When your friend answers the call, Facebook displays the video chat window shown in Figure 20.4. Your friend appears in the main part of the window; your picture is in a smaller window at the top left. All you have to do is talk.

3. When you're ready to close the chat, hover over the chat window and then click the X in the top-right corner.

FIGURE 20.4

Video chatting via Facebook.

THE ABSOLUTE MINIMUM

Here are the key points to remember from this chapter:

- If you have a webcam built into or connected to your PC, you can video chat with friends and family members over the Internet.

- The Skype app, built into Windows 8.1, enables free full-screen video calling.

- Skype also powers the video chat built into Facebook, which lets you connect with your Facebook friends via video.

21

UNDERSTANDING AND USING WINDOWS APPS

When you want to do something on your computer, you need to use the appropriate applications. *Applications*—more commonly called *apps*—are software programs that perform one or more functions. Some apps are work related; others provide useful information; still others are more entertaining in nature. But whatever it is you want to do, you need to launch the right app.

With Windows 8 and 8.1, there are actually two kinds of apps. Old-style software apps run in windows on the traditional desktop, whereas newer Modern-style apps (newly developed for Windows 8/8.1) run full screen from the Start screen. Most people use a mix of traditional and Modern-style apps in their day-to-day use.

Using Apps in Windows 8.1

Both traditional and Modern-style apps have a lot in common, especially in how you find them, launch them, and switch between them. It's a matter of knowing the right commands and operations.

Searching for Apps

When it comes to finding the app you want, you can scroll through the various pages of the Start screen, but not all apps are necessarily tiled there. For example, you may remove little-used apps from the Start screen to make things a little less cluttered. And even if an app is on the Start screen, if there are too many tiles there, you might not be able to quickly find it.

For this reason, Windows enables you to search for apps by name. It's really quite easy to do:

1. From the Windows Start screen, press Windows+Q to display the Search panel.

2. Start typing the name of the app you're looking for into the search box.

3. As you type, Windows suggests apps (and other items) that match your query, as shown in Figure 21.1. If the app you want is listed here, click it to launch it.

FIGURE 21.1

Searching for apps in Windows.

4. If Windows doesn't suggest the app you want, finish entering your query and then click or tap the magnifying glass button to start the search.

Windows now displays apps, files, and web pages that match your query. Click or tap an app to launch it.

Displaying All Apps

On the Windows Apps screen, you can also display all apps and utilities that are installed on your computer. Just go to the Start screen and click or tap the Apps (down arrow) button at the bottom left.

As you can see in Figure 21.2, the Apps screen displays all the apps installed on your PC. You can sort your apps in a number of different ways, by clicking the down arrow next to the Apps title.

FIGURE 21.2

Viewing all installed apps on the Apps screen.

You can sort by

- Name
- Date installed
- Most used
- Category

Scroll to the right to view additional apps; click or tap an app to launch it.

Pinning Apps to the Start Screen

You might find that it's easier to launch a frequently used app by adding it to the Windows Start screen—what's known as "pinning" the app. When you pin an app to the Start screen you create a tile for the app; you can click or tap the tile to launch the app.

To pin an app to the Start screen, follow these steps:

1. Go to the Apps screen and find the app you'd like to pin.

2. Right-click the app or swipe down on the app (if you have a touchscreen device) to display the Options bar at the bottom of the screen, as shown in Figure 21.3.

3. Click or tap Pin to Start.

FIGURE 21.3

Pinning an app to the Start menu.

The app you selected is added to the end of the Start screen. You can then drag it to a different position, if you like.

Switching Between Apps

If you have more than one open app, it's easy to switch between them. In fact, there are several ways to do this:

*   **Press Alt+Tab**—A box displays in the center of the screen, as shown in Figure 21.4, with the current app highlighted. Continue pressing Tab (while holding down the Alt button) to cycle through all open apps.

FIGURE 21.4

Press Alt+Tab to cycle through open apps.

- **Press Windows+Tab**—The Switcher panel displays at the left side of the screen, as shown in Figure 21.5, with the current app highlighted. Continue pressing Tab (while holding down the Windows button) to cycle through all open apps.

FIGURE 21.5

Press Windows+Tab to display the Switcher panel.

- **Display the Switcher panel with your mouse**—Mouse over the top-left corner of the screen and then drag the mouse downward (without clicking the mouse button). Once the Switcher panel displays, click the app you want to switch to.

- **Display the Switcher panel on a touchscreen device**—Touch the left edge of the screen, drag your finger to the right, and then quickly drag it back to the left. You can then tap the app you want to switch to.

Working with Modern-Style Apps

Most Modern-style apps are fairly intuitive to use. You seldom find difficult-to-understand elements such as pull-down menus and toolbars; instead, most operations are front and center for you to click or tap.

There are, however, a few common operations you need to familiarize yourself with. We'll look at these next.

Viewing and Configuring App Options

Many Modern-style apps have options you can or need to configure. For example, the Weather app needs to know where you live so it can deliver the proper weather reports.

To configure an app's options, you need to display the Options bar. Every app has its own unique options, of course. In fact, some Options bars drop down from the top of the screen instead of pull up from the bottom!

To display the Options bar(s), just right-click the screen or swipe up from the bottom of the screen (on a touchscreen device). You can then click or tap the options you want to configure.

Snapping Open Apps

By default, all Modern apps display across your entire computer screen; they're designed for full-screen use. You can, however, display two or more Modern apps side by side, as shown in Figure 21.6. This is called *snapping* the apps. The wider your display, the more apps you can snap; you can snap up to eight apps side by side if your display is wide enough.

Follow these steps to snap your apps:

1. Display the first app in full screen mode; then bump your mouse against the top-left corner of the screen and drag it downward (without pressing the mouse button) to display the Switcher panel.

2. Click and drag the other app you want to display to the right.

3. When the shaded vertical bar appears in the middle of the screen, drop the second app into the blank area. The two apps are now displayed side by side.

FIGURE 21.6

Two Modern apps snapped side by side.

NOTE If your screen is wide enough, you can snap more than two apps side by side. Just repeat steps 1 through 3 to snap additional apps.

To change the width of the displayed apps, click and drag the vertical bar to one side or another. To revert to a single app onscreen, click and drag the vertical bar all the way to the other side of the screen from that app.

Closing an Open App

In older versions of Windows, you needed to close open apps when you were done with them. That's not the case with Windows 8 and 8.1; you can leave any Modern-style app running as long as you like without using valuable system resources. (An open but unused app is essentially paused until you return to it.)

You can still, however, close open apps, if you'd like. There are two ways to do this:

- From the open app, move the mouse cursor to the top of the screen until it changes to a hand shape; then click and drag the top of the screen downward to the bottom of the screen.

- With a touchscreen device, swipe down from the top of the screen toward the center. This reduces the app to a small window and then closes it.

Working with Traditional Software Apps

Modern-style apps are newer apps designed specifically for Windows 8 and 8.1, but there are still lots of older software programs available that you might find useful, such as Microsoft Word (and the entire Office suite), Adobe Photoshop Elements, and even Apple's iTunes media player. You need to learn how these traditional software programs work.

You launch traditional software apps from the Start screen, just like you do with Modern apps. These older apps, however, run on the traditional Windows desktop, within their own windows. As such, you can have multiple open apps onscreen at the same time, with the windows stacked on top of or tiled next to each other.

Most traditional apps have different onscreen elements than do newer Modern apps. We'll look at the more common elements next.

Using Menus

Many software apps use a set of pull-down *menus* to store all the commands and operations you can perform. The menus are aligned across the top of the window, just below the title bar, in what is called a *menu bar*.

You open (or pull down) a menu by clicking the menu's name with your mouse. The full menu then appears just below the menu bar, as shown in Figure 21.7. You activate a command or select a menu item by clicking it with your mouse.

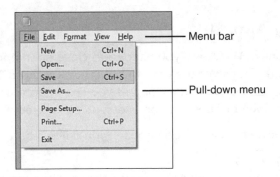

FIGURE 21.7

Navigating the menu system in the Notepad app.

Some menu items have a little black arrow to the right of the label. This indicates that additional choices are available, displayed on a *submenu*. Click the menu item or the arrow to display the submenu.

TIP If an item in a menu, toolbar, or dialog box is dimmed (or grayed), that means it isn't available for the current task.

Other menu items have three little dots (called an ellipsis) to the right of the label. This indicates that additional choices are available, displayed in a dialog box. Click the menu item to display the dialog box.

The nice thing is, after you get the hang of this menu thing in one program, the menus should be similar in all the other programs you use. For example, many apps have a File menu that, when clicked, displays a pull-down menu of common file-oriented operations. Although each program has menus and menu items specific to its own needs, these common menus make it easy to get up and running when you install new software programs on your system.

Using Toolbars and Ribbons

Some apps put the most frequently used operations on one or more *toolbars*, typically located just below the menu bar. (Figure 21.8 shows a typical toolbar.) A toolbar looks like a row of buttons, each with a small picture (called an *icon*) and maybe a bit of text. You activate the associated command or operation by clicking the button with your mouse.

Buttons   Toolbar

FIGURE 21.8

A typical toolbar in Adobe Photoshop.

 TIP If the toolbar is too long to display fully on your screen, you see a right arrow at the far-right side of the toolbar. Click this arrow to display the buttons that aren't currently visible.

Other programs substitute a *ribbon* for the toolbar. For example, all the apps in Microsoft Office have ribbons that contain buttons or controls for the most-used operations. As you can see in Figure 21.10, each ribbon has different tabs, each containing a unique collection of buttons. Click the tab to see the ribbon buttons for that particular type of operation.

Buttons   Tabs   Ribbon

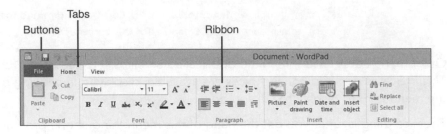

FIGURE 21.9

A ribbon with tabs for different types of operations in the WordPad app.

 TIP If you're not sure which button does what on a toolbar or ribbon, you can mouse over the button to display a ToolTip. A *ToolTip* is a small text box that displays the button's label or other useful information.

Closing an Open App

When you're working with a desktop app, you should close it when you're done. The easiest way to do this is to click the X at the top-right corner of the window, as shown in Figure 21.10. You might also be able to pull down the app's File menu and select Exit, or click the File tab and click Exit from there.

FIGURE 21.10

Click the X to close the app.

THE ABSOLUTE MINIMUM

Here are the key points to remember from this chapter:

- An application, or app, is a software program that performs a specific function.

- You can search for apps by pressing Windows+Q, or view all installed apps from the Windows Apps screen.

- To switch between apps, press Alt+Tab. Alternatively, press Windows+Tab to display the Switcher panel and display all running apps.

- Many Modern-style apps have an Options bar you can display by right-clicking within the app.

- Traditional apps run on the desktop and use some combination of pull-down menus, toolbars, and ribbons.

- Modern-style apps don't have to be officially closed when you're done using them; to close a traditional app, click the X in the top-right corner of the window.

22

EXPLORING WINDOWS 8.1'S BUILT-IN APPS

Windows 8.1 comes with a variety of apps and utilities you can start using as soon as you log onto your system. Most of these are Modern-style apps, but some still run on the traditional desktop.

This chapter describes all the apps and utilities built into Windows 8.1 and explores how you can use some of the more popular ones.

Discovering the Apps and Utilities Included with Windows 8.1

Windows is more than just an operating environment; it's also host to a number of useful apps and utilities. Most of these apps are designed specifically for Windows 8.1's Modern interface, but others run in the traditional desktop environment.

Tables 22.1 details the apps included with Windows 8.1.

TABLE 21.1   Windows 8.1 Apps

Name	Description
Alarms	Functions as an alarm clock, timer, and stopwatch.
Bing Finance	Serves as a hub for financial news and information.
Bing Food and Drink	Offers recipes, cooking tips and advice, and meal planning.
Bing Health and Fitness	Offers a diet tracker, health tracker, exercise tracker, and symptom checker, along with other health-related content.
Bing News	Displays the latest news headlines; customizable to your personal news preferences.
Bing Sports	Displays the latest sports headlines and scores; customizable for your favorite sports and teams.
Bing Travel	Displays favorite travel destinations and top travel stories.
Calculator	Functions as both a standard and a scientific calculator and offers popular conversions of various measures.
Calendar	Manages schedules and appointments.
Camera	Controls your PC's webcam (if it has one) to take still photos and videos.
Internet Explorer	Microsoft's web browser.
Mail	Sends and receives email.
Maps	Displays street maps and driving directions.
People	Serves as a contact manager program and consolidates posts from all your friends across multiple social networks.
Photos	Displays and edits digital photos stored on your PC.
Reading List	Lets you bookmark web content for later reading.
Scan	Manages document and photo scanning (if you have a scanner connected to your PC).

Name	Description
SkyDrive	Cloud-based document storage and online apps.
Skype	Enables video and voice calling over the Internet.
Sound Recorder	Creates audio recordings using your PC's built-in microphone.
Store	Accesses the Windows Store so you can purchase and download new Windows apps.
Weather	Displays local weather conditions and forecasts.
Windows Reader	Offers a Modern-style reader for PDF- and XPS-format files.
Xbox Games	Enables you to purchase, download, and play Xbox games on your PC, as well as interface with fellow gamers.
Xbox Music	Plays music stored on your PC and downloads new music from the Web.
Xbox SmartGlass	Connects your Windows 8.1 PC to your Xbox 360 game console so you can control and interact with games, movies, TV programming, and more.
Xbox Video	Enables you to view movies and TV shows from the Web or view your own videos stored on your PC.

In addition, Windows 8.1 includes a number of apps (dubbed *accessories*) that add extra functionality to the basic operating system. Most of these apps run on the traditional desktop; Table 22.2 details these accessory programs.

TABLE 22.2 Windows 8.1 Accessories

Name	Description
Character Map	Enables you to insert all manner of special characters into your word processing and other documents.
Math Input Panel	Enables you to create handwritten equations (on a tablet or touchscreen PC) that are converted into digital format.
Notepad	Serves as a basic word processor.
Paint	Serves as a basic illustration/coloring tool.
Remote Desktop Connection	Enables you to remotely control other PCs as if you were using them directly—great for accessing your home PC when you're on the road.
Snipping Tool	Enables you to take snapshots of the current computer screen.
Steps Recorder	Typically used for troubleshooting system problems; records a series of screenshots used in performing a given operation.

Name	Description
Sticky Notes	Enables you to create virtual sticky notes on the traditional desktop.
Windows Fax and Scan	Enables you to send and receive faxes, as well as scan printed documents into digital files.
Windows Journal	Enables you to create handwritten notes (on a tablet or touchscreen PC) that are converted into digital format.
Windows Media Player	Serves as a full-featured music and video player.
WordPad	Offers a slightly more fully featured word processor than Notepad (but still not as fully featured as Microsoft Word).
XPS Viewer	Enables you to view XPS-format files.

If you have difficulty seeing what's on the computer screen or typing on a traditional keyboard, Windows 8.1 includes four useful utilities for improved ease of access. Table 22.3 details these utility programs.

TABLE 22.3 Windows 8.1 Ease of Access Utilities

Name	Description
Magnifier	Enlarges all or part of the screen for the visually impaired.
Narrator	"Reads" onscreen text out loud for the visually impaired.
On-Screen Keyboard	Displays a fully functioning onscreen keyboard, like the one shown in Figure 22.1. It's ideal for tablets or other touchscreen devices without a traditional keyboard.
Windows Speech Recognition	Converts speech to digital text, which is ideal for the visually impaired.

FIGURE 22.1

Windows 8.1's onscreen keyboard—for when tablet users need to type.

Finally, Windows 8.1 includes a number of utility programs that help you better manage your computer and the Windows environment. Table 22.4 details these system utilities.

TABLE 22.4 Windows 8.1 System Utilities

Name	Description
Command Prompt	Opens a "DOS window" with a prompt where you can enter system commands.
Control Panel	Enables you to configure various Windows system settings.
Default Programs	Enables you to select which programs Windows uses by default to open specific types of files.
File Explorer	Enables you to manage files on your system.
Help and Support	Accesses Windows 8's help system.
This PC	Opens File Explorer with This PC selected, which enables you to access the different devices connected to your computer. You can then drill down to the folders, subfolders, and files stored on each device.
Run	Displays the Run box, which you can use to open programs directly (by entering their program name or filename).
Task Manager	Displays the Task Manager, which details current system resource usage and enables you to close frozen programs.
Windows Defender	Installed on PCs that do not have other malware protection options, protects your system against computer viruses and spyware.
Windows Easy Transfer	Enables you to transfer files and settings from an older computer to a newer one.
Windows Easy Transfer Reports	Displays reports associated with use of the Easy Transfer Wizard.
Windows PowerShell	For developers, an environment for creating scripts and batch files.

To display all available apps and utilities, click the Apps (down arrow) button on the Start screen. This opens the Apps screen, with all apps and utilities displayed there.

Working with Popular Apps

We've already examined some of these apps in the book and will examine others when appropriate. With that in mind, let's take a quick look at a few additional apps—what they do and how they work.

Weather

Windows 8.1's Weather app is one of the better-looking apps available. It's also quite useful.

The functionality starts before you ever launch the app. The Weather tile displays current weather conditions, "live" right on the Windows Start screen, as you can see in Figure 22.2. (Make the tile larger to display more information.) Click or tap the tile to launch the app.

FIGURE 22.2

Viewing current conditions "live" on the Weather app tile.

Figure 22.3 shows what the Weather app itself looks like. The background image represents current conditions; for example, a sunny spring day is represented by a beautiful image of fresh leaves in the sunlight. Current conditions are on the left—temperature, wind, humidity, and the like. The rest of the screen is devoted to a five-day forecast.

Scroll right to view additional weather information, including an hourly forecast, various weather maps, and a graph for historical weather in your location. Click any item to view it.

Of course, before the Weather app can deliver your weather, it has to know where you're located. To do this, right-click to display the Options bars, and then click or tap Places in the top bar to see a list of places already added. (The app starts with Seattle as the default city, a conceit from Microsoft's Seattle-based programmers.) Click or tap the + tile, and then enter a new location.

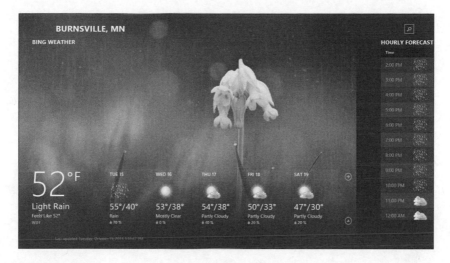

FIGURE 22.3

Viewing current conditions and a five-day forecast in the Weather app.

 TIP You can switch locations at any point by clicking or tapping Places in the Options bar and selecting a different location. You can also view weather around the world by clicking or tapping World Weather in the Options bar.

Maps

The Windows 8.1 Maps app lets you create street maps and driving directions. It's based on Bing Maps, which is Microsoft's web-based mapping service.

You launch the Maps app by clicking or tapping the Maps tile on the Start screen. What you see next is a map of the United States, with controls at the top and bottom of the screen.

To display a street map of your current location, display the Options bar and click or tap My Location. The resulting map is like the one shown in Figure 22.4. You can click and drag your mouse to move the map in any direction—or, if you have a touchscreen device, just drag your finger to move the map. You can zoom in and out of the map by using the zoom controls at the lower left. On a touchscreen device, you can zoom out by pinching the screen with your fingers, or you can zoom in by expanding your fingers on the screen.

FIGURE 22.4

Viewing a street map with the Maps app.

TIP After a brief time, both Options bars on the map disappear. To make them display again, right-click anywhere on the map.

To show current traffic conditions (green is smooth flowing; yellow and red, less so), click or tap Map Style in the Options bar and select Show Traffic. To change from a traditional street map to a satellite map, click or tap Map Style and select Aerial View. To switch back to the traditional map, click or tap Map Style and select Road View.

To generate driving directions, display the Options bar and click or tap Directions. You can then enter the start and end addresses into the Directions panel. Click or tap the right arrow button to display turn-by-turn directions onscreen, as shown in Figure 22.5.

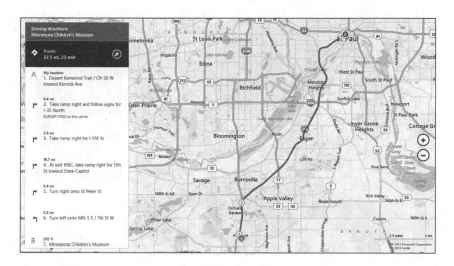

FIGURE 22.5

Generating turn-by-turn driving directions.

Bing News

When you want to read the latest headlines, use the Bing News app. It works great "out of the box," but you can also customize it to display news stories from those sources you personally select.

When you launch the app, you see the Top Story page, like the one shown in Figure 22.6. This is indeed the top story of the day, at least as selected by Microsoft's Bing News. Click or tap anywhere on this page to open the full story for in-depth reading.

Scroll to the right to view stories organized by topic: World, Technology and Science, Politics, Opinion, Business, Entertainment, and Sports. Click or tap any story tile to read that particular story, or click or tap the section header to view more stories about that particular topic.

You can also view news gathered by specific news sources, such as BBC News, CNN, Fox News, or Al Jazeera. (Every viewpoint is covered!) Just go to the Sources section and click the news you want to read.

FIGURE 22.6

Viewing the top story of the day with the Bing News app.

Bing Sports

You can use the Bing Sports app to read the latest headlines from the world of sports, as well as follow your favorite sports and teams. Content is compiled from Microsoft's Bing Sports site.

When you launch the Sports app you see the top story of the day. Click to read the complete story, or scroll right to view more stories, headlines, and videos.

The Sports app makes it easy to follow a particular sport or league (NFL, NBA, MLB, NHA, and so forth). Right-click to display the top and bottom Options bars, and then click the league you follow. As you can see in Figure 22.7, you can then view news, standings, scores, and stats for that league.

FIGURE 22.7

Viewing Major League Baseball news and stats.

Bing Finance

Windows 8.1's Bing Finance app is the perfect way to stay up-to-date on the latest financial news, as well as keep track of your personal investments. Scroll past the top story of the day to view current market information, and then scroll further right to view your own Watch List—those stocks you want to track. Click a stock's tile to view more information about that stock, as shown in Figure 22.8.

FIGURE 22.8

Viewing detailed stock information in the Bing Finance app.

To add a new stock to your Watch List, click the + tile. When the Add to Watchlist panel appears, enter the name or symbol of the stock and then click Add.

Bing Travel

The Bing Travel app is a mini-guidebook to popular travel destinations. It also lets you search for flights and hotels online.

To search for flights, scroll to the Tools and Tasks section and click the Search Flights tile. This displays the Flights page, shown in Figure 22.9; enter information about your trip (departure and arrival locations and dates), and then click Search Flights to view available flights.

FIGURE 22.9

Searching for flights with the Bing Travel app.

To search for hotels, scroll to the Tools and Tasks section, and click the Search Hotels tile. When the Hotels page appears, enter your destination and check-in/check-out dates. Click Search Hotels to view available rooms and rates.

Bing Food and Drink

The Bing Food and Drink app offers a wealth of information for home cooks and gourmands. There are tons of online recipes, cooking tips and techniques, advice from chefs such as Wolfgang Puck and Marcus Samuelsson, and articles about various aspects of food culture. You'll even find lots of information about wine and cocktails. (Figure 22.10 shows some of the famous chefs included.)

FIGURE 22.10

Advice and recipes from celebrity chefs in the Bing Food and Drink app.

The navigation panel to the right of the main story leads you into even more useful content. Click or tap the following options:

- Collections, to create and view your collected recipes.
- Add a Recipe, to create your own recipe.
- Shopping List, to create a shopping list of items for a recipe.
- Today's Meal Plan, to edit and view your daily meal planner.

Bing Health and Fitness

The Bing Health and Fitness app includes numerous tools to help you lead a healthier life, including a Diet Tracker, Exercise Tracker, and Health Tracker. It also includes online workouts and useful information about medical conditions and prescription drugs, as shown in Figure 22.11.

FIGURE 22.11

Viewing fitness and medical information in the Bing Health and Fitness app.

Click or tap an option in the Quick Access section to go directly to specific sections of the app—Diet Tracker, Nutrition and Calories, Exercise Tracker, Exercises, Health Tracker, Symptoms, Drugs, and Conditions. Or, if you're looking for specific health-related information, just use the search box.

Alarms

The Alarms app turns your computer into a digital alarm clock. It also includes timer and stopwatch functions.

To set an alarm in the app, click or tap Alarm to enter the alarm function, shown in Figure 22.12, and then click or tap the + button. Click and drag the outer circle to set the minutes, click and drag the inner circle to set the hour, and then click or tap AM or PM. Click or tap Once to make this a one-time only alarm or, to have this alarm repeat, click or tap Repeats and check those days you want the alarm to go off. Click or tap the down arrow in the Sound section to set the alarm sound, and then click or tap the Alarm header to enter a new name for this alarm. Finally, click or tap the Save button to save the alarm.

To use the app's timer function, click or tap Timer. To use the app as a stopwatch, click or tap Stopwatch.

FIGURE 22.12

Setting an alarm in the Alarms app.

THE ABSOLUTE MINIMUM

Here are the key points to remember from this chapter:

- Windows 8.1 contains a variety of apps and utilities that expand the functionality of the basic operating system.

- Most apps included with Windows 8.1 take full advantage of the Modern environment; most system utilities run on the older desktop.

- The Weather app displays current weather conditions and a five-day forecast.

- The Maps app displays street maps and driving directions.

- The various Bing apps (News, Sports, Finance, Travel, Food and Drink, and Health and Fitness) offer a combination of up-to-date information and useful tools.

- The Alarms app can be used as a desktop alarm, timer, or stopwatch.

23

FINDING AND INSTALLING NEW APPS

Your new computer system probably came with a bunch of programs preinstalled on its hard disk. Some of these are the apps that come with Windows 8.1, some are preview or limited-use versions provided by the PC manufacturer (included in the hope you'll purchase the full version if you like what you see), and some are real, honest-to-goodness fully functional applications. The more the merrier.

As useful as some of these programs might be, at some point you're going to want to add something new. Maybe you want to install the full version of Microsoft Office or purchase a full-featured photo editing program, such as Adobe Photoshop Elements. Maybe you want to add some educational apps for the kids or a productivity program for yourself. Maybe you just want to play some new computer games.

Whatever type of app you're considering, installing it on your computer system is easy. In fact, you might find just what you're looking for in the Microsoft Windows Store. Wherever you find a new app, however, installing it on your system is relatively easy, as you'll soon discover.

Finding and Installing Apps from the Windows Store

With Windows 8, Microsoft plunged headfirst into the app model popularized by Apple's iPhone and Google's Android smartphones. In this model, applications are designed specifically for the given operating system and sold through a central "app store." You search or browse the app store for the apps you want and then purchase and download them directly to your device.

This new app model is consumer friendly, especially when it comes to pricing. A traditional computer software program can cost hundreds of dollars, whereas most apps cost just a few bucks—and many are free. In addition, you can download and install the apps you want without ever leaving home; you install apps directly from the app store to your device.

Opening the Windows Store

For Windows 8.1, Microsoft has a Windows Store offering Modern apps from a variety of publishers. You access the Windows Store by clicking or tapping the Store tile on the Windows desktop.

As you can see in Figure 23.1, the Windows Store offers all manner of free and paid apps. You see a rotating selection of spotlighted apps first, but you can then scroll right to view specific offerings.

FIGURE 23.1

Shopping for apps in the Windows Store.

In particular, the Windows Store offers the following "departments":

- Picks for You

- Trending

- New & Rising

- Top Paid

- Top Free

Click a department header to view more similar selections.

Browsing the Windows Store

You can also browse the Windows Store by category, although it isn't obvious how to do so. The "secret" is to right-click the screen to display the Options bar, which in this instance drops down from the top to display a listing of app categories, as you can see in Figure 23.2. Click a category to view apps within that category.

FIGURE 23.2

Browsing apps by category.

Within a category, apps are organized by New and Rising, Top Paid, and Top Free. To view all the apps in a category, scroll to and click the See All section. The resulting list of apps can be filtered by price (free or paid) and sorted by noteworthy, newest, lowest price, or highest price.

Searching the Windows Store

If you know the app you're looking for, the easiest way to find it is to use the Store's search function. Just enter the name or description of the app into the search box at the top-right corner of the screen and press Enter. The app you're looking for should be somewhere on the search results screen.

Downloading an App

When you find an app you want, click or tap it to view the app's page in the Store, like the one shown in Figure 23.3. Scroll right to read more about the app, as well as view consumer reviews.

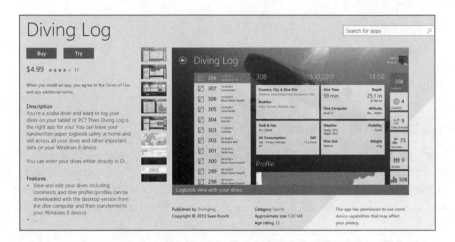

FIGURE 23.3

Getting ready to download and install a new app from the Windows Store.

If it's a free app, click or tap the Install button to download it to your computer. If it's a paid app, click or tap the Try button to download a limited-time free trial. To purchase the app, click or tap the Buy button. You'll be prompted for your payment information; then you're good to go.

 NOTE   In Windows 8, you had to manually update any installed apps. In Windows 8.1, updating is automatic. If an app has been updated, that update is downloaded and installed automatically the next time you connect your computer to the Internet.

Finding and Installing Apps from Your Local Retailer

The majority of apps in the Windows Store are optimized for use with Windows 8.1's Modern interface. However, there are a great many more traditional software programs available that work just fine with your version of Windows—albeit on the desktop, not in Modern full-screen mode.

You can find these software programs at just about any consumer electronics store, office store, or computer store. (For that matter, mass merchants such as Target and Walmart also carry a selection of computer software.) Traditional software programs run the gamut from rather generic sub-$10 apps to more sophisticated productivity apps priced several hundred dollars or more.

Most software programs today come on either a CD-ROM or a DVD disc; these disks typically come with their own built-in installation utilities. All you have to do is insert the program's disc into your computer's CD/DVD drive. The installation utility should run automatically.

When the installation utility launches, you usually see some sort of notification window asking if you want to install the new software. Assuming you do, click or tap the appropriate install or setup option.

The program's installation program should then proceed apace. All you have to do from here is follow the onscreen instructions—and, if instructed, reboot your computer at the end of the installation process.

Finding and Installing Apps Online

Nowadays, many software publishers make their products available via download from the Internet. Some users like this because they can get their new programs immediately without having to make a trip to the store.

 TIP Most software publishers that offer downloadable software also let you order CD or DVD versions of their software—although you might have to pay extra to get a physical copy.

When you download a program from a major software publisher, the process is generally easy to follow. You probably have to read a page of do's and don'ts, agree to the publisher's licensing agreements, and then click a button to start the download. If you're purchasing a commercial program online, you also need to provide your credit card information, of course. Then, after you specify where (which folder on your hard disk) you want to save the downloaded file, the download begins.

When the download is complete, you should be notified via an onscreen dialog box. When prompted, choose to run the program you just downloaded. Follow the onscreen instructions from there.

Sometimes, programs you download from the Internet require the use of something called ActiveX controls—a technology that Internet Explorer normally blocks, for security reasons. If you try to install a program and nothing happens, look for a message at the bottom of the Internet Explorer screen. If you're sure that this is a legitimate part of the program you're installing, click or tap the message and select Install ActiveX Control from the pop-up menu. The installation should proceed normally from this point.

CAUTION Limit your software downloads to reputable download sites and software publisher sites. Programs downloaded from unofficial sites might contain computer viruses or spyware, which can damage your computer. Learn more in Chapter 29, "Protecting Your PC from Computer Attacks, Malware, and Spam."

Understanding Cloud Computing Apps

There is another type of app that's becoming increasingly popular. You don't actually install this type of app on your computer; instead, it runs over the Web from what we call the *cloud*.

In essence, the cloud is that nebulous assemblage of computers and servers on the Internet. Cloud-based computing involves storing your files on and running apps from the cloud. The apps aren't located on your PC; they're located in the cloud, and you run them from within Internet Explorer or a similar web browser.

Because of this, cloud apps are sometimes called web-based apps. They're just like traditional software-based apps, except they run over the Internet.

With traditional software applications, you have to install a copy of the application on each computer you own; the more computers you use, the more expensive that gets. Web-based applications, on the other hand, are typically free to use. That's always appealing.

Then there's the issue of the documents you create. With traditional software applications, your documents are stored on the computer on which they were created. If you want to edit a work document at home, you have to transfer that document from one computer to another—and then manage all the different "versions" you create.

TIP Cloud apps are also great for group collaboration. Multiple users from different locations can access the same document over the Internet, in real time.

Document management is different with a web-based application. That's because your documents aren't stored on your computer; instead, they're stored on the Internet, just like the applications are. You can access your web-based documents from any computer, wherever you might be. So it's a lot easier to edit that work document at home or access your home budget while on the road.

Some other advantages of cloud apps are that they can run on any computer at any location, and they don't take up hard disk space. This is especially important if you have a device without traditional hard disk storage, such as a tablet, ultrabook, or smartphone. Just point your web browser to the cloud app and start running—no installation required.

It isn't all positive, however. The primary downside of running cloud apps is that you need a stable Internet connection to do so. If you can't connect to the Internet, you can't access the cloud, and you can't run any apps. So if you're planning on getting work done on your next plane trip, cloud apps might not be the way to go.

For most other uses, however, cloud apps represent a viable alternative to traditional hard disk–based computer programs. Most cloud apps are low cost or free to use, and they offer much the same functionality as their more traditional software cousins.

What types of cloud apps are available? Some of the more popular apps are traditional office apps in the cloud, such as Google Drive apps (drive.google.com) and similar apps from Zoho (www.zoho.com). For that matter, the Microsoft Office Web Apps (skydrive.live.com) are popular cloud-based applications.

But there's more than that out there. So if you're into universal document access and online collaboration, keep an eye open!

THE ABSOLUTE MINIMUM

Here are the key points to remember from this chapter:

- You can purchase, download, and install Modern-style apps from Microsoft's Windows Store.

- Traditional software apps come on either CD or DVD and install automatically when you insert the installation disc into your computer's CD/DVD drive.

- You can download many software apps from the Internet just by clicking a button (and providing your credit card number).

- Web-based or cloud apps don't install on your PC; instead, they run over the Internet within your web browser.

24

DOING OFFICE WORK

When it comes to doing office work—writing letters and reports, crunching budgets, and creating presentations—you need a particular type of app called an *office suite*. In reality, an office suite is a combination of different programs, each designed to perform a specific task.

The most common office suite components are a *word processor* (for writing letters and memos), a *spreadsheet* (for crunching your numbers), and a *presentation program* (for creating and giving presentations to small and large groups). With these office apps installed on your computer, you're ready to do just about anything you might be asked to do in the workplace.

What kind of office suite should you use? It all depends on how often and for what purposes you'll be using it.

Working with Microsoft Office

The most popular office suite today is Microsoft Office, which comes to you from the same folks who produce Microsoft Windows. The latest version is called Office 365, and it's available as traditional desktop software for purchase, as desktop software available on a subscription plan (kind of like leasing it), and as web-based apps. The web-based version, dubbed Office Web Apps, is available for free but isn't as fully featured as the desktop version.

Microsoft Office contains several productivity applications; which apps are included depends on the version of Office you have. Most versions include Word (word processing), Excel (spreadsheet), and PowerPoint (presentations); the desktop version also includes the Outlook email app.

You can learn more about Office at office.microsoft.com. You can even purchase and subscribe to Office there.

Using Office on the Desktop

The version of Office that reigns supreme is the traditional desktop software version—whether purchased outright or leased on a subscription basis. This is a software program—actually, a group of programs—that you install on your computer, typically from an installation CD or DVD. (Microsoft also offers online installation, which is actually quite convenient.)

There are several different editions of the Microsoft Office suite, each containing its own unique bundle of programs. Which Office programs you get depends on the edition of Office you have. Table 24.1 details the different editions for the current version, Microsoft Office 2013.

TABLE 23.1 Microsoft Office 2013 Editions

Edition	Applications Included	Price
Office 365 Home Premium	Word (word processing)	$99.99/year (or $9.99/month) subscription
	Excel (spreadsheet)	
	PowerPoint (presentations)	
	OneNote (notes)	
	Outlook (email and calendar)	
	Access (database)	
	Publisher (desktop publishing	

Edition	Applications Included	Price
Office Home and Student 2013	Word (word processing) Excel (spreadsheet) PowerPoint (presentations) OneNote (notes)	$139.99 one-time purchase
Office Home and Business 2013	Word (word processing) Excel (spreadsheet) PowerPoint (presentations) OneNote (notes) Outlook (email)	$219.99 one-time purchase
Office Professional 2013	Word (word processing) Excel (spreadsheet) PowerPoint (presentations) OneNote (notes) Outlook (email and calendar) Access (database) Publisher (desktop publishing)	$399.99 one-time purchase

For my money, the most attractive version is the Office 365 Home Premium subscription. It comes with all the available apps and costs just $99.99 per year. That subscription enables me to install Office on up to five different PCs, which means I can run Office on just about every PC in my home without paying extra for additional software. Of course, I do have to pay that subscription price every year, but it's still a pretty good deal—especially considering I have multiple Windows PCs in my home.

 NOTE Many new PCs come with a trial version of Office preinstalled. You can use this version for 90 days at no charge; at that point, you have the option of purchasing the software or having the trial version deactivated.

Using Office on the Web

If you don't want to go to all the trouble of purchasing and installing an expensive piece of software, you can still use Microsoft Office on the Web. Microsoft offers a web-based version of Office, dubbed Microsoft Office Web Apps, via its SkyDrive cloud-based storage system.

This web-based version of Office is free, which is always appealing. The individual apps, however, don't come with all the sophisticated functionality of the software versions, so there's a trade-off. Bottom line: If you're not a power user, you might be able to get by with the free Office Web Apps instead of purchasing and installing the traditional software version of Office.

You access Office Web Apps from within Internet Explorer. Launch the web browser and go to skydrive.live.com. You now see all the files you've previously uploaded to SkyDrive, organized in the folders you created, as shown in Figure 24.1. Note that Word, Excel, and PowerPoint files are displayed with icons that include the app graphics, so you can quickly see what kind of file you're looking at.

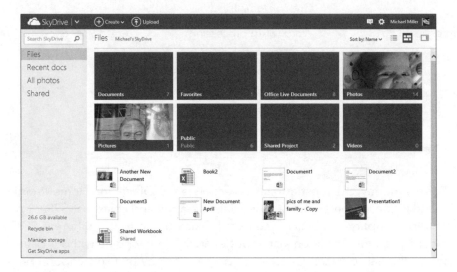

FIGURE 24.1

Working with Office documents in Microsoft SkyDrive.

 NOTE You can also open and edit existing documents using the SkyDrive app in Windows 8.1. However, at this writing, you can't use the SkyDrive app to create new documents; you have to do this from within Internet Explorer.

To open an existing document, click it with your mouse. To open a new document of a given type (Word, Excel, PowerPoint, or OneNote), click the appropriate icon in the Create bar at the top of the screen.

The designated app opens in Internet Explorer. You can begin to enter text and numbers to create the content of the new document. We'll look at each of the three major Office Web Apps next.

NOTE   The next few sections of this chapter focus on the Web-based versions of Microsoft Word, Microsoft Excel, and Microsoft PowerPoint. You can learn more about Office Web Apps at office.microsoft.com/en-us/web-apps/.

Which Version of Office Should You Use?

Given the choice of a free web-based version of Microsoft Office or a somewhat expensive desktop version, many users choose the web-based Office. There's a good argument for that—free is always more attractive than paid.

In the case of Office Web Apps, what you get is kind of a basic version of the full-featured Office you can buy in a store. For most users, Office Web Apps offers all the needed features; it's great for doing letters and memos, home budgets and planning, and even basic presentations. There's the added plus that you can run Office Web Apps on any Windows-based PC or tablet without having to install anything. Getting up and running is as quick and easy as clicking a few buttons.

If your needs are more sophisticated, however, the paid desktop version of Office is the way to go. There are so many advanced functions in the Office software that it's unlikely you'll ever use them all. But if your work involves creating brochures or newsletters, fancy comparison spreadsheets, or sophisticated presentations with animations and such, you have to go the Office software route; you just can't do some of this stuff in the web-based version.

Word Processing with Microsoft Word

When you want to write a letter, fire off a quick memo, create a report, or create a newsletter, you use a word processing app. For most computer users, that means Microsoft Word—in either its web-based or traditional desktop versions.

Exploring the Word Workspace

Before we get started, let's take a quick tour of the Word workspace—so you know what's what and what's where.

If you're using the web-based version of Word, dubbed Word Web App, you see the screen shown in Figure 24.2. At the top of the screen is the Ribbon, which provides all the buttons and controls you need to create and edit a document. Different tabs on the Ribbon display different collections of functions; click a tab, such as File, Home, Insert, or View, to access commands associated with that particular operation.

Beneath the Ribbon is the document itself. Begin typing at the cursor.

FIGURE 24.2

The Word Web App workspace—all functions are on the Ribbon.

Click a tab on the Ribbon to access all the related commands. For example, the File tab contains basic file opening and saving operations; the Home tab contains most of the editing and formatting functions you use on a daily basis; the Insert tab contains commands to add images and tables to a document; and the View tab contains commands that enable you to change how a document is viewed or displayed.

 TIP If you're not sure just what button on a Ribbon or toolbar does what, you're not alone—those little graphics are sometimes difficult to decipher. To display the name of any specific button, just hover your cursor over the button until the descriptive *ScreenTip* appears.

Working with Documents

Anything you create with Word is called a *document*. A document is nothing more than a computer file that can be copied, moved, and deleted—or edited—from within Word.

To create a new document in the Word Web App, follow these steps:

1. From the main SkyDrive page (skydrive.live.com), click Create on the menu bar and then select Word Document.

2. When the New Microsoft Word Document dialog box appears, enter a name for this new document and click the Create button.

Opening an existing document is just as easy. Just go to the main SkyDrive page, navigate to the document, and click it.

When it comes to saving your work, don't worry about it. One of the advantages of using the web-based version of Word is that all your work is saved automatically, in the cloud. You don't have to manually save a thing.

Entering Text

You enter text in a Word document at the *insertion point*, which appears onscreen as a blinking cursor. When you start typing on your keyboard, the new text is added at the insertion point.

You move the insertion point with your mouse by clicking a new position in your text. You move the insertion point with your keyboard by using your keyboard's arrow keys.

Editing Text

After you've entered your text, it's time to edit. With Word you can delete, cut, copy, and paste text—or graphics—to and from anywhere in your document, or between documents.

Before you can edit text, though, you have to *select* the text to edit. The easiest way to select text is with your mouse; just hold down your mouse button and drag the cursor over the text you want to select. You also can select text using your keyboard; use the Shift key—in combination with other keys—to highlight blocks of text. For example, Shift+left arrow selects one character to the left; Shift+End selects all text to the end of the current line.

Any text you select appears as white text against a black highlight. After you've selected a block of text, you can then edit it in a number of ways, as detailed in Table 24.2.

TABLE 24.2 Word Editing Operations

Operation	Keystroke
Delete	Del
Copy	Ctrl+Ins or Ctrl+C
Cut	Shift+Del or Ctrl+X
Paste	Shift+Ins or Ctrl+V

Formatting Text

After your text is entered and edited, you can use Word's numerous formatting options to add some pizzazz to your document. Fortunately, formatting text is easy.

When you want to format your text, select the Home Ribbon. This Ribbon includes buttons for bold, italic, and underline, as well as font, font size, and font color. To format a block of text, highlight the text and then click the desired format button.

Checking Spelling and Grammar

If you're not a great speller, you'll appreciate Word's automatic spell checking. You can see it right onscreen; just deliberately misspell a word, and you see a squiggly red line under the misspelling. That's Word telling you you've made a spelling error.

When you see that squiggly red line, position your cursor on top of the misspelled word and then right-click your mouse. Word displays a pop-up menu with its suggestions for spelling corrections. You can choose a replacement word from the list or return to your document and manually change the misspelling.

Sometimes Word meets a word it doesn't recognize, even though the word is spelled correctly. In these instances, you can add the new word to Word's spelling dictionary by right-clicking the word and selecting Add from the pop-up menu.

Printing Your Document

When you've finished editing your document, you can instruct Word to send a copy to your printer. To print a document, select the File tab and click Print. The document is converted to PDF format, which you can then open in any PDF-reader program (such as Adobe Reader) and then send to your printer.

NOTE   The desktop version of Word prints directly to your printer, no PDF involved.

Working with Pictures

Although memos and letters might look fine if they contain nothing but text, you might want to jazz up other types of documents—newsletters, reports, and so on.

The easiest way to add a graphic to your document is to use Word's built-in Clip Art Gallery. The Clip Art Gallery is a collection of ready-to-use illustrations and photos, organized by topic, that you can paste directly into your Word documents.

To insert a piece of clip art, select the Insert Ribbon and click the Clip Art button; the Insert Clip Art dialog box displays.

Enter one or more keywords into the search box and then press the Enter key. Pictures matching your criteria display, as shown in Figure 24.3. Double-click a graphic to insert it into your document.

FIGURE 24.3

Searching for clip art.

You're not limited to using graphics from the Clip Art Gallery. Word enables you to insert any type of graphics file into your document—including GIF, JPG, BMP, TIF, and other popular graphics formats.

To insert a graphics file into your document, select the Insert Ribbon and click the Picture button. When the Files page appears, navigate to and select the picture you want to insert. Click the Open button.

 TIP To move your picture to another position in your document, use your mouse to drag it to its new position. You also can resize the graphic by clicking the picture and then dragging a selection handle to resize that side or corner of the graphic.

Number Crunching with Microsoft Excel

When you're on your computer and want to crunch some numbers, you use a program called a *spreadsheet*. Microsoft Excel is the spreadsheet program in the Microsoft Office suite, and it's available in both web-based and traditional desktop versions.

Exploring the Excel Workspace

A spreadsheet is nothing more than a giant list. Your list can contain just about any type of data you can think of—text, numbers, and even dates. You can take any of the numbers on your list and use them to calculate new numbers. You can sort the items on your list, pretty them up, and print the important points in a report. You can even graph your numbers in a pie, line, or bar chart!

In a spreadsheet, everything is stored in little boxes called *cells*. Your spreadsheet is divided into lots of these cells, each located in a specific location on a giant grid made of *rows* and *columns*. Each cell represents the intersection of a particular row and column.

As you can see in Figure 24.4, each column has an alphabetic label (A, B, C, and so on). Each row, on the other hand, has a numeric label (1, 2, 3, and so on). The location of each cell is the combination of its column and row locations. For example, the cell in the upper-left corner of the spreadsheet is in column A and row 1; therefore, its location is signified as A1. The cell to the right of it is B1, and the cell below A1 is A2.

Formula bar   Column

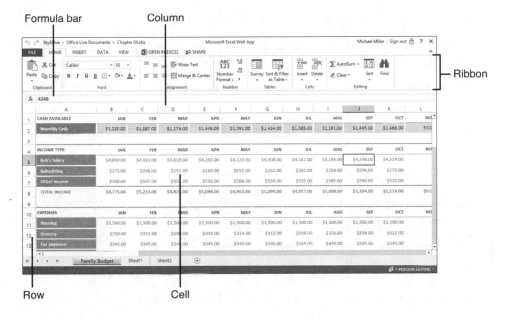

Row   Cell

FIGURE 24.4

An Excel spreadsheet—divided into many rows and columns.

Entering Data

Entering text or numbers into a spreadsheet is easy. Just remember that data is entered into each cell individually—then you can fill up a spreadsheet with hundreds or thousands of cells filled with their own data.

To enter data into a specific cell, follow these steps:

1. Select the cell you want to enter data into.

2. Type your text or numbers into the cell; what you type is echoed in the Formula bar at the top of the screen.

3. When you're done typing data into the cell, press Enter.

 TIP You can enter numbers and text directly into the selected cell or into the Formula bar at the top of the spreadsheet. The Formula bar echoes the contents of the active cell.

Inserting and Deleting Rows and Columns

Sometimes you need to go back to an existing spreadsheet and insert some new information.

To insert a new row or column in the middle of your spreadsheet, follow these steps:

1. Click the row or column header *after* where you want to make the insertion.

2. Select the Home Ribbon and click the down arrow below the Insert button; then select either Insert Rows or Insert Columns.

Excel now inserts a new row or column either above or to the left of the row or column you selected.

To delete an existing row or column, follow these steps:

1. Click the header for the row or column you want to delete.

2. Select the Home Ribbon and click the Delete button.

The row or column you selected is deleted, and all other rows or columns move up or over to fill the space.

Adjusting Column Width

If the data you enter into a cell is too long, you see only the first part of that data—there'll be a bit to the right that looks cut off. It's not cut off, of course; it just can't be seen because it's longer than the current column is wide.

You can fix this problem by adjusting the column width. Wider columns allow more data to be shown; with narrow columns you can display more columns per page.

To change the column width, move your cursor to the column header, and position it on the dividing line on the right side of the column you want to adjust. When the cursor changes shape, click the left button on your mouse and drag the column divider to the right (to make a wider column) or to the left (to make a smaller column). Release the mouse button when the column is the desired width.

 TIP To make a column the exact width for the longest amount of data entered, position your cursor over the dividing line to the right of the column header and double-click your mouse. This makes the column width automatically "fit" your current data.

Calculating with Formulas

Excel lets you enter just about any type of algebraic formula into any cell. You can use these formulas to add, subtract, multiply, divide, and perform any nested combination of those operations.

Excel knows that you're entering a formula when you type an equal sign (=) into any cell. You start your formula with the equal sign and enter your operations *after* the equal sign.

For example, if you want to add 1 plus 2, enter this formula into a cell: **=1+2**. When you press Enter, the formula disappears from the cell—and the result, or *value*, is displayed.

Table 24.3 shows the algebraic operators you can use in Excel formulas.

TABLE 24.3 Excel Operators

Operation	Operator
Add	+
Subtract	−
Multiply	*
Divide	/

So if you want to multiply 10 by 5, enter **=10*5**. If you want to divide 10 by 5, enter **=10/5**.

Including Other Cells in a Formula

If all you're doing is adding and subtracting numbers, you might as well use a calculator. Where a spreadsheet becomes truly useful is when you use it to perform operations based on the contents of specific cells.

To perform calculations using values from cells in your spreadsheet, you enter the cell location into the formula. For example, if you want to add cells A1 and A2, enter this formula: **=A1+A2**. And if the numbers in either cell A1 or A2 change, the total automatically changes, as well.

An even easier way to perform operations involving spreadsheet cells is to select them with your mouse while you're entering the formula. To do this, follow these steps:

1. Select the cell that will contain the formula.

2. Type **=**.

3. Click the first cell you want to include in your formula; that cell location is automatically entered in your formula.

4. Type an algebraic operator, such as +, –, *, or /.

5. Click the second cell you want to include in your formula.

6. Repeat steps 4 and 5 to include other cells in your formula.

7. Press Enter when your formula is complete.

Quick Addition with AutoSum

The most common operation in any spreadsheet is the addition of a group of numbers. Excel makes summing up a row or column of numbers easy via the AutoSum function.

All you have to do is follow these steps:

1. Select the cell at the end of a row or column of numbers, where you want the total to appear.

2. Select the Home Ribbon and click the AutoSum button.

Excel automatically sums all the preceding numbers and places the total in the selected cell.

Excel's AutoSum also includes a few other automatic calculations. When you click the down arrow on the bottom of the AutoSum button, you can perform the following operations:

- **Average**, which calculates the average of the selected cells

- **Count Numbers**, which counts the number of selected cells

- **Max**, which returns the largest value in the selected cells

- **Min**, which returns the smallest value in the selected cells

TIP When you're referencing consecutive cells in a formula, you can just enter the first and last number of the series separated by a colon. For example, cells A1 through A4 can be entered as A1:A4.

Using Functions

In addition to the basic algebraic operators previously discussed, Excel includes a variety of *functions* that replace the complex steps present in many formulas. For example, if you want to total all the cells in column A, you could enter the formula **=A1+A2+A3+A4**. Or, you could use the SUM function, which lets you sum a column or row of numbers without having to type every cell into the formula. (And when you use AutoSum, it's simply applying the SUM function.)

In short, a function is a type of prebuilt formula.

You enter a function in the following format: **=function(argument)**, where **function** is the name of the function and **argument** is the range of cells or other data you want to calculate. Using the last example, to sum cells A1 through A4, you'd use the following function-based formula: **=sum(A1,A2,A3,A4)**.

Excel includes hundreds of functions. You can access and insert any of Excel's functions by following these steps:

1. Select the cell where you want to insert the function.

2. Select the Home Ribbon. Then click the down arrow beneath the AutoSum button and select More Functions.

3. When the Insert Function dialog box appears, as shown in Figure 24.5, pull down the Select a Category list to display the functions of a particular type.

4. Click the function you want to insert.

5. If the function has related arguments, a Function Arguments dialog box displays; enter the arguments and click OK.

6. The function you selected is inserted into the current cell. You can manually enter the cells or numbers into the function's argument.

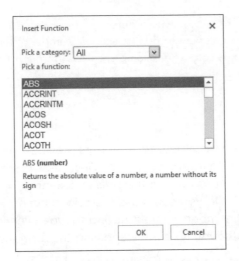

FIGURE 24.5

Choose from hundreds of functions in Excel.

TIP In the desktop version of Excel, you can access more functions directly from the Formula Ribbon.

Formatting Your Spreadsheet

You don't have to settle for boring-looking spreadsheets. You can format the way the data appears in your spreadsheet—including the format of any numbers you enter.

When you enter a number into a cell, Excel applies what it calls a "general" format to the number—it just displays the number, right-aligned, with no commas or dollar signs. You can, however, select a specific number format to apply to any cells in your spreadsheet that contain numbers.

All of Excel's number formatting options are in the Number section of the Home Ribbon. Click the Dollar Sign button to choose an accounting format, the Percent button to choose a percentage format, the Comma button to choose a comma format, or the General button to choose from all available formats. You can also click the Increase Decimal and Decrease Decimal buttons to move the decimal point left or right.

In addition, you can apply a variety of other formatting options to the contents of your cells. You can make your text bold or italic, change the font type or size, or even add shading or borders to selected cells.

These formatting options are found in the Font and Alignment sections of the Home Ribbon. Just select the cell(s) you want to format; then click the appropriate formatting button.

Creating a Chart

Numbers are fine, but sometimes the story behind the numbers can be better told with a picture. The way you take a picture of numbers is with a *chart,* such as the one shown in Figure 24.6.

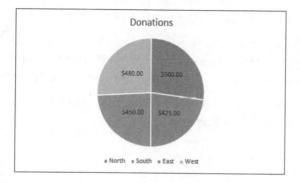

FIGURE 24.6

Some numbers are better represented via a chart.

You create a chart based on numbers you've previously entered into your Excel spreadsheet. It works like this:

1. Select the range of cells you want to include in your chart. (If the range has a header row or column, include that row or column when selecting the cells.)

2. Select the Insert Ribbon, shown in Figure 24.7.

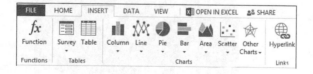

FIGURE 24.7

Select the type of chart you want to insert.

3. In the Charts section of the Ribbon, click the button for the type of chart you want to create.

4. Excel displays a variety of charts within that general category. Select the type of chart you want.

5. When the chart appears in your worksheet, select the Design Ribbon to edit the chart's type, layout, and style.

Giving Presentations with Microsoft PowerPoint

When you need to present information to a group of people, the hip way to do it is with a PowerPoint presentation. Microsoft PowerPoint is a presentation program—that is, an app you can use to both create and give presentations.

If you work in an office, you probably see at least one PowerPoint presentation a week—if not one a day. Teachers use PowerPoint to present lesson materials in class. Kids even use PowerPoint to prepare what used to be oral reports.

So get with the program—and learn how to create your own great-looking presentations with PowerPoint!

Exploring PowerPoint Workspace

As you can see in Figure 24.8, PowerPoint looks like the other Office apps. The workspace is dominated by the Ribbon at the top of the screen, with the current slide displayed in the middle.

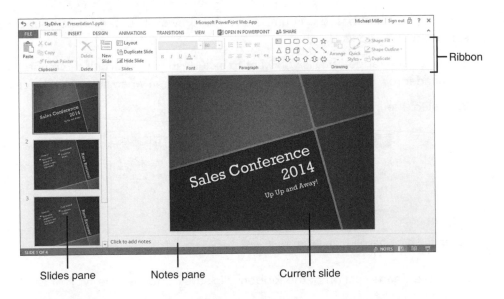

FIGURE 24.8

The PowerPoint workspace.

On the left side of the workspace is something unique to PowerPoint—the Slides pane, which displays all the slides in your presentation, one after another. Below the current slide is a Notes pane, which lets you enter presentation notes.

Applying a Theme

You don't have to reinvent the wheel when it comes to designing the look of your presentation. PowerPoint includes a number of slide *themes* that you can apply to any presentation, blank or otherwise. A theme specifies the color scheme, fonts, layout, and background for each slide you create in your presentation.

 NOTE In the desktop version of PowerPoint, themes are located on the Design Ribbon.

To apply a new theme to your current presentation, select the Design Ribbon. Available themes are displayed in the Themes section, as shown in Figure 24.9; click a theme to apply it to your presentation.

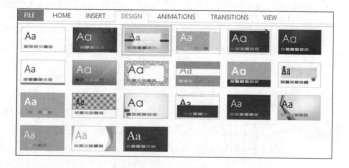

FIGURE 24.9

Selecting a new theme in the PowerPoint Web App.

It's that simple. All the colors, fonts, and everything else from the theme are automatically applied to all the slides in your presentation—and every new slide you add carries the selected design.

 NOTE Don't confuse the slide *layout*, which defines which elements appear on the slide, with the slide *template*, which defines the colors and fonts used.

Inserting New Slides

When you create a new presentation, PowerPoint starts with a single slide—the *title slide*. Naturally, you need to insert additional slides to create a complete presentation. PowerPoint lets you insert different types of slides, with different types of layouts for different types of information.

To insert a new slide, all you have to do is select the Home Ribbon and click the New Slide button. This displays the New Slide dialog box; select the slide layout you want, and then click the Add Slide button.

Adding and Formatting Text

You can enter text for a slide directly into that slide. When PowerPoint creates a new slide, the areas for text entry are designated with boilerplate text—"Click to add title" (for the slide's title) or "Click to add text" (for regular text or bullet points). Adding text is as easy as clicking the boilerplate text and then entering your own words and numbers. Press Enter to move to a new line or bullet. To enter a subbullet, press the Tab key first; to back up a level, press Shift+Tab.

Formatting text on a slide is just like formatting text in a word processing document. Select the text you want to format and then click the appropriate button in the Font section of the Home Ribbon.

 TIP The desktop version of PowerPoint enables you to add animated transitions between slides. The PowerPoint Web App does not have this feature. If you want to use slide transitions, you'll have to switch to the desktop PowerPoint software.

Start the Show!

To run your slideshow, select the View tab and click the Slide Show button. (In the desktop version, click the Slide Show button at the bottom of the workspace.) To move from one slide to the next, all you have to do is click your mouse.

Exploring Other Office Suites

Microsoft Office is just one of several office suites on the market today. You might also want to check out the following competing suites:

- **Google Drive** (drive.google.com, free)—This is the primary web-based competitor to Office Web Apps. It's free to use and based totally in the cloud. It includes Google Docs (word processor), Google Spreadsheets, and Google Presentations.

- **OpenOffice** (www.openoffice.org, free)—This is an open-source office suite, similar to Office in terms of features but completely free to use. It's a software-based suite, so you download to your PC the office apps you want to use. The apps include Writer (word processor), Calc (spreadsheet), Impress (presentations), Draw (drawing), Base (database), and Math (equation creator).

- **WordPerfect Office X6 Home and Student Edition** (www.corel.com, $99.99)—This is a set of traditional desktop programs, including WordPerfect (word processor), Quattro Pro (spreadsheet), Presentations, and Corel WordPerfect Lightning (notes). Also available in Standard, Professional, and Legal editions.

- **Zoho Office** (www.zoho.com, free)—This is another popular web-based office suite. It includes word processor, spreadsheet, presentations, and other apps.

THE ABSOLUTE MINIMUM

Here are the key points to remember from this chapter:

- To perform common work-related tasks, you need the individual apps that make up an office suite.

- The most popular office suite today is Microsoft Office, which is available in either web-based or traditional desktop software versions.

- Microsoft Word is the word processor in Microsoft Office, used to write letters and reports.

- Microsoft Excel is Office's spreadsheet program, used for budgets and other number crunching.

- Microsoft PowerPoint is used to create and give presentations.

- Other popular office suites include the OpenOffice WordPerfect Office X6 software, as well as the web-based Google Drive and Zoho Office suites.

25

STAYING ORGANIZED

In today's hectic world, you need to stay organized. Fortunately, you can use your new computer to help you plan your schedule—to track appointments, manage your to-do list, and such. It's all a matter of entering the proper information into the appropriate app and letting your computer do its thing.

There are a number of different ways to use your computer to organize your day. Windows 8 includes a pretty good Calendar app that a lot of people like; there are also various web-based calendars and task management apps you might find worthwhile.

Using the Windows Calendar App

Let's start with the Calendar app included with Windows 8.1. Like most Modern Windows apps, it's integrated well into the operating system.

This integration starts on the Start screen. The Calendar tile is "live"—that is, it displays a scrolling list of upcoming appointments. This way you can see what's coming up, without even having to launch the app.

Displaying Different Views

When you click or tap the Calendar tile, you see the What's Next view, with your upcoming appointments listed. To display a traditional monthly calendar, like the one in Figure 25.1, right-click to display the top and bottom Options bars, and then click Month. To scroll backward or forward through the months, use your keyboard's left and right arrow keys or swipe the screen (on a touchscreen device). To recenter the calendar on the current day, display the Options bar and then click or tap Today.

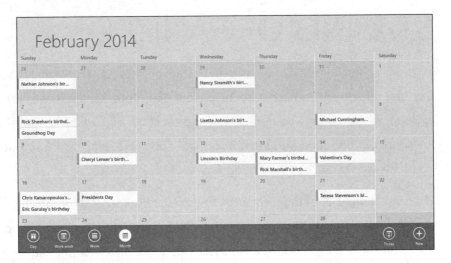

FIGURE 25.1

The Calendar app in monthly view.

You can also display your calendar in weekly or daily views. Right-click anywhere on the screen to display the Options bar, and then click or tap the desired view— Day, Work Week, Week, Month, or What's Next.

To view more details about an appointment, click or tap the item. The appointment screen opens; you can then edit anything about the appointment. Click or tap the Save button to save your changes.

Creating a New Appointment

To create a new appointment, click or tap the day of the appointment. (If you're in daily or weekly views, click or tap the day and time you want the appointment to start.) The appointment screen displays, as shown in Figure 25.2.

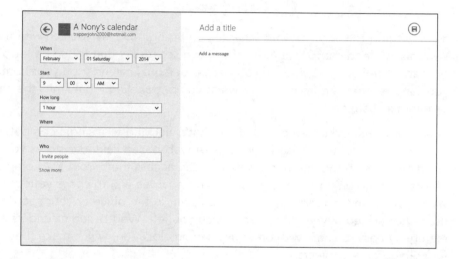

FIGURE 25.2

Creating a new appointment.

On the appointment screen, enter the following information:

- Event name, into the Add a Title field at the top right of the form.

- Information about the event, into the Add a Message section on the right.

- When (what date) the event takes place.

- What time the event starts.

- How long the event lasts, in hours and minutes. If it's an all-day event, pull down the How Long list and select All Day.

- Where the event takes place (into the Where box).

- If you want to invite others to this event, enter their email addresses into the Who box.

You can enter other details by clicking or tapping the Show More link. This expands the pane so that you can enter how often the event occurs, set a reminder (so Windows will remind you before the event), and set your status for this event (the default status is Busy). You can even keep this event private, by checking the Private box.

When you're done entering information about this event, click or tap the Save button on the top right.

Using Web-Based Calendars

It's one thing to keep a private schedule on a single PC, as you can with the Windows Calendar app, but most of us have schedules that include a lot of public or shared events. In addition, if you keep a personal calendar on your home PC, you can't reference it from work or when you're traveling. That limits the calculator program's usefulness.

This is why, instead of using a calendar that's wedded to a single computer, many users prefer web-based calendars. A web-based calendar stores your appointments on the Internet, where you can access them from any computer or device that has an Internet connection. This enables you to check your schedule when you're on the road, even if your assistant in the office or your spouse at home has added new appointments since you left. Web-based calendars are also extremely easy to share with other users in any location, which make them great for collaborative projects.

Most web-based calendars are free and offer similar online sharing and collaboration features. The most popular of these calendars include

- 30Boxes (www.30boxes.com)
- Google Calendar (calendar.google.com), shown in Figure 25.3.
- Windows Live Calendar (calendar.live.com)
- Yahoo! Calendar (calendar.yahoo.com)
- Zoho Calendar (calendar.zoho.com)

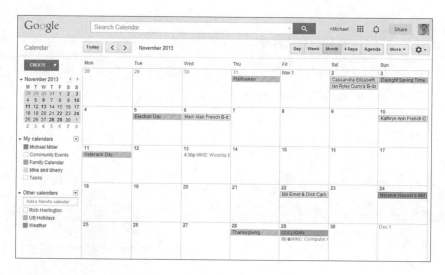

FIGURE 25.3

Google Calendar—one of the most popular web-based calendars.

Using Web-Based To-Do Lists

Just as you can track your appointments with a web-based calendar, you can track your to-do lists with web-based to-do lists. These apps enable you to manage everything from simple to-do lists to complex group tasks, and you can do it over the Internet so you can collaborate with other users.

The most popular of these web-based task management applications include the following:

- Bla-bla List (www.blablalist.com)
- hiTask (www.hitask.com)
- Hiveminder (www.hiveminder.com)
- iPrioritize (www.iprioritize.com)
- Remember the Milk (www.rememberthemilk.com)
- Vitalist (www.vitalist.com)
- voo2do (www.voo2do.com)

 TIP Some web-based calendars, such as Google Calendar, also offer task management and to-do list functions.

THE ABSOLUTE MINIMUM

Here are the key points to remember from this chapter:

- The Windows Calendar app is a good, basic way to manage your schedule and appointments.

- Web-based calendars enable you to access your schedule from any computer, and you can collaborate with others on public calendars.

- Web-based task management services help you manage your to-do lists.

26

VIEWING AND SHARING DIGITAL PHOTOS

In the old days, if you wanted to share your photos with friends and family, you had to have extra prints made and then hand them out or mail them off, as appropriate. This approach is not only time-consuming, it's costly; you have to pay money for each extra print you make.

In today's age of digital photography, it's a whole lot easier to view and share your photos on your computer, over the Internet. In fact, you can even edit your digital photos to eliminate red-eye and such before you share them. It's a whole new digital world out there. All you need is a digital camera and a computer.

Transferring Pictures from Your Camera, Smartphone, or Tablet

If you want to edit or print your digital photos, you need to connect that digital camera to your PC—which is relatively easy to do. You can transfer digital photos directly from your camera's memory card, download pictures from your camera via a USB connection, or even scan existing photo prints.

Connecting via USB

Connecting a digital camera to your PC is easy. All you have to do is connect a USB cable from your camera to a USB port on your computer. With this type of setup, Windows recognizes your camera or scanner as soon as you plug it in and installs the appropriate drivers automatically.

When you connect a USB cable between your camera and your PC, Windows should recognize when your camera is connected and automatically download the pictures in your camera, while displaying a dialog box that notifies you of what's going on. That is, of course, unless you have another photo management program installed.

Some digital cameras come with their own proprietary picture management programs. If you've installed such a program on your PC, this is the program that probably launches when you connect your camera to your computer. If this program launches and asks to download the pictures from your camera, follow the onscreen instructions to proceed.

You might also have installed a third-party photo editing program, such as Adobe Photoshop Elements. If so, this might be the program that launches when you connect your camera to your PC. Again, just follow the onscreen instructions to proceed.

 CAUTION   Depending on the apps you have installed on your system, you might get multiple prompts to download photos when you connect your camera. If this happens, pick the program you'd prefer to work with and close the other dialog boxes.

Transferring Pictures from a Memory Card

Copying digital pictures via USB cable is nice—if your camera supports this method. For many users, an easier approach is to use a memory card reader. Many PCs have memory card readers built in; if yours doesn't, you can always add a low-cost external memory reader via USB. You then insert the memory card from your digital camera into the memory card reader, and your PC recognizes the card as if it were another hard disk.

In many cases Windows recognizes a memory card full of photos and asks if you want to download them. If not, you can use File Explorer to copy files from the memory card to your computer. Just open File Explorer and click the drive icon for the memory card. This displays the card's contents, typically in a subfolder labeled DCIM. You can then move, copy, and delete the photos stored on the card, as you would with any other type of file in Windows.

Transferring Photos from an iPhone or iPad

Many people are ditching dedicated digital cameras and instead taking pictures with the cameras built into their smartphones and tablets. It's certainly more convenient to whip out your phone or tablet to take a quick picture than it is to lug around a digital camera everywhere you go.

If you have an iPhone or iPad, you can configure your device to use Apple's iCloud service to back up your photos and other data. With iPhone backup enabled, the photos you take will automatically be transferred from your device to your home computer whenever your device is connected to your home Wi-Fi network.

You can also manually transfer photos from your iPhone or iPad to your PC, using Apple's standard connection cable. Just connect your i-device to your computer, using the appropriate Apple-approved cable, and then launch File Explorer on your PC. Click the This PC icon in the Navigation pane, select the iPhone or iPad icon, the Internal Storage folder, and then select the DCIM folder to display one or more subfolders that contain your device's pictures. Double-click each of these folders to display their contents.

Now hold down the Ctrl key and click each photo you want to transfer. Select the Home tab, click the Move To button, and then click Pictures. All the photos you've selected will be moved from your iPhone or iPad to the Pictures folder on your PC.

If you have an Android phone or tablet, use this same method to move pictures from your mobile device to your PC. Just connect your device, open File Explorer, navigate to the DCIM or Camera folder, and start moving.

Scanning a Picture

If your photos are of the old-fashioned print variety, you can still turn them into digital files using a flatbed scanner. The scanning starts automatically when you press the Scan button on your scanner. Your print photo is saved as a digital file for future use.

Note that some third-party software programs, such as Adobe Photoshop Elements, also let you scan photos from the program. In most instances, scanning via one of these programs offers more options than scanning via Windows; you can change the resolution (in dots per inch) of the scanned image, crop the image, and even adjust brightness and contrast if you want. If you're scanning a lot of old, washed-out prints, this approach might produce better results.

 NOTE By default, Windows stores all your pictures in the Pictures folder, which you can access from File Explorer. This folder includes a number of features specific to the management of picture files, as well as all the normal file-related tasks, such as copying, moving, or even deleting your photos.

Viewing Your Photos with the Windows Photos App

Viewing photos in Windows 8.1 is a snap. All you have to do is click or tap the Photos tile on the Start page. This launches the Modern-style Photos app, which you use for viewing and editing your digital photos.

 NOTE If you used the Photos app in Windows 8, get ready for a big surprise; the Windows 8.1 Photos app has significantly changed. Whereas the Windows 8 version of the app let you view photos stored on Facebook, Flickr, and SkyDrive, the Windows 8.1 app is limited to viewing photos stored on your PC. The new app, however, adds photo-editing features not found in the Windows 8 version of the app—which is a much-desired improvement.

As you can see in Figure 26.1, the Photos app displays all the photos and subfolders stored in your Pictures folder. To view photos stored in a specific folder, click or tap the tile for that folder.

Click through the folders and subfolders until you find a photo you want to view, and then click that photo to view it full screen, as shown in Figure 26.2. To enlarge the picture, click the + button at the lower-right corner of the screen. To make a picture smaller, click the − button.

To move to the next picture in the folder, click the right arrow onscreen or press the right arrow key on your keyboard. To return to the previous picture, click the left arrow onscreen or press the left arrow key on your keyboard.

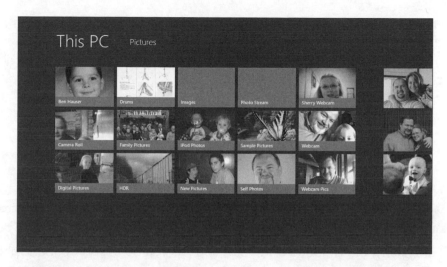

FIGURE 26.1

Viewing the contents of your Pictures folder in the Photos app.

FIGURE 26.2

Viewing a photo full screen.

You can also view a slide show of all the pictures in the current folder, starting with the current picture. Right-click the full-screen photo to display the Options bar, and then click or tap Slide Show. Windows now displays your photos one at a time, full screen, in random order. Playing a slide show can be quite relaxing when the rest of your work is done.

Finally, if you want to delete the current picture, display the Options bar and then click or tap Delete.

 TIP To use the current picture as the image on the Windows Lock screen, display the photo full screen, display the Options bar, and click Set As, Lock Screen.

Editing Your Photos with the Photos App

Not all the digital photos you take turn out perfectly. Some pictures are too light, while others are too dark. Some have bad color, and some need to be cropped to highlight the important area.

Fortunately, the Windows 8.1 Photos app lets you do this sort of basic photo editing. With Windows 8.1, a better-looking photo is only a click or a tap away!

Auto Fixing a Photo

When you want to quickly touch up a photo, use the Photos app's Auto Fix command. Auto Fix delivers several possible variations of your original photo; just choose the one that looks best to you.

Here's how to use the Auto Fix tool:

1. From within the Photos app, navigate to and display the photo you want to edit.

2. Display the Options bar and click Edit to display the editing screen, shown in Figure 26.3.

3. Click the Auto Fix button on the left side of the screen.

4. Click the best suggested result on the right side of the screen.

FIGURE 26.3

Choosing from several Auto Fix options.

Rotating a Photo

Is your picture sidewise? To turn a portrait into a landscape or vice versa, use the Photos app's Rotate control. Follow these steps:

1. From within the Photos app, navigate to and display the photo you want to edit.

2. Display the Options bar and click Rotate to rotate the picture 90 degrees clockwise.

3. Continue clicking to further rotate the picture.

Cropping a Photo

Sometimes you don't get close enough to the subject for the best effect. When you want to zoom in, use the Photos app's Crop control to remove the edges you don't want.

Here's how it works:

1. From within the Photos app, navigate to and display the photo you want to edit.

2. Display the Options bar and click Crop to display the crop screen, shown in Figure 26.4.

FIGURE 26.4

Cropping a photo.

3. Use your mouse or fingers (on a touchscreen display) to drag the corners of the white border until the picture appears as you like.

4. Click Apply.

 NOTE By default, Windows maintains the original aspect ratio when you crop a photo. To crop to a different aspect ratio, click the Aspect Ratio button and make a new selection.

Removing Red-Eye

Red-eye is caused when a camera's flash causes the subject's eyes to appear a devilish red. The Photos app lets you remove the red-eye effect by changing the red color to black in the edited photo.

To remove red-eye from a photo, follow these steps:

1. From within the Photos app, navigate to and display the photo you want to edit.

2. Display the Options bar, and then click Edit to display the editing screen.

3. Click Basic Fixes on the left side of the screen.

4. Click Red Eye on the right side of the screen; the cursor changes to a blue circle.

5. Move the circle to the eye(s) you want to fix, and then click the mouse button to remove red-eye.

Retouching a Photo

Does someone in your photo have a blemish or a loose hair, or is there a rough or scratched area in the photo you want to get rid of? Use the Photos app's Retouch control to smooth out or remove blemishes from your photos.

Follow these steps:

1. From within the Photos app, navigate to and display the photo you want to edit.

2. Display the Options bar, and then click Edit to display the editing screen.

3. Click Basic Fixes on the left side of the screen.

4. Click Retouch on the right side of the screen; the cursor changes to a blue circle.

5. Move the circle to the area you want to repair, and then click the mouse button to do so.

Adjusting Brightness and Contrast

When a photo is too dark or too light, use the Photos app's Light controls. There are four controls available:

- Brightness makes the picture lighter or darker.

- Contrast increases or decreases the difference between the photo's darkest and lightest areas.

- Highlights brings out or hides detail in too-bright highlights.

- Shadows brings out or hides detail in too-dark shadows.

Follow these steps to use these controls:

1. From within the Photos app, navigate to and display the photo you want to edit.

2. Display the Options bar, and then click Edit to display the editing screen.

3. Click Light on the left side of the screen.

4. Click the control you want to adjust—Brightness, Contrast, Highlights, or Shadows.

5. The selected control changes to a circular control, as shown in Figure 26.5. Click/tap and drag the control clockwise to increase the effect, or counterclockwise to decrease the effect.

FIGURE 26.5

Adjusting a photo's brightness levels.

Adjusting Color and Tint

The Photos app lets you adjust various color-related settings. There are four color controls available:

- Temperature affects the color characteristics of lighting; you can adjust a photo so that it looks warmer (reddish) or cooler (bluish).

- Tint affects the shade of the color.

- Saturation affects the amount of color in the photo; completely desaturating a photo makes it black and white.

- Skype also powers the video chat built into Facebook, which lets you connect with your Facebook friends via video.

Follow these steps to adjust a photo's color and tint:

1. From within the Photos app, navigate to and display the photo you want to edit.

2. Display the Options bar, and then click Edit to display the editing screen.

3. Click Color on the left side of the screen.

4. Click the control you want to adjust—Temperature, Tint, Saturation, or Color Enhance.

5. The selected control changes to a circular control. Click/tap and drag the control clockwise to increase the effect, or counterclockwise to decrease the effect.

 NOTE   If, when you're editing a photo, you decide you don't want to keep the changes you've made, simply display the Options bar and select Cancel to return to the original version of the photo.

Applying Special Effects

You can also use the Photos app to apply various vignette and selective focus effects to a picture. Follow these steps:

1. From within the Photos app, navigate to and display the photo you want to edit.

2. Display the Options bar, and then click Edit to display the editing screen.

3. Click Effects on the left side of the screen.

4. To apply a vignette to your photo, click Vignette on the right side of the screen, and then rotate the control clockwise for a dark (positive) vignette or counterclockwise for a light (negative) vignette.

5. To apply a selective focus effect, like the one shown in Figure 26.6, click Selective Focus. On the next screen, use your mouse to move or resize the circle in the middle of the screen; the center of this circle will be in focus, while the area outside the circle will be blurred. To change the strength of the selective focus effect, click Strength and select a new value, from Minimum to Maximum.

6. Click Apply to apply the effect.

FIGURE 26.6

Applying a selective focus effect.

Using Other Photo-Editing Programs

When it comes to editing your digital photos, you're not limited to the Windows Photos app. In fact, there are many photo-editing apps available that provide more powerful editing tools.

If you're looking for an alternative photo editor, you can choose from low-priced, consumer-oriented programs to high-priced programs targeted at professional photographers. For most users, the low-priced programs do everything you need. The most popular of these include the following:

- Adobe Photoshop Elements (www.adobe.com), $99.99

- Paint Shop Pro (www.corel.com), $79.99

- Photo Explosion Deluxe (www.novadevelopment.com), $49.95

- Picasa (www.picasa.com), free

 NOTE Don't confuse the affordable Adobe Photoshop Elements with the much higher-priced (and more sophisticated) Adobe Photoshop CS, which is used by most professional photographers.

You can also find photo-editing programs in the Windows Store. Look in the Photo section of the store.

Printing Your Photos

After you've touched up (or otherwise manipulated) your photos, it's time to print them.

Choosing the Right Printer and Paper

If you have a color printer, you can make good-quality prints of your image files. Even a low-priced color inkjet can make surprisingly good prints, although the better your printer, the better the results.

Some manufacturers sell printers specifically designed for photographic prints. These printers use special photo print paper and output prints that are almost indistinguishable from those you get from a professional photo processor. If you take a lot of digital photos, one of these printers might be a good investment.

The quality of your prints is also affected by the type of paper you use. Printing on standard laser or inkjet paper is okay for making proofs, but you'll want to use a thicker, waxier paper for those prints you want to keep. Check with your printer's manufacturer to see what type of paper it recommends for the best quality photo prints.

Making the Print

You can print photos directly from the Windows Photos app. Here's how to do it:

1. From within the Photos app, navigate to and display the photo you want to edit.

2. Display the Options bar and select Devices.

3. When the Devices panel appears, click Print.

4. When the Print panel appears, click the printer you want to use.

5. You now see the printer panel, like the one in Figure 26.7. Pull down the Copies list to select how many copies to print.

6. Pull down the Orientation list and select either Portrait (vertical) or Landscape (horizontal).

7. Click the Print button to print the photo.

FIGURE 26.7

Printing a photo from the Photos app.

Printing Photos Professionally

If you don't have your own photo-quality printer, you can use a professional photo-processing service to print your photos. You can create prints from your digital photos in two primary ways:

- Copy your image files to CD or memory card and deliver the CD or card by hand to your local photo finisher.

- Go to the website of an online photo-finishing service, and transfer your image files over the Internet.

The first option is convenient for many people, especially because numerous drugstores, supermarkets, and discount stores (including Target and Walmart) offer onsite photo-printing services. Often the printing service is via a self-serve kiosk; just insert your CD or memory card, follow the onscreen instructions, and come back a half hour later for your finished prints.

The second option is also convenient, if you don't mind waiting a few days for your prints to arrive. You never have to leave your house; you upload your photo files from your computer over the Internet and then receive your prints in your postal mailbox.

TIP Some photo services, particularly those associated with retail chains, offer the option of picking up your prints at a local store—often with same-day service!

There are a number of photo-printing services online, including the following:

- dotPhoto (www.dotphoto.com)

- Nations Photo Lab (www.nationsphotolab.com)

- Shutterfly (www.shutterfly.com)

- Snapfish (www.snapfish.com)

To print a photo online, you start by using Internet Explorer or another browser to go to the site and sign up for a free account. After you create your account, choose which photos on your PC you want to print. After the photos are selected, the site automatically uploads them from your PC to the website. You can then select how many and what size prints you want. Enter your shipping information and credit card number, and you're good to go.

For example, Shutterfly makes it easy to order prints at a variety of sizes, from 4"×6" to 20"×30", in either matte or glossy finish. Choose the size and quantity you want for each print, and then enter your payment and shipping information.

Most sites ship within a day or two of receiving your order; add shipping time, and you should receive your prints in less than a week. Shipping is typically via the U.S. Postal Service or some similar shipping service.

Sharing Photos at an Online Photo Site

You don't have to print your photos to share them with friends. There are a number of photo-sharing websites that let you upload your photos and then share them with the people you love.

These photo-sharing sites let you store your photos in online photo albums, which can then be viewed by any number of visitors via their web browsers—for free. Some of these sites also offer photo-printing services, and some sell photo-related items, such as picture tee shirts, calendars, and mugs. Most of these sites are free to use; they make their money by selling prints and other merchandise.

To use a photo-sharing site, you start by signing up for a free account. After your account is created, choose which photos on your PC you want to share. After you select the photos, the site automatically uploads them from your PC to the website. You then organize the photos into photo albums, each of which has its own unique URL. You can then email the URL to your friends and family; when they access the photo site, they view your photos on their computer screens.

The most popular of these photo-sharing sites include

- DropShots (www.dropshots.com)
- Flickr (www.flickr.com)
- Fotki (www.fotki.com)
- FotoTime (www.fototime.com)
- Photobucket (www.photobucket.com)
- Picturetrail (www.picturetrail.com)
- Webshots (www.webshots.com)

Emailing Digital Photos

There's another way to share your digital photos that doesn't involve uploads or websites. I'm talking about sharing via email; all you have to do is attach your photos to an email message you create in your regular email program and then send that message to as many recipients as you want.

You learned how to attach files to email messages in Chapter 16, "Sending and Receiving Email." Because a digital photo is just another type of computer file, the process is the same when you want to send a photo. Create a new message in your email program or web mail service, click the Attach button, and then select those photos you want to attach. Click the Send button, and your message is sent on its way, complete with the photos you selected.

As easy as this process is, you need to be aware of one issue before you start emailing your photos far and wide—the size of the photo files you're emailing.

If you're emailing photos pretty much as they were shot with your camera, you're probably emailing some large files. This can be a problem if you or your recipients are using a slow dial-up Internet connection; the larger the attached files, the longer it takes to send or receive an email message. In addition, some ISPs have trouble handling messages that are too large; you want to avoid messages more than 1 or 2MB in size.

 NOTE You can use most third-party photo-editing programs (but not the Windows Photos app) to resize your pictures.

For this reason, you probably want to resize your photos before you email them. If your recipients will be viewing your photos only on their computer screens, you should make your photos no larger than the typical screen—no more than 1024 pixels wide or 768 pixels tall. Anything larger won't fit on a typical computer screen.

On the other hand, if your recipients will be printing the photos, you probably don't want to resize them—or at least not that much. A photo resized to 1024×768 pixels doesn't have enough picture resolution to create a detailed print. You should keep your photos at or near their original size if someone is going to print them; any significant resizing results in fuzzy prints.

THE ABSOLUTE MINIMUM

Here are the key points to remember from this chapter:

- You can transfer photos from your digital camera to your PC via a USB connection or by using your camera's memory card.

- The Windows 8.1 Photos app enables you to view and edit digital photos stored on your computer.

- You can also use the Photos app to print photos on your home printer.

- You can order photo prints from a variety of online printing services, or from your local drugstore, supermarket, or department store.

- You can share your photos with multiple people by uploading them to an online photo-sharing website.

- You can also send photos as email attachments—as long as the files aren't too big.

27

PLAYING MUSIC

Your personal computer is a full-featured digital music machine. You can use your PC to play music from CDs, create your own digital music library, and download music from the Web. You can even stream music in real time over the Internet, at little or no cost.

There are actually several different ways to do all this, depending on which apps you choose to use. We'll examine two of the most popular full-featured music applications—Windows 8.1's Xbox Music app and Apple's iTunes program.

Using the Xbox Music App

Windows 8.1 features a central hub for all your music-related activities. That hub is the Xbox Music app, which you open by clicking or tapping the Music tile on the Windows Start screen.

The Xbox Music app enables you to listen to any tunes you've previously downloaded or ripped from a CD, and purchase and download new tracks from the Xbox Music Store. It also lets you stream music in real time over the Internet, using the Xbox Music Pass service.

 NOTE   If you need more fully featured music playback and management, check out the Windows Media Player app that runs on the traditional Windows desktop. To launch this app, go to the Apps screen, and then scroll to and click the Windows Media Player icon.

You navigate the Xbox Music app via the Navigation pane on the left side of the screen, shown in Figure 27.1. From here you click to view your personal music library (Collection), listen to streaming music online (Radio), or purchase new music from the Xbox Music Store (Explore).

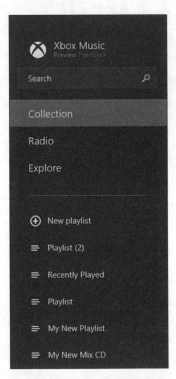

FIGURE 27.1

Navigating the Xbox Music app.

Playing Music from Your Library

All the music you've purchased and downloaded online, as well as music you've ripped from your own CDs, is stored in the Music folder on your computer's hard drive. You can use the Xbox Music app to view and play music from your music library.

After you launch the Xbox Music app, click or tap Collection in the Navigation pane to view the music stored on your computer. As you can see in Figure 27.2, you can display your collection organized by Albums, Artists, or Songs by clicking the appropriate button at the top of the screen.

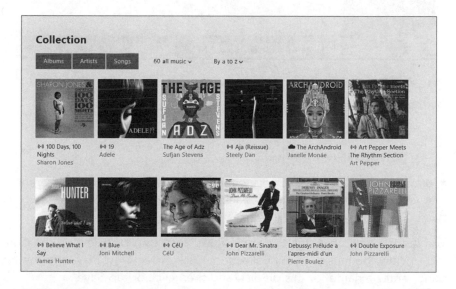

FIGURE 27.2

Viewing your music collection by Albums.

TIP To view information about a given artist, right-click an album or track to display the Options bar at the bottom of the screen, and then click Explore Artist.

To view all the tracks in an album, click or tap an album cover. As you can see in Figure 27.3, you can then play the album by clicking or tapping the Play button next to the album cover or at the bottom of the screen. To play an individual track, click or tap that track and then click that track's Play button. You can then use the playback controls at the bottom of the screen to pause or restart playback, move to the next or previous track, or adjust the volume.

FIGURE 27.3

Playing an album in the Xbox Music app.

Creating and Playing Playlists

A *playlist* is a collection of tracks, either from the same artist or different artists, that you assemble for future playback. Playlists are great for creating music mixes based on mood or individual taste.

To create a new playlist in the Xbox Music app, start by selecting the Collection tab to view the music in your collection. Click or tap New Playlist in the Navigation pane, enter a name for this playlist, and then click or tap Save.

To add a track to a playlist, navigate to and right-click that track to display the Options bar. Click or tap Add To, and then select the name of the playlist.

All your playlists are listed at the bottom of the Navigation pane, as shown in Figure 27.4. To play an existing playlist, click or tap the playlist's name, and then click or tap the Play button. Use the playback controls to pause or restart playback, as well as move to the next or previous track in the playlist.

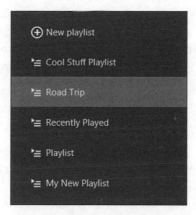

FIGURE 27.4

Viewing your playlists.

Purchasing and Downloading Music

Looking for some new music? Want an entire album or just a single track? Chances are you can find the music you want in the Xbox Music Store.

You access the Xbox Music Store from the Xbox Music app. Click Explore in the Navigation pane, and you'll see a selection of albums to purchase, as shown in Figure 27.5.

FIGURE 27.5

Viewing music to purchase in the Xbox Music Store.

To view more albums, scroll to the Top Albums section and click View All. Click the down arrow next to All Genres to view a selection of musical genres, and then pick a genre to view all music in that genre. Click the All Subgenres down arrow to view and select additional subgenres within the main genre.

You can also search for a particular song, album, or artist by entering the name or title into the search box in the Navigation pane. When the search results page appears, click to view only Artists, Albums, or Songs. Click an album cover to view the Album page.

To purchase an album or tracks from that album, click the album to display the album's page, like the one in Figure 27.6. Click the Buy Album (shopping cart) button to purchase the entire album. To purchase an individual track, right-click that track to display the Options bar, and then click Buy Song.

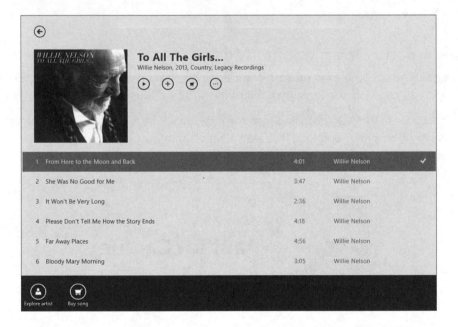

FIGURE 27.6

Purchasing an album from the Xbox Music Store.

When you make a purchase, you'll be prompted to sign into your Microsoft Account. Click Confirm to purchase with your currently registered credit card; click Change Payment Options to pay with a different card.

Streaming Music Online

For decades, consumers have purchased the music they love to listen to, whether on vinyl, cassette tape, compact disc, or via digital download. But there's an entire world of music on the Internet that you don't have to purchase and download. It's called *streaming music*, and it gives you pretty much all you can listen to for a low monthly subscription price—or even for free. There's nothing to download; the music is streamed to your computer in real time, over the Internet.

Microsoft's streaming music service is called Xbox Music Pass, and it offers 30 million or so songs for your listening pleasure. You can listen to individual tracks on demand or create your own personalized online radio stations.

Xbox Music Pass comes in both free and premium versions. The free version makes you listen to occasional ads and limits you to just 10 hours of music a month. Xbox Music Pass Premium costs $9.99/month but gets rid of the ads and gives you unlimited music streaming. A yearly subscription and 30-day free trial are also available.

There are a number of ways to listen to streaming music in the Xbox Music app. The easiest way is to click Explore in the Navigation pane, navigate to the track or album you want to listen to, and then click the Play button. Xbox Music now starts playing that selection, streamed in real time over the Internet.

You can also use Xbox Music Pass to create personalized "radio stations," based on an artist you select. To do this, select Radio from the Navigation pane to display the Radio page shown in Figure 27.7, Click Start a Station and, when prompted, enter the name of an artist. As you type, Xbox Music lists matching artists; click the name of the artist you want. Xbox Music now creates a radio station based on this artist and begins playback.

To listen to a radio station you've previously created, click Radio in the Navigation pane and then click the image for that station. The currently playing track is displayed in the playback bar at the bottom of the screen. Press Pause to pause playback; press Play to resume playback.

FIGURE 27.7

Listening to and creating new radio stations in the Xbox Music app.

Using iTunes

The Xbox Music app isn't the only way to play music on your PC. If you're the proud owner of an iPod, iPad, or iPhone, you're probably already familiar with the iTunes program, which functions as both a desktop music player and a front end for Apple's iTunes Store. It lets you play, download, rip, and burn digital music on your PC—and synchronize that music to your Apple device.

 NOTE The iTunes player runs on the traditional Windows desktop. To download and install the iTunes software on your PC, go to www.apple.com/itunes/. It's free.

Playing Your Digital Music

You can use the iTunes software to play any music you've downloaded to your PC or that you've ripped from your own personal CDs. As you can see in Figure 27.8, iTunes displays all the music tracks stored on your PC. You can view your music by album, recording artist, or genre; just click the appropriate button at the top of the window.

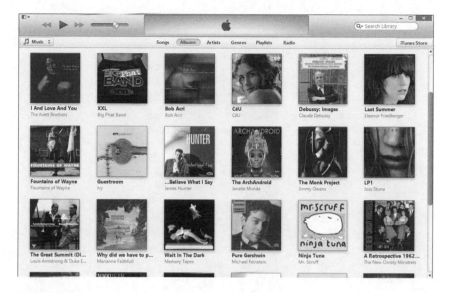

FIGURE 27.8

Viewing and playing digital music in the iTunes player.

To play an individual track or album, double-click that item. A mini-player displays at the top of the iTunes window, along with a set of playback controls. Click the Pause button to pause playback; click the Play button to resume playback.

 NOTE   If you have an iPhone, iPod, or iPad, you use the iTunes software to synchronize ("sync") music from your computer to your portable device. If you've downloaded or ripped new music to your PC, it will be automatically copied to your portable device the next time you connect your device to your computer.

Creating and Playing Playlists

The iTunes program also lets you combine multiple songs into a single playlist. To create a new playlist, start by clicking the Playlists button to display the Playlists pane, shown in Figure 27.9. Click the + button at the bottom of the Playlists pane and then click New Playlist. When the new Playlists pane appears on the right side of the window, enter a title for this playlist into the first text box.

FIGURE 27.9

Playing and creating playlists in iTunes.

To add a song to this playlist, drag it from the Content pane into the Playlists pane. Repeat this step to add multiple songs to the playlist and, when you're finished adding tracks to the playlist, click the Done button.

To play a playlist, click the Playlists button to display the Playlists pane, and then click that playlist. The contents of the selected playlist are displayed in the Content pane; click the Play button to begin playback.

TIP To play the tracks in the playlist in random order, click the Shuffle icon in the mini-player. (When activated, the Shuffle icon turns blue.)

Playing a CD

If your PC has a CD/DVD drive, it's easy enough to use iTunes to play the music on that CD. Just launch iTunes and then insert your music CD into the PC's CD/DVD drive.

The CD should automatically appear in the iTunes window, with all the tracks listed. Click the Play button to begin playback; click Pause to pause playback. You can also click the Forward arrow to skip to the next track on the CD or the Back arrow to skip to the previous track. Double-click a specific track to jump directly to that track.

Ripping a CD to Your PC

You can use also iTunes to copy songs from any CD to your PC's hard drive for future listening on your computer. Start by launching iTunes and then inserting the music CD into your PC's CD/DVD drive.

The CD should automatically appear in the iTunes window, with all the tracks listed. Leave checked those tracks you want to copy to your computer, and uncheck those you don't want to copy.

Next, click the Import CD button. (If the Import Settings dialog box appears at this point, click OK to proceed.) The selected tracks are now copied to your PC's hard disk and automatically added to the iTunes library.

 NOTE   The process of copying music from a CD to a computer's hard drive, in digital format, is called *ripping*. The reverse process, copying music from your PC to a blank CD, is called *burning*.

Burning Your Own CDs

You might prefer to take CDs with you to play in your car or on the go. Did you know that you can use iTunes to create your own "mix" CDs, with tracks from multiple artists and albums? It's called *burning* a CD, and it's relatively easy to do.

Start by using iTunes to create a new playlist containing all the songs you want to burn to CD. Make sure that your playlist is less than 80 minutes long, because that's the maximum length you can put on a CD.

Next, insert a blank CD into your PC's CD drive. Select the playlist that contains the songs you want to burn, and make sure that all the songs in the playlist are checked. Then click the Gear button and select Burn Playlist to Disc. iTunes copies the selected tracks to the blank CD and ejects the disc when it's done.

Downloading Music from the iTunes Store

When you want to add new music to your library, you can either rip music from a CD, as just discussed, or purchase new digital music online—which you can do from Apple's iTunes Store. The iTunes Store is the largest online music store today, with more than 20 million tracks available for downloading at prices ranging from 69 cents to $1.29 each. (It also offers complete albums for download.) It's a much bigger store than any local music store you've ever seen in your life.

 NOTE The iTunes Store offers more than just music for download. iTunes also sells (or rents) movies, TV shows, music videos, podcasts, audiobooks, and eBooks (in the ePub format). You even get access to iTunes U, which offers all manner of textbooks, courses, and educational materials, and Apple's App Store for the iPhone and iPad.

To access the Store, open the iTunes software and click the iTunes Store button in the top-right corner. This connects you to the Internet and displays the Store's home page, as shown in Figure 27.10.

FIGURE 27.10

Shopping for music in the iTunes Store.

To view only music items, click Music in the iTunes toolbar. Then, to browse music by category, click the All Categories list and select a category. Alternatively, you can search for a given song, album, or artist by entering the appropriate query into the search box at the top of the iTunes window.

Once you see a list of albums, click an album cover to view all the tracks in that album, as shown in Figure 27.11. To purchase an individual track, click the Buy (price) button for that track; to purchase an entire album, click the Buy button for that album.

FIGURE 27.11

Purchasing music from the iTunes Store.

Listening to Streaming Music via iTunes Radio

Just as Microsoft offers the Xbox Music Pass streaming music service, Apple offers its own online streaming music plan, dubbed iTunes Radio. The iTunes Radio service is free (and ad supported), with 27 million or so tracks in its library.

 NOTE If you want to nix the ads in iTunes Radio, subscribe to Apple's iTunes Match service. For $24.99/year you get ad-free iTunes Radio, plus the ability to listen to your own music library on your mobile devices via the cloud.

You can listen to iTunes Radio on your iPhone, iPad, iPod, Apple TV box, or any personal computer via the iTunes software. To listen to iTunes Radio, shown in Figure 27.12, click the Radio button at the top of the iTunes window.

To listen to one of iTunes Radio's featured stations, just click the station, and playback starts right up. To create your own personal radio station, go to the My Stations section and click the + button. When you see the new station pane, shown in Figure 27.13, click a genre or enter the name of an artist, genre, or song. You now see a list of matching stations; click the one you want to listen to.

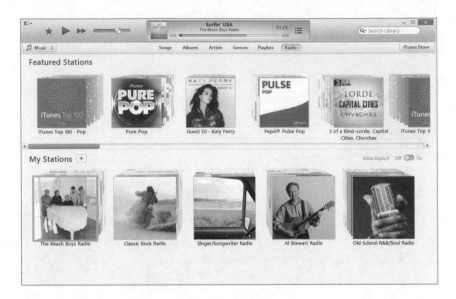

FIGURE 27.12

Listening to Apple's iTunes Radio.

FIGURE 27.13

Creating a new station in iTunes Radio.

Listening to Streaming Music Online

As noted previously, you don't have to own a song or album to play it on your PC. There's another way to listen to music on your computer—online, via streaming music services, such as Microsoft's Xbox Music Pass and Apple's iTunes Radio.

A streaming music service is the online equivalent of listening to AM or FM radio. In some instances you choose the specific songs you want to listen to; in other cases, you just sit back and listen to whatever's served up—just like old-school radio.

What makes streaming music different from downloading or ripping music is that you don't store files on your computer; it all comes at you in real time, over the Internet. It's a great way to hear a lot of music at relatively low cost.

There are two primary types of delivery services for streaming audio over the Internet. You can listen to music from a streaming music service or from an Internet radio station. (And, yes, there is some overlap between the two.)

Exploring Streaming Music Services

A streaming music service is typically a paid service that enables you to listen to an unlimited amount of music, which is streamed over the Internet, for a flat monthly subscription fee. (Some call this an "all you can eat" plan.) Most services let you browse or search for specific tracks or albums, or music by a given artist or in a given genre. Some services let you create playlists of your favorite tracks; some even create custom "radio stations" based on your listening habits. A few services are social in nature, in that they let you share your favorite music with friends on Facebook and other social networks.

You access most streaming music services from Internet Explorer or another web browser. In most instances, listening is as easy as going to the music service's website, searching for the music you want, and clicking the Play button.

 NOTE Some online music services, such as Spotify, require you to install an app on your computer to access their music.

There are a lot of similarities between the major streaming music services. Many offer free services that are supported by occasional ads; you'll also find a lot of subscription services (most between $5 to $10 per month) that do away with those annoying commercials.

Most of these services offer 15 million or more tracks for your listening pleasure. And most let you create online "radio stations" on the fly, based on the tracks or artists you select.

Table 27.1 compares the most popular streaming music services today.

TABLE 27.1   Streaming Music Services

Service	URL	Price	Selection (Number of Tracks Available)
Google Play Music All Access	play.google.com/about/music/	Subscription ($9.99/month)	18 million
Grooveshark	www.grooveshark.com	Free (ad supported) Subscription ($9.00/month)	15 million
iTunes Radio	www.apple.com/itunes/itunes-radio/	Free (ad supported) Subscription ($24.99/year)	27 million
Last.fm	www.last.fm	Free (ad supported)	12 million
MOG	www.mog.com	Free (ad supported) Subscription ($4.99–$9.99/month)	16 million
Pandora Radio	www.pandora.com	Free (ad supported) Subscription ($3.99/month or $36/year)	1 million
Raditaz	www.raditaz.com	Free (ad supported)	23 million
Rdio	www.rdio.com	Free (ad supported) Subscription ($4.99–$9.99/month)	20 million
Rhapsody	www.rhapsody.com	Subscription ($9.99–$14.99/month)	20 million
Slacker Radio	www.slacker.com	Free (ad supported) Subscription ($3.99–$9.99/month)	13 million
Spotify	www.spotify.com	Free (ad supported) Subscription ($4.99–$9.99/month)	20 million
Xbox Music Pass	music.xbox.com	Free (ad supported) Subscription ($9.99/month)	30 million

Listening to Internet Radio

The other form of streaming music is so-called Internet radio. This is the online equivalent of terrestrial AM/FM radio, full of all sorts of radio stations that operate over the Web using streaming audio technology.

Some Internet radio stations exist solely online. Others simulcast existing AM/FM stations. And some let you create own personal stations, just for you, in real time. It's an interesting way to hear old favorites and new music alike, town to town and up and down the dial—over the Internet, on your own PC, through Internet Explorer or a similar web browser.

There are a large number of Internet radio stations that create their own original radio programming and beam it over the Internet. This programming is typically genre-specific music; many of these sites offer dozens (or hundreds) of channels, each devoted to a specific type of music. So whether you're interested in '70s pop hits or classic polka tunes, one of these sites probably has a channel just for you!

Here's a short list of some of the most popular Internet-only radio sites:

- **AccuRadio** (www.accuradio.com)—Listen to programmed stations (typically by genre) or create your own custom stations.

- **AOL Radio** (music.aol.com/radioguide/)—A large number of genre-specific radio stations, created specifically for online listening.

- **Goom Radio** (www.goomradio.us)—A variety of genre-specific Internet radio stations, as well as user-created stations.

- **Jango** (www.jango.com)—A mix of genre-based stations and user-personalized programming.

- **Live365** (www.live365.com)—One of the largest Internet radio sites, with more than 5,000 stations in more than 260 different genres.

- **RadioMOI** (www.radiomoi.com)—Features a mix of programmed channels (browsable by genre) and on-demand content.

- **SHOUTcast** (www.shoutcast.com)—Part of the AOL empire and one of the oldest and most reliable Internet radio sites. Amalgamates more than 50,000 free Internet radio stations in a single site. You can browse by genre or search by station, artist, or genre.

Listening to AM/FM and Satellite Radio Online

Most traditional AM and FM radio stations simulcast their programming over the Internet. This is a great way to get local news and views or listen to your local DJs while you're on your computer. Of course, you're not limited to listening to just *your* local stations; via the magic of the Internet, you can listen to local stations from anywhere in the world, in real time.

Here's a list of resources for AM/FM stations online:

- **iHeartRadio** (www.iheart.com)—Presents more than 850 terrestrial and web-only stations, plus user-created custom stations.

- **Live Radio on the Internet** (www.live-radio.net)—A great guide to AM/FM simulcasts from all around the globe.

- **Online Radio Stations** (www.webradios.com)—Listings of local radio stations online, by location or genre.

- **radio-locator** (www.radio-locator.com)—A search engine with links to more than 10,000 AM and FM stations, searchable by city or ZIP Code, country, or call letters.

- **Sirius/XM Radio** (www.siriusxm.com/player/)—Satellite radio online, with more than 130 channels of music, news, and talk—including several web-only channels that aren't available via normal satellite radio. (Available by subscription only.)

- **TuneIn Radio** (www.tunein.com)—This site lets you browse local stations in any city or state, as well as listen to local police and fire bands. TuneIn Radio and iHeartRadio are arguably the most popular sources of terrestrial radio on the Internet.

All you have to do is point Internet Explorer to your website of choice and search for stations in a specific locale. Listening in is a matter of clicking the station you want.

THE ABSOLUTE MINIMUM

Here are the key points to remember from this chapter:

- The Xbox Music app included with Windows 8.1 lets you listen to music stored on your PC, purchase and download new tunes online, and listen to streaming music over the Internet.

- If you have an iPhone, iPad, or iPod, use the iTunes program to listen to your digital music, buy and download music from the iTunes Store, rip and burn CDs, and listen to streaming music via Apple's iTunes Radio service.

- There are a number of other streaming music services available online that offer free or low-cost access to tens of millions of tracks in your web browser.

- You can also listen to traditional AM and FM radio stations on your computer, over the Internet.

WATCHING MOVIES, TV SHOWS, AND OTHER VIDEOS

As you've learned, your Windows PC is great for listening to your favorite music. It's also great for watching videos—movies, TV shows, and homemade movies—either downloaded to your PC or streamed over the Internet.

That's right, you can fire up your PC, connect to the Internet, and watch that episode of *Grey's Anatomy* or *Chopped* that you missed last week. Or you can go on a binge and watch all five seasons of *Breaking Bad* in a single (long) sitting. Or you can purchase or rent the latest fresh-from-the-theaters blockbuster and watch it at your own convenience in your own home.

It's all a matter of knowing where to look for the videos you want—and launching the right app for viewing them.

Watching Streaming Video Online

There's a ton of programming on the Web that you don't have to purchase or download separately to your computer. This programming is available via a technology called *streaming video*. Streaming video is a lot like the streaming music we discussed previously; the movie or TV show you pick is streamed over the Internet in real time to your computer. You watch the programming in your web browser or in a dedicated Modern-style app. Assuming you have a fast enough Internet connection, you can find tens of thousands of free and paid videos to watch at dozens of different websites.

Viewing Movies and TV Shows on Netflix

When it comes to watching movies and TV shows online, you can't beat Netflix, a streaming video service with more than 38 million subscribers. Netflix lets you watch all the movies and TV shows you want, all for a low $7.99/month subscription. It's tough to beat that price.

As to what you can watch, Netflix offers a mix of both classic and newer movies, as well as a surprising amount of classic and newer television programming. There's a wide range of TV shows, from *Cheers* to *Arrested Development*, and movies old and new (and domestic and foreign, too).

 NOTE Netflix also offers a separate DVD-by-mail rental service, with a separate subscription fee. That's not what we're talking about here, however.

On a Windows 8.1 PC, the best way to watch Netflix is via the full-screen Modern-style Netflix app. (You can also watch Netflix in your web browser, if you like, but the full-screen experience is best.) To download and install the Netflix app, just go to the Windows Store and search for **netflix**. It's free.

The first time you open the Netflix app, you're prompted to either create a new Netflix account or log into an existing one. Each subsequent time you open the app, it automatically logs in to this account and displays the appropriate content tailored exclusively to your viewing habits.

Once you open the app and sign into your Netflix account, you can browse or search for movies and TV shows to watch, and then you can start playback directly on your PC. The Netflix home screen, shown in Figure 28.1, is personalized based on your viewing habits. Scroll right to view Netflix's Instant Queue, your personal Top 10, Popular movies, and more. There are also links to your top 10 shows (Top 10 for You) and New Releases.

FIGURE 28.1

Stream movies and TV series from Netflix.

NOTE If you have multiple users on your Netflix account, you may see a Who's Watching prompt when you sign in. This way Netflix can customize its recommendations for each user.

To view programming by type, click Genres. You can then click a genre to view all items within that category.

If you have a specific movie or TV series in mind, click the Search (magnifying glass) icon to display the Search panel. Enter the name of the movie or show into the search box and then press Enter.

Once you find a movie or show you want to watch, click it. You now see the detail page for that show, like the one in Figure 28.2.

If it's a movie you want to watch, just click the Play button on the movie image to start playback. If you choose to watch a TV show, you typically can choose from different episodes in different seasons. Select a season to see all episodes from that season, and then click the episode you want to watch.

Once Netflix begins playing the movie or show you selected, right-click anywhere on the screen to display the Options bar, shown in Figure 28.3. Click the Pause button to pause playback; the Pause button then changes to a Play button, which you can click again to resume playback. You can also click and drag the slider control to move directly to another part of the program.

FIGURE 28.2

Getting ready to watch a TV show on Netflix.

FIGURE 28.3

Viewing a program on Netflix.

Viewing TV Shows on Hulu Plus

As good as Netflix is, it isn't the best place to find recent television programming. If you want to watch the current season of most TV shows, your best bet is Hulu, which is a streaming service similar to Netflix but with slightly different programming.

Hulu offers episodes from a number of major-network TV shows, as well as some new and classic feature films. (There are also a fair number of programs from Canada, England, and other countries.) The standard free membership offers access to a limited number of videos; Hulu Plus ($7.99/month) offers a larger selection of newer shows. A Hulu Plus subscription is necessary to use the Hulu Plus app—which happens to be the best way to watch Hulu on your Windows 8.1 PC.

The Hulu Plus app is available from the Windows Store for free. The app runs full screen in Windows, which is the way you want to watch your shows anyway.

After you've installed the Hulu Plus app, you can create a new Hulu Plus account or log into an existing one. Once you've launched the app and logged in, Hulu displays a series of featured programs on its main screen, as shown in Figure 28.4. Scroll right to view recommended programming by type, and then click TV to view available TV shows.

FIGURE 28.4

Selected TV programs available on Hulu Plus.

To search for specific shows, click the Search (magnifying glass icon) to display the Search pane. Enter the name of the program into the Search box and press Enter. When the search results appear, click the show you want to watch.

You now see a detailed program page for your selection, like the one in Figure 28.5. Scroll right to view episodes by season, and then click the episode you want to watch.

FIGURE 28.5

A detailed program page on Hulu Plus.

Hulu begins playing the program you selected, as shown in Figure 28.6. Move your mouse over the screen (or tap the screen on a touchscreen) to display the playback controls. Click the Pause button to pause playback; the Pause button changes to a Play button, which you can click again to resume playback. Click and drag the slider control to move directly to another part of the program.

FIGURE 28.6

Viewing a program on Hulu Plus.

Viewing Videos on Network Websites

Unfortunately, not all television programming is available from Netflix or Hulu. Some programs are available only on their networks' websites, which you can view in the Internet Explorer web browser.

For example, you can go to the ABC website (abc.go.com) to view episodes of your favorite prime-time and late-night series. Missed this week's episode of *Modern Family* or *Dancing with the Stars*? They're available online, for free, as you can see in Figure 28.7.

FIGURE 28.7

Watch ABC shows on the ABC website.

Similarly, the NBC website (www.nbc.com) is the place for the latest episodes of your favorite NBC series, such as *The Voice* and *Saturday Night Live*. You can watch other network programming on the CBS (www.cbs.com), Fox (www.fox.com), CW (www.cwtv.com), and Comedy Central (www.comedycentral.com) websites. And to get your daily sports fix, check out the videos on the ESPN website (espn.go.com).

Using the Xbox Video App

Windows 8.1 includes its own Modern-style app for downloading and viewing videos on your PC. The Xbox Video app enables you to play videos you've downloaded to your PC, as well as purchase new videos from the Xbox Video Store.

Purchasing Videos

Microsoft appears to have designed the Xbox Video app to be a front end to the Xbox Video Store. It's all about purchasing—or "renting" for a limited time—new and bestselling movies and TV shows.

 TIP There are lots of other sites online that let you purchase or "rent" movies and TV shows for viewing on your PC. Some of the most popular online video stores include Amazon Instant Video (www.amazon.com), Apple's iTunes Store (www.apple.com/itunes/), CinemaNow (www.cinemanow.com), and Vudu (www.vudu.com).

When you launch the Xbox Video app (by clicking the Video tile on the Start screen), you see the Home section, shown in Figure 28.8, with recommendations just for you. Scroll right to purchase movies (click New Movies or Featured Movies) and TV shows (click New TV Shows or Featured TV Shows).

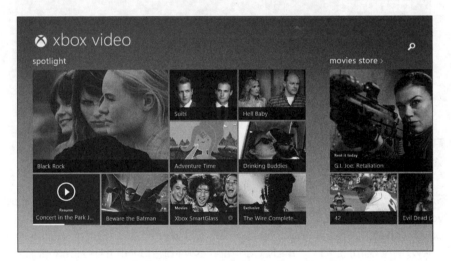

FIGURE 28.8

The Home screen of the Xbox Video app.

When you find an item you want to purchase, click or tap the tile for that item. From the next panel, shown in Figure 28.9, click or tap the Buy button to purchase and download the selected item. Or, if you prefer to rent the item for a specific number of days, click or tap the Rent button.

FIGURE 28.9

Purchasing a movie from the Xbox Video Store.

 NOTE Many movies can be "rented" for a limited time (14 days), in addition to being available for permanent purchase. If you rent a movie, you have to start watching within 14 days, and then have 24 hours to finish watching it once you've started.

Viewing Videos

All the items you've purchased or rented are displayed within the Xbox Video app, and you can view them within the app. You can also use the Xbox Video app to view home movies you've recorded yourself, as well as any other videos you've downloaded to your computer.

To view all the videos in your collection, scroll *left* from the app's home screen and click either Personal Videos (your own videos stored on your PC), My TV (televisions shows you've purchased), or My Movies (movies you've purchased), as shown in Figure 28.10. You now see all the videos of that type stored on your PC.

Click or tap the video, program, or movie you want to view. (If you selected a television program, you can now click the episode you want to watch.) When the video begins to play, move your mouse to display program information and playback controls, shown in Figure 28.11. Click the Pause control to pause playback; click the Play control to resume playback. Or click and drag the slider bar to move to any specific part of the program.

FIGURE 28.10

Viewing your video collection in the Xbox Video app.

FIGURE 28.11

Watching a program in the Xbox Video app.

Viewing Videos on YouTube

Then there's YouTube (www.youtube.com), which is the biggest video site on the Web. What's cool about YouTube is that the majority of the videos are uploaded by other users, so you get a real mix of professional-quality and amateur clips, as you can see in Figure 28.12.

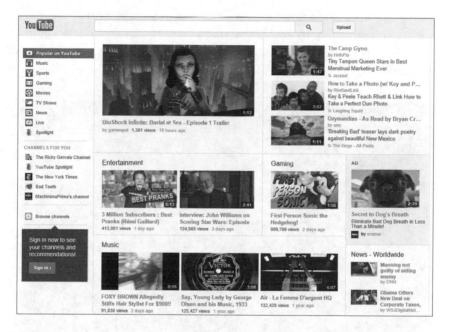

FIGURE 28.12

View user-uploaded videos at YouTube.

Searching for Videos

Looking for an early performance clip of the Beatles? Or a classic toy commercial from the 1970s? Or maybe a homemade mash-up of news clips with a hip hop soundtrack? Or something to do with dancing monkeys? What you're looking for is probably somewhere on YouTube; all you have to do is search for it, using the top-of-page search box.

The results of your search are shown on a separate page. Each matching video is listed with a representative thumbnail image, the length of the video, a short description (and descriptive tags), the name of the user who uploaded the video, and a viewer rating (from zero to five stars).

CAUTION Although YouTube has strict content policies and a self-policing community, there are no parental controls on the site—so it's viewer beware!

Viewing Videos

When you find a video you like, click the image or title, and a new page appears. As you can see in Figure 28.13, this page includes an embedded video player, which starts playing the video automatically. Use the Pause and Play controls as necessary.

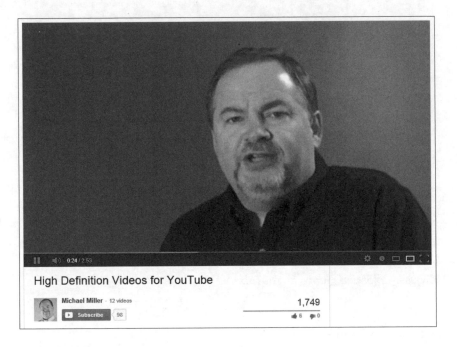

FIGURE 28.13

Watching a video on YouTube.

TIP Most YouTube videos can also be watched full screen; just click the Full-Screen button beneath the video. If a video is available in high definition, click the Change Quality button to view it in all its high-resolution, widescreen glory.

Sharing Videos

Videos become viral when they're shared between hundreds and thousands of users—and the easiest way to share a YouTube video is via email. YouTube enables you to send an email containing a link to the video you like to your friends. When a friend receives this email, he can click the link in the message to go to YouTube and play the video.

When you want to share a video, go to that video's page and click the Share button underneath the YouTube video player. When the Share tab expands, click the Email button, and then enter the email addresses of the intended recipients into the To box. (Separate multiple addresses with commas.) Enter a personal message if you want, and then click the Send button. In a few minutes your recipients will receive the message, complete with a link to the selected video.

You can also share a given video via Facebook, Twitter, Pinterest, and other social media. Click the Share button and then the button for your social network of choice.

Uploading Your Own Videos to YouTube

Anyone can upload a movie or video to the YouTube site. After the video is uploaded, users can view the video—and if you're lucky, the video will go viral!

You can shoot YouTube videos with any computer webcam or consumer camcorder. YouTube accepts videos in just about any format, as long as each video is no more than 15 minutes long. (You can apply to upload longer videos, if you like.)

Uploading is easy. Just follow these steps:

1. Click the Upload link at the top of any YouTube page.

2. When the next page appears, click Select Files from Your Computer.

3. When the Upload page appears, navigate to and select the file to upload and then click the Open button.

4. While the video uploads, you're prompted to enter information about the video, including title, description, tags, category, and privacy level. Do so, and then click the Save Changes button.

That's it. After the video uploads, YouTube converts it to the proper viewing format and creates a viewing page for the video. To view your video, click the My Videos link on any YouTube page, and then click the thumbnail for your new video.

Watching Online Videos on Your Living Room TV

Watching movies and other online videos on your PC is fine if you're on the go, but it's not the same as watching programming on the flat screen TV you have in your living room. Some newer TVs (sometimes called "smart" TVs) have built-in Internet, so you can watch Netflix and Hulu directly from the TV itself. Older TVs, however, don't have Internet connections, which means you're limited to over-the-air and cable/satellite programming.

You can, however, connect many PCs to your TV to watch Internet-based programming. All you need is the right connections on your PC and the right connecting cable.

If your computer has an HDMI connector, it's an easy task. HDMI is the cable technology used to connect high-definition Blu-ray players, cable boxes, and other equipment to flatscreen TVs; the HDMI cable carries both audio and video signals. Just connect an HDMI cable from your PC to a similar HDMI input on your TV, and you're ready to go. Start Netflix, Hulu, or YouTube on your PC, as you would normally, and then switch your TV to the corresponding HDMI input. The programming you're playing on your PC is displayed on your TV. Sit back and start watching.

Making Your Own Home Movies

If you have a video camcorder or smartphone with built-in video camera, it's easy to download movies from your device to your PC and then edit them into professional-looking videos. The movies you shoot are actually video files that can be transferred to your Windows PC with File Explorer, and stored on your computer's hard disk.

You can then edit the raw video files into more professional-looking productions. You might, for example, want to cut out some boring footage, combine two or more clips, insert transitions between clips, and even add titles and credits to your movie.

You can do all of these things—and more—with a PC-based video-editing program. These programs perform many of the same functions as the professional editing consoles you might find at your local television station. Today's video-editing programs are surprisingly easy to use—and the results are amazing!

The most popular Windows-compatible video-editing programs are quite affordable—typically $100 or less. The most popular of these include the following:

- Adobe Premiere Elements (www.adobe.com, $99.99)

- Pinnacle Studio HD (www.pinnaclesys.com, $59.95)

- Sony Vegas Movie Studio HD (www.sonycreativesoftware.com, $44.95)

- VideoStudio Pro (www.corel.com, $79.99)

- Windows Movie Maker (windows.microsoft.com/en-us/windows-live/movie-maker, free)

Most of these video-editing programs work in much the same fashion. You select the video files you want to include in your movie and then drag and drop the clips onto a timeline of some sort. You can then rearrange and trim the clips and add transitions from clip to clip. You can create titles and insert them at the front of the video; likewise, you can insert credits at the end. Depending on the program, additional special effects and editing functions might be available.

It's all easier to do than you'd think, and the results can approach professional quality. Naturally, all the home movies you create in this fashion can be viewed with the Windows Xbox Video app.

Playing DVD Movies on Your PC

What about watching old-fashioned DVD movies on your PC? Well, previous versions of Windows included the necessary technology to play DVDs, but Windows 8 and 8.1 do not. This means that you can't use Windows itself to play DVDs on your computer—although DVD playback is still possible.

If you want to watch DVDs on a Windows 8.1 computer, you need to use a third-party media player program. You might already have such a program installed; many PC manufacturers include DVD or media player programs as part of the package with new computers. Look on the Start screen for a tile labeled "movies," "movie player," "media player," or something like that.

If your computer did not come with a movie player app, you can easily install such a program to play DVD movies. There are a number of popular programs out there, including the following:

- BlazeDVD (www.blazevideo.com, $49.95)

- PowerDVD (www.cyberlink.com, $49.95)

- Roxio CinePlayer (www.roxio.com, $29.99)

- WinDVD (www.corel.com, $49.99)

- Zoom Player (www.inmatrix.com, free)

All these players work in pretty much the same fashion. Insert your DVD, and the player should launch automatically. Playback controls are typically at the bottom of the playback window; you can choose to watch a movie in a window on the desktop or full screen.

THE ABSOLUTE MINIMUM

Here are the key points to remember from this chapter:

- If you want to watch movies and classic TV programming, use the Netflix app available for Windows 8.1.

- If you want to watch recent episodes of current TV shows, use the Hulu Plus app available for Windows 8.1.

- If you want to watch recent Hollywood movies, you'll need to purchase or rent from an online video store, such as the Xbox Video Store. You can access the Xbox Video Store from Windows 8.1's Xbox Video app.

- You can also use the Xbox Video app to watch videos downloaded to or stored on your PC.

- If you want to watch videos uploaded by other users, check out YouTube.

- You can upload your own videos to YouTube—after you've used a video-editing program to make them look more professional.

29

PROTECTING YOUR PC FROM COMPUTER ATTACKS, MALWARE, AND SPAM

As you've seen, a lot of what you'll do on your computer revolves around the Internet. Unfortunately, when you connect your computer to the Internet, you open a whole new can of worms—literally. Computer worms, viruses, spyware, spam, and the like can attack your computer and cause it to run slowly or not at all. In addition to these malicious software programs (called *malware*) that can infect your computer, you're likely to come across all manner of inappropriate content that you'd probably rather avoid. It can be a nasty world online if you let it be.

Fortunately, it's easy to protect your computer and your family from these dangers. All you need are a few software utilities—and a lot of common sense!

Safeguarding Your System from Computer Viruses

A *computer virus* is a malicious software program designed to do damage to your computer system by deleting files or even taking over your PC to launch attacks on other systems. A virus attacks your computer when you launch an infected software program, launching a "payload" that oftentimes is catastrophic.

Watching for Signs of Infection

How do you know whether your computer system has been infected with a virus?

In general, whenever your computer starts acting different from normal, it's possible that you have a virus. You might see strange messages or graphics displayed on your computer screen or find that normally well-behaved programs are acting erratically. You might discover that certain files have gone missing from your hard disk or that your system is acting sluggish—or failing to start at all. You might even find that your friends are receiving emails from you (that you never sent) that have suspicious files attached.

If your computer exhibits one or more of these symptoms—especially if you've just downloaded a file from the Internet or received a suspicious email message—the prognosis is not good. Your computer is probably infected.

 NOTE   Many computer attacks today are executed using personal computers compromised by a computer virus. These so-called *zombie computers* are operated via remote control in an ad hoc attack network called a *botnet*. A firewall program protects against incoming attacks and botnet controllers.

Catching a Virus

Whenever you share data with another computer or computer user (which you do all the time when you're connected to the Internet), you risk exposing your computer to potential viruses. There are many ways you can share data and transmit a virus:

- Opening an infected file attached to an email message or instant message or sent to you from within a social network
- Launching an infected program file downloaded from the Internet
- Sharing a USB memory drive or data CD that contains an infected file
- Sharing over a network a computer file that contains an infection

Of all these methods, the most common means of virus infection is via email—with instant messaging close behind. Whenever you open a file attached to an email message or instant message, you stand a good chance of infecting your computer system with a virus—even if the file was sent by someone you know and trust. That's because many viruses "spoof" the sender's name, thus making you think the file is from a friend or colleague. The bottom line is that no email or instant message attachment is safe unless you were expressly expecting it.

Practicing Safe Computing

Because you're not going to completely quit doing any of these activities, you'll never be 100% safe from the threat of computer viruses. There are, however, some steps you can take to reduce your risk:

- Don't open email attachments from people you don't know—or even from people you *do* know, if you aren't expecting them. That's because some viruses can hijack the address book on an infected PC, thus sending out infected email that the owner isn't even aware of. Just looking at an email message won't harm anything; the damage comes when you open a file attached to the email.

- Don't accept files sent to you via instant messaging; like email attachments, files sent via IM can be easily infected with viruses and spyware.

- Download files only from reliable file archive websites, such as Download.com (www.download.com) and Tucows (www.tucows.com/downloads), or from legitimate online stores, such as the Windows Store.

- Don't access or download files from music and video file-sharing networks, which are notoriously virus and spyware-ridden. Instead, download music and movies from legitimate sites, such as the iTunes Store and Amazon MP3 Store.

- Don't execute programs you find posted to web message boards or blogs.

- Don't click links sent to you from strangers via instant messaging or in a chat room.

- Share USB drives, CDs, and files only with users you know and trust.

- Use antivirus software—and keep it up-to-date with the most recent virus definitions.

These precautions—especially the first one about not opening email attachments—should provide good insurance against the threat of computer viruses.

CAUTION   If you remember nothing else from this chapter, remember this: Never open an unexpected file attachment. Period!

Disinfecting Your System with Antivirus Software

Antivirus software programs are capable of detecting known viruses and protecting your system against new, unknown viruses. These programs check your system for viruses each time your system is booted and can be configured to check any programs you download from the Internet. They're also used to disinfect your system if it becomes infected with a virus.

Fortunately, Windows 8.1 comes with its own built-in antivirus utility. It's called Windows Defender, and you can see it in action by clicking or tapping the Windows Defender tile on the Windows Apps page.

 NOTE   Windows Defender may or may not be activated on your new PC. Some computer manufacturers prefer to include third-party antivirus software and thus disable Windows Defender by default.

As you can see in Figure 29.1, Windows Defender runs in the background, monitoring your computer against all sorts of malware, including both viruses and spyware. Although Defender automatically scans your system on its own schedule, you can opt to perform a manual scan at any time by clicking the Scan Now button.

Of course, you're not locked into using Microsoft's antimalware solution. There are a lot of third-party antivirus programs available, including the following:

- AVG Anti-Virus (www.avg.com)
- Avira Antivirus (www.avira.com)
- Kaspersky Anti-Virus (www.kaspersky.com)
- McAfee AntiVirus Plus (www.mcafee.com)
- Malwarebytes (www.malwarebytes.org)
- Norton AntiVirus (www.symantec.com)
- Trend Micro Titanium (www.trendmicro.com)

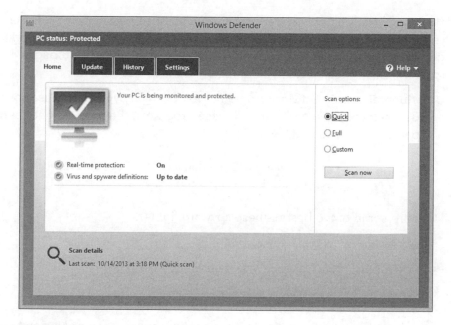

FIGURE 29.1

Windows Defender—the built-in antimalware utility for Windows.

 CAUTION   Your antivirus software is next to useless if you don't update it at least weekly. An outdated antivirus program won't be capable of recognizing—and protecting against—the latest computer viruses.

Whichever antivirus program you choose, you need to configure it to go online periodically to update the virus definition database the program uses to look for known virus files. Because new viruses are created every week, this file of known viruses must be updated accordingly.

Hunting Down Spyware

Even more pernicious than computer viruses is the proliferation of *spyware*. A spyware program installs itself on your computer and then surreptitiously sends information about the way you use your PC to some interested third party. Spyware typically gets installed in the background when you're installing another program. Peer-to-peer music-trading networks (*not* legitimate online music stores, such as the iTunes Store) are one of the biggest sources of spyware; when you install the file-trading software, the spyware is also installed.

Having spyware on your system is nasty—almost as bad as being infected with a computer virus. Some spyware programs even hijack your computer and launch pop-up windows and advertisements when you visit certain web pages. If there's spyware on your computer, you definitely want to get rid of it.

Unfortunately, many antivirus programs won't catch spyware because spyware isn't a virus. To track down and uninstall these programs, then, you might need to run a separate antispyware utility.

 NOTE Windows Defender, included free in Windows 8.1, guards against both viruses and spyware.

Here are some of the best of these spyware fighters:

- Ad-Aware (www.lavasoftusa.com)
- Spybot Search & Destroy (www.safer-networking.org)
- Webroot Spy Sweeper (www.webroot.com)

In addition, some of the major Internet security suites, such as Norton Internet Security and McAfee Total Protection, include antispyware modules. Check the program's feature list before you buy.

Defending Against Computer Attacks

Connecting to the Internet is a two-way street—not only can your PC access other computers online, but other computers can access *your* PC. This means that, unless you take proper precautions, malicious hackers can read your private data, damage your system hardware and software, and even use your system (via remote control) to cause damage to other computers.

You protect your system against outside attack by blocking the path of attack with a *firewall*. A firewall is a software program that forms a virtual barrier between your computer and the Internet. The firewall selectively filters the data that is passed between both ends of the connection and protects your system against outside attack.

Using the Windows Firewall

Fortunately for all of us, Microsoft builds a firewall utility into Windows. The Windows Firewall is activated by default, although you can always check to make sure that it's up and working properly. You do this by pressing Win+Q and searching for **firewall**; click to launch the Windows Firewall program.

Using Third-Party Firewall Software

For most users, the Windows Firewall is more than enough protection against computer attacks. That said, a number of third-party firewall programs also are available, most of which are more robust and offer more protection than the Windows built-in firewall. The best of these programs include

- McAfee Total Protection (www.mcafee.com)

- Norton Internet Security (www.symantec.com)

- ZoneAlarm Free Firewall (www.zonelabs.com)

 NOTE If you're running a third-party firewall program, you might need to turn off the Windows Firewall so the two don't interfere with each other.

Fighting Email Spam

If you're like most users, well over half the messages delivered to your email inbox are unsolicited, unauthorized, and unwanted—in other words, *spam*. These spam messages are the online equivalent of the junk mail you receive in your postal mailbox and are a huge problem.

Although it's probably impossible to do away with 100% of the spam you receive (you can't completely stop junk mail, either), there are steps you can take to reduce the amount of spam you have to deal with. The heavier your spam load, the more steps you can take.

Protecting Your Email Address

Spammers accumulate email addresses via a variety of methods. Some use high-tech methods to harvest email addresses listed on public web pages and message board postings. Others use the tried-and-true approach of buying names from list brokers. Still others automatically generate addresses using a "dictionary" of common names and email domains.

One way to reduce the amount of spam you receive is to limit the public use of your email address. It's a simple fact: The more you expose your email address, the more likely it is that a spammer will find it—and use it.

To this end, you should avoid putting your email address on your web page or your company's web page. You should also avoid including your email address in postings you make to web-based message boards or Usenet newsgroups. In addition, you should most definitely not include your email address in any of the conversations you have in chat rooms or via instant messaging.

Another strategy is to actually use *two* email addresses. Take your main email address (the one you get from your ISP) and hand it out only to a close circle of friends and family; do *not* use this address to post public messages or to register at websites. Then obtain a second email address (you can get a free one at Outlook.com or Gmail) and use that one for all your public activity. When you post on a message board or newsgroup, use the second address. When you order something from an online merchant, use the second address. When you register for website access, use the second address. Over time, the second address will attract the spam; your first email address will remain private and relatively spam-free.

 TIP If you do have to leave your email address in a public forum, you can insert a spamblock into your address—an unexpected word or phrase that, although easily removed, will confuse the software spammers use to harvest addresses. For example, if your email address is johnjones@myisp.com, you might change the address to read johnSPAMBLOCKjones@myisp.com. Other users will know to remove the SPAMBLOCK from the address before emailing you, but the spam harvesting software will be foiled.

Blocking Spammers in Your Email Programs

Most email software and web-based email services include some sort of spam filtering. You should always enable the antispam features in your email program or service. Doing so should block most of the unwanted messages you might otherwise receive.

 TIP It's a good idea to review messages in your spam folder periodically to make sure no legitimate messages have been accidentally sent there.

Resisting Phishing Scams

Phishing is a technique used by online scam artists to steal your identity by tricking you into disclosing valuable personal information, such as passwords, credit card numbers, and other financial data. If you're not careful, you can mistake a phishing email for a real one—and open yourself up to identity theft.

A phishing scam typically starts with a phony email message that appears to be from a legitimate source, such as your bank, eBay, PayPal, or another official institution. When you click the link in the phishing email, you're taken to a fake website masquerading as the real site, complete with logos and official-looking text. You're encouraged to enter your personal information into the forms on the web page; when you do so, your information is sent to the scammer, and you're now a victim of identity theft. When your data falls into the hands of criminals, it can be used to hack into your online accounts, make unauthorized charges on your credit card, and maybe even drain your bank account.

Until recently, the only guard against phishing scams was common sense. That is, you were advised never to click through a link in an email message that asks for any type of personal information—whether that be your bank account number or eBay password. Even if the email *looks* official, it probably isn't; legitimate institutions and websites never include this kind of link in their official messages. Instead, access your personal information only by using your web browser to go directly to the website in question. Don't link there!

Fortunately, Windows now offers some protection against phishing scams, in the form of a SmartScreen Filter that alerts you to potential phishing sites. When you attempt to visit a known or suspected phishing site, the browser displays a warning message. Do not enter information into these suspected phishing sites— return to your home page instead! But even with these protections, you still need to use your head. Don't click through suspicious email links, and don't give out your personal information and passwords unless you're sure you're dealing with an official (and not just an official-looking) site!

Shielding Your Children from Inappropriate Content

The Internet contains an almost limitless supply of information on its tens of billions of web pages. Although most of these pages contain useful information, it's a sad fact that the content of some pages can be quite offensive to some people—and that there are some Internet users who prey on unsuspecting youths.

As a responsible parent, you want to protect your children from any of the bad stuff (and bad people) online, while still allowing access to all the good stuff. How do you do this?

Using Content-Filtering Software

If you can't trust your children to always click away from inappropriate web content, you can choose to install software on your computer that performs filtering functions for all your online sessions. These safe-surfing programs guard against either a preselected list of inappropriate sites or a preselected list of topics—and then block access to sites that meet the selected criteria. After you have the software installed, your kids won't be able to access the really bad sites on the Web.

The most popular filtering programs include the following:

- CyberPatrol (www.cyberpatrol.com)

- CYBERsitter (www.cybersitter.com)

- Net Nanny (www.netnanny.com)

In addition, many of the big Internet security suites (such as those from McAfee and Norton/Symantec) offer built-in content-filtering modules.

Kids-Safe Searching

If you don't want to go to all the trouble of using content-filtering software, you can at least steer your children to some of the safer sites on the Web. The best of these sites offer kid-safe searching so that all inappropriate sites are filtered out of the search results.

The best of these kids-safe search and directory sites include

- Ask Kids (www.askkids.com)

- Fact Monster (www.factmonster.com)

- Google SafeSearch (www.google.com; go to the Preferences page and then choose a SafeSearch Filtering option)

 TIP A kids-safe search site is often good to use as the start page for your children's browser because it is a launching pad to guaranteed safe content.

Encouraging Safe Computing

Although using content-filtering software and kids-safe websites are good steps, the most important thing you can do, as a parent, is to create an environment that encourages appropriate use of the Internet. Nothing replaces traditional parental supervision, and at the end of the day, you have to take responsibility for your children's online activities. Provide the guidance they need to make the Internet a fun and educational place to visit—and your entire family will be better for it.

Here are some guidelines you can follow to ensure a safer surfing experience for your family:

- Make sure that your children know never to give out identifying information (home address, school name, telephone number, and so on) or to send their photos to other users online. This includes not putting overly personal information (and photos!) on their Facebook or Twitter pages.

- Provide each of your children with an online pseudonym so they don't have to use their real names online.

- Don't let your children arrange face-to-face meetings with other computer users without parental permission and supervision. If a meeting is arranged, make the first one in a public place, and be sure to accompany your child.

- Teach your children that people online might not always be who they seem; just because someone says that she's a 10-year-old girl doesn't necessarily mean that she really is 10 years old, or a girl.

- Consider making Internet surfing an activity you do together with your younger children—or turn it into a family activity by putting your kids' PC in a public room (such as a living room or den) rather than in a private bedroom.

- Set reasonable rules and guidelines for your kids' computer use. Consider limiting the number of minutes/hours they can spend online each day.

- Monitor your children's Internet activities. Ask them to keep a log of all websites they visit or check their browser history; oversee any chat sessions they participate in; check out any files they download; even consider sharing an email account (especially with younger children) so that you can oversee their messages.

- Don't let your children respond to messages that are suggestive, obscene, belligerent, or threatening—or that make them feel uncomfortable in any way. Encourage your children to tell you if they receive any such messages, and then report the senders to your ISP.

- Install content-filtering software on your PC, and set up one of the kid-safe search sites (discussed earlier in this section) as your browser's start page.

Teach your children that Internet access is not a right; it should be a privilege earned by your children and kept only when their use of it matches your expectations.

THE ABSOLUTE MINIMUM

Here are the key points to remember from this chapter:

- Avoid computer viruses by not opening unsolicited email attachments and by using an antivirus software program.

- Use antispyware tools to track down and remove spyware programs from your computer.

- Windows 8.1 has its own Windows Defender antimalware utility that guards against computer viruses and spyware.

- Protect your computer from an Internet-based attack by turning on the Windows Firewall or using a third-party firewall program.

- Fight email spam by keeping your email address as private as possible and utilizing your email program's spam filter.

- Avoid falling for phishing scams characterized by fake—but official-looking—email messages.

- To protect against inappropriate content on the Internet, install content-filtering software—and make sure that your children use kid-safe websites.

30

PERFORMING PREVENTIVE MAINTENANCE AND DEALING WITH COMMON PROBLEMS

"An ounce of prevention is worth a pound of cure."

That old adage might seem trite and clichéd, but it's also true—especially when it comes to your computer system. Spending a few minutes a week on preventive maintenance can save you from costly computer problems in the future.

To make this chore a little easier, Windows includes several utilities to help you keep your system running smoothly. You should use these tools as part of your regular maintenance routine—or if you experience specific problems with your computer system.

And if you experience more serious problems—well, try not to panic. There are ways to fix most issues you encounter, without necessarily calling in the tech support guys.

Maintaining Your Computer

Most computers these days, especially those running Windows 8, don't require a lot of handholding to keep them up and running. That said, there's a little bit of routine maintenance you might want to undertake—just to make sure your system remains in its optimal operating condition.

Cleaning Up Unused Files

Most desktop and notebook computers have pretty big hard disks; ultrabooks and tablets do not. But even if your computer has a tremendous amount of storage, it's still easy to end up with too many useless files and programs taking up too much disk space.

Fortunately, Windows includes a utility that identifies and deletes unused files. The Disk Cleanup tool is what you want to use when you need to free up extra hard disk space for more frequently used files.

To use Disk Cleanup, follow these steps:

1. From the Windows desktop, open File Explorer.

2. Navigate to the This PC section, right-click the drive you want to clean up (usually the C: drive), and click Properties to open the Properties dialog box.

3. Select the General tab (displayed by default), and then click the Disk Cleanup button.

4. Disk Cleanup automatically analyzes the contents of your hard disk drive. When it's finished analyzing, it presents its results in the Disk Cleanup dialog box, shown in Figure 30.1.

5. You have the option of permanently deleting various types of files: downloaded program files, temporary Internet files, offline web pages, deleted files in the Recycle Bin, and so forth. Select which files you want to delete.

6. Click OK to begin deleting.

 NOTE   You can safely choose to delete all the files found by Disk Cleanup except the setup log files, which the Windows operating system sometimes needs.

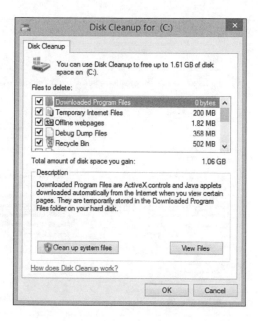

FIGURE 30.1

Use Disk Cleanup to delete unused files from your hard disk.

Removing Unused Programs

Another way to free up valuable hard disk space is to delete those programs you never use. This is accomplished using the Uninstall or Change a Program utilities in Windows. Use the following steps.

 TIP Most brand-new PCs come with unwanted programs and trial versions installed at the factory. Many users choose to delete these "bloatware" programs when they first run their PCs.

1. From the Windows Start screen, right-click in the lower-left corner to display the Quick Access menu, and then click Programs and Features.

2. When the next screen appears, as shown in Figure 30.2, click the program you want to delete.

3. Click Uninstall.

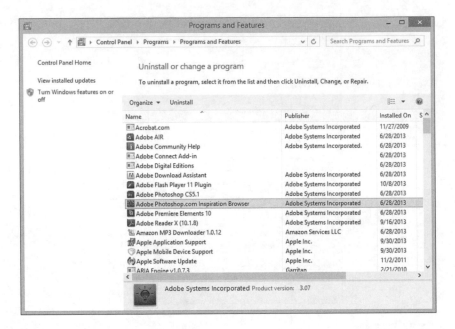

FIGURE 30.2

Uninstall any program you're no longer using.

Performing a Hard Disk Checkup with ScanDisk

Any time you run an application, move or delete a file, or accidentally turn the power off while the system is running, you run the risk of introducing errors to your hard disk. These errors can make it harder to open files, slow down your hard disk, or cause your system to freeze when you open or save a file or an application.

Fortunately, you can find and fix most of these errors directly from within Windows. All you have to do is run the built-in ScanDisk utility.

To find and fix errors on your hard drive, follow these steps:

1. From the Windows desktop, click the File Explorer icon in the taskbar to open File Explorer.

2. Click This PC in the Navigation pane.

3. Right-click the icon for the drive you want to scan, and then select Properties from the pop-up menu. The Properties dialog box displays.

4. Select the Tools tab.

5. Click the Check button in the Error-Checking section.

6. When the Error Checking dialog box appears, click Scan Drive.

Windows now scans your hard disk and attempts to fix any errors it encounters. Note that you might be prompted to reboot your PC if you're checking your computer's C: drive.

Keeping Your Hardware in Tip-Top Condition

There's also a fair amount of preventive maintenance you can physically perform on your computer hardware. It's simple stuff, but it can really extend the life of your PC.

System Unit

The system unit on a traditional desktop PC—or the entire unit of an all-in-one, notebook, or tablet computer—has a lot of sensitive electronics inside, from memory chips to disk drives to power supplies. Check out these maintenance tips to keep your system unit from flaking out on you:

- Position your computer in a clean, dust-free environment. Keep it away from direct sunlight and strong magnetic fields. In addition, make sure that your system unit and your monitor have plenty of air flow around them to keep them from overheating.

- Hook up your system unit to a surge suppressor to avoid damaging power spikes.

- Avoid turning on and off your system unit too often; it's better to leave it on all the time than incur frequent "power on" stress to all those delicate components. However...

- Turn off your system unit if you're going to be away for an extended period—anything longer than a few days.

- Check all your cable connections periodically. Make sure that all the connectors are firmly connected and all the screws properly screwed—and make sure that your cables aren't stretched too tight or bent in ways that could damage the wires inside.

Keyboard

Even something as simple as your computer keyboard requires a little preventive maintenance from time to time. Check out these tips:

- Keep your keyboard away from young children and pets—they can get dirt and hair and Play-Doh all over the place, and they have a tendency to put way too much pressure on the keys.

- Keep your keyboard away from dust, dirt, smoke, direct sunlight, and other harmful environmental stuff. You might even consider putting a dust cover on your keyboard when it's not in use.

- Use a small vacuum cleaner to periodically sweep the dirt from your keyboard. (Alternatively, you can use compressed air to *blow* the dirt away.) Use a cotton swab or soft cloth to clean between the keys. If necessary, remove the keycaps to clean the switches underneath.

- If you spill something on your keyboard, disconnect it immediately and wipe up the spill. Use a soft cloth to get between the keys; if necessary, use a screwdriver to pop off the keycaps and wipe up any seepage underneath. Let the keyboard dry thoroughly before trying to use it again.

Display

If you think of your computer display as a little television set, you're on the right track. Just treat your screen as you do your TV, and you'll be okay. That said, look at these preventive maintenance tips:

- As with all other important system components, keep your monitor away from direct sunlight, dust, and smoke. Make sure that it has plenty of ventilation, especially around the back; don't cover the rear cooling vents with paper or any other object, and don't set anything bigger than a small plush toy on top of the cabinet.

- Don't place strong magnets in close proximity to your monitor. (This includes external speakers.)

- With your monitor turned off, periodically clean the monitor screen. For an LCD flat-panel monitor, use water to dampen a lint-free cloth, and then wipe the screen; do not spray liquid directly on the screen. Do not use any cleaner that contains alcohol or ammonia; these chemicals may damage an LCD screen. (You can, however, use commercial cleaning wipes specially formulated for LCD screens.)

- Don't forget to adjust the brightness and contrast controls on your monitor every now and then. Any controls can get out of whack—plus, your monitor's performance will change as it ages, and simple adjustments can often keep it looking as good as new.

Printer

Your printer is a complex device with a lot of moving parts. Follow these tips to keep your printouts in good shape:

- Use a soft cloth, mini-vacuum cleaner, or compressed air to clean the inside and outside of your printer on a periodic basis. In particular, make sure that you clean the paper path of all paper shavings and dust.

- If you have an inkjet printer, periodically clean the inkjets. Run your printer's cartridge cleaning utility, or use a small pin to make sure they don't get clogged.

- If you have a laser printer, replace the toner cartridge as needed. When you replace the cartridge, remember to clean the printer cleaning bar and other related parts, per the manufacturer's instructions.

- Don't use alcohol or other solvents to clean rubber or plastic parts—you'll do more harm than good!

Maintaining a Notebook PC

All the previous tips hold for both desktop and notebook PCs. If you have a notebook PC, however, there are additional steps you need to take to keep everything working in prime condition.

Using the Windows Mobility Center

Let's start with all the various settings that are unique to a notebook PC—power plan, display brightness, presentation settings, and so forth. Windows puts all these settings into a single control panel called the Windows Mobility Center. As you can see in Figure 30.3, you can use the Mobility Center to configure and manage just about everything that makes your notebook run better.

To access the Windows Mobility Center, right-click the Start button to display the Quick Access menu, and then click Mobility Center. Click or tap the button or adjust the slider for whichever option you need to change.

 NOTE Some notebook manufacturers add their own mobile configuration settings to the Windows Mobility Center.

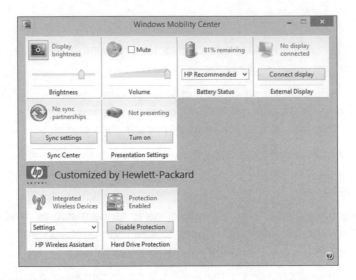

FIGURE 30.3

Manage key notebook PC settings with the Windows Mobility Center.

Conserving Battery Life

One of the key issues with a notebook PC is battery life. It's especially important if you use your notebook a lot on the road.

Any notebook, even a desktop replacement model, gives you at least an hour of operation before the battery powers down. If you need more battery life than that, here are some things you can try:

- **Change your power scheme**—Windows includes several built-in power schemes that manage key functions to provide either longer battery life or better performance. (It's always a trade-off between the two.) You can switch power schemes from the Windows Mobility Center (in the Battery Status section) or by clicking the Power icon in the notification area of the Windows taskbar on the traditional desktop.

- **Dim your screen**—The brighter your screen, the more power your PC uses. Conserve on power usage by dialing down the brightness level of your notebook's screen.

- **Turn it off when you're not using it**—A PC sitting idle is still using power. If you're going to be away from the keyboard for more than a few minutes, turn off the notebook to conserve power—or put the PC into sleep mode, which also cuts power use.

- **Don't do anything taxing**—Anytime you write or read a file from your notebook's hard disk, you use power. The same goes with using the CD or DVD drive; every spin of the drive drains the battery. If you use your notebook to watch DVD movies, don't expect the batteries to last as long as if you were just checking email or surfing the Web.

- **Buy a bigger battery**—Many notebook manufacturers sell batteries that have various capacities. You might be able to buy a longer-lasting battery than the one that came in the box.

- **Buy a second battery**—When the first battery is drained, remove it and plug in a fresh one.

- **Buy a smaller notebook**—Ultrabook models use less power and have longer battery life than do traditional notebooks, which in turn are less power-hungry than desktop replacement models. The smaller the screen and the less powerful the CPU, the longer the notebook's battery life.

If worse comes to worst, keep an eye out for an available power outlet. Most coffee shops and airport lounges have at least one seat next to a power outlet; just carry your notebook's AC adapter with you and be ready to plug in when you can.

Securing Your Notebook

One of the great things about a notebook PC is that it's small and easily portable. One of the bad things about a notebook PC is that's it's small and easily portable—which makes it attractive to thieves. Take care to protect your notebook when you're using it in public, which may mean investing in a notebook lock or some similar sort of antitheft device. Of course, just being vigilant helps; never leave your notebook unattended in a coffee shop or airport terminal.

In addition, be careful about transmitting private data over a public Wi-Fi network. Avoid the temptation to do your online shopping (and transmit your credit card number) from your local coffee shop; wait until you're safely connected to your home network before you send your private data over the Wi-Fi airwaves.

Troubleshooting Computer Problems

Computers aren't perfect. It's possible—although unlikely—that at some point in time, something will go wrong with your PC. It might refuse to start, it might freeze up, it might crash and go dead. Yikes!

When something goes wrong with your computer, there's no need to panic (even though that's what you'll probably feel like doing). Most PC problems have easy-to-find causes and simple solutions. The key thing is to keep your wits about you and attack the situation calmly and logically—following the advice you'll find in this chapter.

No matter what kind of computer-related problem you're experiencing, there are six basic steps you should take to track down the cause of the problem. Work through these steps calmly and deliberately, and you're likely to find what's causing the current problem—and then be in a good position to fix it yourself:

1. **Don't panic!**—Just because there's something wrong with your PC is no reason to fly off the handle. Chances are there's nothing seriously wrong. Besides, getting all panicky won't solve anything. Keep your wits about you and proceed logically, and you can probably find what's causing your problem and get it fixed.

2. **Check for operator errors**—In other words, *you* might have done something wrong. Maybe you clicked the wrong button, pressed the wrong key, or plugged something into the wrong jack or port. Retrace your steps and try to duplicate your problem. Chances are the problem won't recur if you don't make the same mistake twice.

3. **Check that everything is plugged into the proper place and that the system unit itself is getting power**—Take special care to ensure that all your cables are *securely* connected—loose connections can cause all sorts of strange results.

4. **Make sure you have the latest versions of all the software installed on your system**—While you're at it, make sure you have the latest versions of device drivers installed for all the peripherals on your system.

5. **Try to isolate the problem by when and how it occurs**—Walk through each step of the process to see if you can identify a particular program or driver that might be causing the problem. If you've just installed a new app (or updated an old one), consider that that might be the cause of your problem.

6. **When all else fails, call in professional help**—If you think it's a Windows-related problem, contact Microsoft's technical support department. If you think it's a problem with a particular program, contact the tech support department of the program's manufacturer. If you think it's a hardware-related problem, contact the manufacturer of your PC or the dealer you bought it from. The pros are there for a reason—when you need technical support, go and get it.

CAUTION   Not all tech support is free. Unless you have a brand new PC or brand new software, expect to pay a fee for technical support.

Troubleshooting in Safe Mode

If you're having trouble getting Windows to start, it's probably because some setting is wrong or some driver is malfunctioning. The problem is, how do you get into Windows to fix what's wrong when you can't even start Windows?

The solution is to hijack your computer before Windows gets hold of it and force it to start *without* whatever is causing the problem. You do this by watching the screen as your computer boots up and pressing the F8 key just before Windows starts to load. This displays the Windows startup menu, where you select Safe mode.

Safe mode is a special mode of operation that loads Windows in a very simple configuration. When in Safe mode, you can look for device conflicts, restore incorrect or corrupted device drivers, or restore your system to a prior working configuration (using the System Restore utility, discussed later in this chapter).

NOTE   Depending on the severity of your system problem, Windows might start in Safe mode automatically.

Reacting When Windows Freezes or Crashes

Probably the most common computer trouble is the freeze-up. That's what happens when your PC just stops dead in its tracks. The screen looks normal, but nothing works—you can't type onscreen, you can't click any buttons, nothing's happening. Even worse is when Windows crashes on you—just shuts down with no warning.

If your system freezes or crashes, the good news is that there's probably nothing wrong with your computer hardware. The bad news is that there's probably something funky happening with your operating system.

This doesn't mean your system is broken. It's just a glitch. And you can recover from glitches. Just remember not to panic and to approach the situation calmly and rationally.

What Causes Windows to Freeze?

If Windows up and freezes, what's the likely cause? There can be many different causes of a Windows freeze, including the following:

- You might be running an older software program or game that isn't compatible with your version of Windows. If so, upgrade the program.

- A memory conflict might exist between applications or between an application and Windows. Try running fewer programs at once or running problematic programs one at a time to avoid potential memory conflicts.

- You might not have enough memory installed on your system. Upgrade the amount of memory in your PC.

- You might not have enough free hard disk space on your computer. Delete any unnecessary files from your hard drive.

- Your hard disk might be developing errors or bad sectors. Check your hard disk for errors, as described in the "Performing a Hard Disk Checkup with ScanDisk" section earlier in this chapter.

Dealing with Frozen Windows

When Windows freezes, you need to get it unfrozen and up and running again. The way to do this is to shut down your computer.

In older versions of Windows, you could force a shutdown by holding down the Ctrl+Alt+Del keys. That doesn't work in Windows 8; instead, you need to press the Windows key and your PC's power button simultaneously. If that doesn't work, just press and hold the power button until the PC shuts down.

If your system crashes or freezes frequently, however, you should call in a pro. These kinds of problems can be tough to track down by yourself when you're dealing with Windows.

Dealing with a Frozen Program

Sometimes Windows works fine but an individual software program freezes. Fortunately, recent versions of Windows present an exceptionally safe environment; when an individual application crashes or freezes, it seldom messes up your entire system. You can use a utility called the Windows Task Manager to close the problem application without affecting other Windows programs.

When a Windows application freezes or crashes, press Ctrl+Alt+Del, and when the next screen appears, click or tap Task Manager; this opens the Windows Task

Manager, shown in Figure 30.4. Select the Processes tab, go to the Apps section, and click the task that's frozen. Click the End Task button and wait for the app to close.

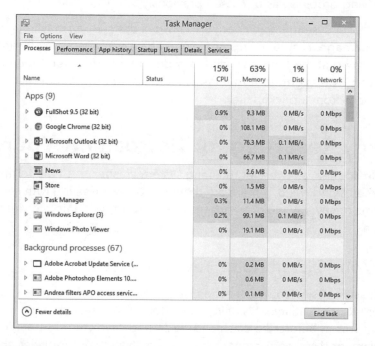

FIGURE 30.4

Use the Windows Task Manager to end nonresponding programs.

If you have multiple applications that crash on a regular basis, the situation can often be attributed to insufficient memory. See your computer dealer about adding more RAM to your system.

Dealing with a Major Crash

Perhaps the worst thing that can happen to your computer system is that it crashes—completely shuts down—without warning. If this happens to you, start by not panicking. Stay calm, take a few deep breaths, and then get ready to get going again.

You should always wait about 60 seconds after a computer crashes before you try to turn on your system again. This gives all the components time to settle down and—in some cases—reset themselves. Just sit back and count to 60 (slowly); then press your system unit's "on" button.

Nine times out of ten, your system will boot up normally, as if nothing unusual has happened. If this is what happens for you, great! If, on the other hand, your system doesn't come back up normally, you'll need to start troubleshooting the underlying problem, as discussed previously.

Even if your system comes back up as usual, the sudden crash might have done some damage. A system crash can sometimes damage any software program that was running at the time, as well as any documents that were open when the crash occurred. You might have to reinstall a damaged program or recover a damaged document from a backup file.

Restoring, Resetting, or Refreshing Your System

If you experience severe or recurring system crashes, it's time to take serious action. In Windows 8.1, there are three options for dealing with serious problems. In terms of severity, you can opt to restore, reset, or completely refresh your system.

Restoring Your System to a Previous State

The least intrusive course of action when your system crashes is to use Microsoft's System Restore utility. This utility can automatically restore your system to the state it was in before the crash occurred—and save you the trouble of reinstalling any damaged software programs. It's a great safety net for when things go wrong.

System Restore works by monitoring your system and noting any changes that are made when you install new applications. Each time it notes a change, it automatically creates what it calls a *restore point*. A restore point is basically a "snapshot" of key system files (including the Windows Registry) just before the new application is installed.

If something in your system goes bad, you can run System Restore to set things right. Pick a restore point before the problem occurred (such as right before a new installation), and System Restore will undo any changes made to monitored files since the restore point was created. This restores your system to its preinstallation—that is, *working*—condition.

To restore your system from a restore point, follow these steps:

1. From the Windows Start screen, right-click in the lower-left corner to display the Quick Access menu and then click System to display the System window.

2. Click System Protection in the Navigation pane to open the System Properties dialog box.

3. Make sure the System Protection tab is selected.

4. Click the System Restore button to display the System Restore window, shown in Figure 30.5.

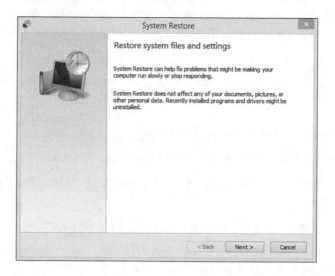

FIGURE 30.5

Use the System Restore utility to restore damaged programs or system files.

5. Click the Next button.

6. Click the restore point you want to return to, and then click the Next button.

7. When the confirmation screen appears, click the Finish button.

 CAUTION System Restore helps you recover any damaged programs and system files, but it doesn't help you recover damaged documents or data files.

Windows now starts to restore your system. You should make sure that all open programs are closed because Windows needs to be restarted during this process.

When the process is complete, your system should be back in decent working shape. Note, however, that it might take a half hour or more to complete a system restore—so you'll have time to order a pizza and eat dinner before the operation is done!

Refreshing System Files

When a system file gets corrupted or deleted, Windows 8.1 provides the ability to "refresh" your system with the current versions of important system files. The Refresh PC utility works by checking whether key system files are working properly or not. If it finds any issues, it attempts to repair those files—and only those files.

 NOTE The Refresh PC utility doesn't remove any of your personal files or documents. It only refreshes Windows system files.

To refresh your system, follow these steps:

1. Display the Charms bar and select Settings.

2. When the next panel appears, click or tap Change PC Settings to display the PC Settings page.

3. Select the Update & Recovery tab, and then click Recovery.

4. Go to the Refresh Your PC Without Affecting Your Files section, shown in Figure 30.6, and click or tap Get Started.

5. Windows tells you what it's going to do. Click or tap Next to proceed.

FIGURE 30.6

Getting ready to refresh your system.

Windows prepares your system for the refresh, which might take a few minutes. Your computer eventually restarts. When you see the Start screen, your system is refreshed.

Resetting Your System to Its Original Condition

Resetting your system is more drastic than simply refreshing it. The Reset PC utility wipes your hard disk clean and reinstalls Windows from scratch. That leaves you with a completely reset system—but without any of the apps you've installed or the files you created.

 CAUTION   The Reset PC utility completely deletes any files, documents, and programs you have on your system. Back up your files before taking this extreme step, and then restore your files from the backup and reinstall all the apps you use.

To reset your system, follow these steps:

1. Display the Charms bar and select Settings.

2. When the next panel appears, click or tap Change PC Settings to display the PC Settings page.

3. Select the Update & Recovery tab, and then click Recovery.

4. Go to the Reset Your PC and Start Over section, and click or tap Get Started.

5. Windows tells you what it's going to do. Click or tap Next to proceed.

6. If your PC has more than one drive, you're prompted to remove files from all drives or only the drive where Windows is installed. Make your choice.

7. Windows asks how you want to remove your personal files—thoroughly or quickly. For most situations, quickly is fine.

Windows begins resetting your system by deleting everything on your hard drive and reinstalling the Windows operating system. This might take some time. When the process is complete, you need to re-enter your Windows product key and other personal information—but you'll have a like-new system, ready to start using again.

THE ABSOLUTE MINIMUM

Here are the key points to remember from this chapter:

- Dedicating a few minutes a week to PC maintenance can prevent serious problems from occurring in the future.

- Windows includes a number of utilities you can use to keep your hard drive in tip-top shape.

- Make sure that you keep all your computer hardware away from direct sunlight, dust, and smoke, and make sure that your system unit has plenty of ventilation.

- If you have a notebook PC, take appropriate steps to conserve battery life—and keep your PC safe from thieves!

- You can shut down frozen programs from the Windows Task Manager, which you display by pressing Ctrl+Alt+Del.

- Some problems can be fixed from Windows Safe mode; to enter Safe mode, restart your computer and press F8 before the Windows Start screen appears.

- If your system has serious problems, you can opt to restore, refresh, or completely reset Windows to its original factory condition.

Index

C

Y

Z

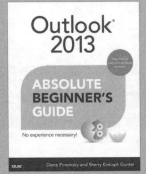

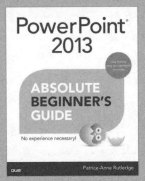
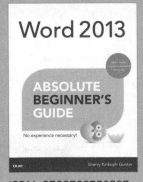

Computer Basics

ABSOLUTE BEGINNER'S GUIDE

Windows 8.1 Edition

No experience necessary!

Seventh Edition

Michael Miller

Safari
Books Online

FREE
Online Edition

Your purchase of Computer Basics Absolute Beginner's Guide includes access to a free online edition for 45 days through the **Safari Books Online** subscription service. Nearly every Que book is available online through **Safari Books Online**, along with thousands of books and videos from publishers such as Addison-Wesley Professional, Cisco Press, Exam Cram, IBM Press, O'Reilly Media, Prentice Hall, Sams, and VMware Press.

Safari Books Online is a digital library providing searchable, on-demand access to thousands of technology, digital media, and professional development books and videos from leading publishers. With ~~~~ed access to learning tools and inform~~~~ ~~~~ment, tips and tricks on using your fa~~~~ ~~~~esign, and much more.

24.99

8/28/14.

STEP

STEP

~~~~t

~~~~on form.

Addison Wesley · Peachpit Press · PRENTICE HALL · que · Redbooks · SAMS · SAS Publishing · vmware PRESS · WILEY · wrox · New Riders · O'REILLY